Family and Childbearing in Canada
A Demographic Analysis

Recent trends and changes in family patterns and childbearing in Canada will have a profound impact on future economic and social formations in the country. To discover the nature and extent of these changes and trends, the three authors of this book directed the National Fertility Study in 1984 to acquire relevant data. *Family and Childbearing in Canada* outlines the findings of this study.

Based on telephone interviews with women between 18 and 49, the book covers marriage and cohabitation history, child-bearing, demographic and socio-economic backgrounds, contraceptive practice, fertility expectations, attitudes towards family, marriage, and abortion, and relations among generations. The book places the findings in the context of other studies done in the industrialized world.

One of the most important gaps this study fills is in providing data on expected fertility needed for future fertility projections. The study also provides new insight regarding the timing and spacing of children, hitherto poorly documented in Canada, and the unique family-planning patterns of Canadian women. Better understanding of declining fertility, marital dissolutions, and living arrangements, and of the ethnic, social, economic, and cultural factors affecting these areas should be invaluable for policy decisions concerning child care, family allowance, the setting of immigration levels, and the development of programs for the aged.

T.R. BALAKRISHNAN is Professor in the Department of Sociology, University of Western Ontario. EVELYNE LAPIERRE-ADAMCYK is Professor and Director of the Département de démographie, Université de Montréal. KAROL J. KRÓTKI is University Professor Emeritus of Sociology, University of Alberta.

T.R. BALAKRISHNAN,
EVELYNE LAPIERRE-ADAMCYK,
AND KAROL J. KRÓTKI

Family and Childbearing in Canada: A Demographic Analysis

UNIVERSITY OF TORONTO PRESS

Toronto Buffalo London

© University of Toronto Press Incorporated 1993
Toronto Buffalo London
Printed in Canada

ISBN-0-8020-2856-X (cloth)
ISBN 0-8020-7356-5 (paper)

∞

Printed on acid-free paper

Canadian Cataloguing in Publication Data

Balakrishnan, T. R.
Family and childbearing in Canada : a demographic analysis

Includes bibliographical references and index.
ISBN 908020-2856-X (bound)   ISBN 0-8020-7356-5 (pbk.)

1. Fertility, Human – Canada.   2. Women – Canada –
Attitudes.   3. Family – Canada.   I. Lapierre-Adamcyk,
Evelyne, 1940–   . II. Krotki, Karol J., 1922–   .
III. Title.

HB939.B35 1993   304.6'32'0971   C93-093050-9

76658

This book has been published with the help of a grant
from the Social Science Federation of Canada,
using funds provided by the Social Sciences and
Humanities Research Council of Canada.

Contents

Preface

Though the National Fertility Survey was done only in 1984, its origins go a long way back. Actually, the Toronto study of 1968 by researchers at the University of Western Ontario was done as a pilot for a nation-wide survey. Various circumstances prevented a follow-up at that time. Though during the period 1971–6 many researchers, mostly university-based, discussed the need for in-depth fertility research using data collected from national samples, no concrete proposal was developed. It is important to note, however, that during this period pathbreaking regional surveys were done in Alberta and Quebec. By providing valuable information, these studies underscored not only the need for a national study but the dangers of generalizing from regional samples, given the great diversity of Canada's population. A major attempt at a national fertility survey was made by a consortium of researchers from the University of Western Ontario, Carleton University, University of Montreal, York University, University of Alberta, Statistics Canada, and the International Development Research Centre. The members were G.E. Ebanks, T.R. Balakrishnan, Ian Pool, Victor Piche, Michael Lanphier, P. Krishnan, Anatole Romaniuc, and Alan Simmons. The consortium received a feasibility grant from the Department of National Health and Welfare during 1976/7 to develop a detailed proposal for a national study. Though the detailed proposal went through the initial stages of approval, final funding was denied. Another proposal for a national fertility study was developed by the researchers at the University of Western Ontario as part of the strategic grants programme of the Social Sciences and Humanities Research Council of Canada. This also went through a long process of appraisal but had an unsuccessful end.

The present study has its origins in a 1981 meeting of remarkable vision arranged by G.E. Ebanks, who was then the president-elect of Planned Parenthood Federation of Canada. He brought together senior officials from various government agencies such as Statistics Canada,

Health and Welfare, the International Development Research Centre, the Social Sciences and Humanities Research Council of Canada, and the Social Science Federation of Canada for a one-day meeting in Ottawa to discuss the importance of a national fertility survey for Canada and the necessity of funding such a major project. Following this meeting, the Social Sciences and Humanities Research Council of Canada (SSHRCC) agreed to entertain a proposal for a feasibility grant subject to its usual review processes. Ebanks followed this up by approaching the investigators of this study, Professors T.R. Balakrishnan of the University of Western Ontario, Karol Krótki of the University of Alberta, and Evelyne Lapierre-Adamcyk of the University of Montreal, to prepare such a proposal. It is doubtful whether this study would have materialized without Ebank's initiative and foresight.

A large project such as this is possible only with the help of dedicated people who have worked at various stages on different aspects of the study. Those who have worked as research assistants include K.V. Rao, Bea Chapman, Jiajian Chen, Dave Dewit, Dorothy Worth, Paul-Marie Huot, Marianne Kempeneers, René Houle, Paola Colozzo, Vijaya Krishnan, and David Odynak. We have also benefited from discussions with our professional colleagues in the three different universities, as well as from the graduate students in courses where the survey data were used as teaching materials and for term papers. That three doctoral dissertations have been completed and another two (as well as many master's theses) are under preparation using Canadian Fertility Survey (CFS) data is an indication of the wide impact of a study such as this. Besides, about nine copies of the public-use tapes have been acquired by scholars both in Canada and in the United States since the data have been in the public domain. Thus, while we feel fortunate in having conducted the study itself and been able to analyse the data first, the study's raison d'être and its wider use have to be credited to the social-science community at large.

We are grateful to the Social Sciences and Humanities Research Council of Canada for the funding of this study. In addition, the three universities, the University of Western Ontario, University of Montreal, and the University of Alberta have provided various facilities in terms of space, computer facilities, and other infrastructure needed for such a large project. They deserve our sincere thanks. Finally, we would like to express our appreciation to Denise Statham and Cheryl McNeill for the able secretarial services in preparing the final manuscript.

T.R. Balakrishnan   March 1992
Evelyne Lapierre-Adamcyk
Karol J. Krótki

List of tables

List of Figures

FAMILY AND CHILDBEARING IN CANADA

1

Introduction

The most important demographic changes in Canada, as in the rest of the developed world, in the latter half of this century are clearly the trends in family formation and, more specifically, in reproductive behaviour. By the end of the 1950s fertility in Canada reached a peak. Starting with 1958, period fertility in Canada declined at a rapid rate. It is convenient to think of 1966 as the end of the baby boom. The total fertility rate, the number of births per woman, fell from 3.9 in 1958 to 1.6 by 1987. The net reproduction rate, the number of daughters per woman, went below unity, the replacement level, for the first time in 1972, and stood by 1989 at 0.78. That such sustained fertility decline is more than a timing effect and is due to a true decline in the number of children various age cohorts of women were having is now beyond doubt.

While some of the causes and consequences of this profound change in fertility have been studied extensively in Canada, much remains to be explored in depth. For example, we know that the aging of the Canadian population in the last two decades is a result more of fertility decline than of other causes. But we know much less about the ways in which the lives of the elderly are directly affected by the declining fertility rates. In the immediate family environment, declining family size will have considerable influence on the population entering the older ages. The increasing number of older persons living alone is not only a function of the need for privacy and economic resources but also of the number of children available to live with, especially in a highly mobile society such as Canada. Social and emotional needs of the elderly which are met by their interactions with their children are dependent on the number of children they have.

Fertility trends affect housing markets in a number of ways. Though

economic factors such as land costs and mortgage rates, and the effect
of demography upon the economic factors, cannot be ignored, the demand for housing is ultimately a function of household composition.
Declining fertility rates in conjunction with increased marital dissolutions and widening sex differences in mortality have moved large numbers of persons outside the traditional nuclear-family situation. Not only
has the number of households increased faster than the overall population, but the type of housing desired in terms of structure has undergone substantial change. The increase in the proportion of people living
in apartments and attached dwellings is as much due to demographic
causes as to economic factors. As the structure of housing is related to
location and zoning laws in a city, the fertility declines also contribute
indirectly to population distributions. There have been instances in some
cities of zoning regulations changing to accommodate the needs of the
elderly, such as allowing the conversion of houses into apartments and
allowing older persons to take in boarders.

Fertility differentials affect the proportion of ethnic and linguistic
groups in Canada, especially the foreign-born component. Fertility declines in Quebec, greater than the national average, have created a possibility of a declining French ethnic proportion that is not being offset
by immigration. While there is a convergence in the reproductive behaviour of ethnic and cultural groups, the extent of this phenomenom
is not well known. Fertility more than anything else will determine the
future ethnic and cultural composition of the country, should immigration levels decline. On the other hand, low fertility is likely to be followed by increasing levels of immigration and in this way will affect
the composition of the society. Much of the earlier Canadian interest in
ethnicity has been superseded in the last two decades by concern with
the country's linguistic composition, not only in the context of Quebec,
but also as an aspect of multiculturalism. Here again, fertility, more than
ethnicity, is likely to affect the linguistic composition of the society.

The increase in female labour-force participation in Canada is closely
related to fertility behaviour. Work outside the home is both a cause
and consequence of childbearing in the contemporary Canadian society.
Past studies have shown that, of all the variables, work status is more
closely correlated to number of children. The traditional pattern of women
stopping work after marriage to have children and later entering the
labour force after the children have grown up is changing in North
America. More women continue to work after marriage and a substantial
proportion work even if they have young children. It is necessary to
investigate the relationship between work and childbearing in greater

depth than before. Work experience outside the home, changing expectations of women from work, and the social and psychological satisfactions derived from work are probably some of the reasons for a decreased emphasis on having a large number of children. Higher female labour-force participation is also at least partly due to changing sex roles within marriage and increased insecurity in an unstable marriage situation. A study of family and marriage as modern social institutions should provide insights into female work outside the home.

Changes in fertility rates have an important impact on the planning of education, health, and other social services. The decline in primary-school enrolments, and its effects on the closing of schools and training of teachers, is already a widely observed phenomenon. Health-care delivery services have also been influenced by the declining birth rates. All types of projections – such as those for school and university enrolments, labour-force size, and family allowances – depend to a large extent on future fertility trends. In-depth data on fertility expectations by age, parity, and other characteristics of women are necessary so that more informed extrapolations can be made than in the past.

Finally, it is not well appreciated that a substantial part of the fertility decline is not due to a drastic decline in marital fertility but rather to the proportion marrying and remaining married. Though net reproduction rates in Canada have been below replacement level for some time, there is no evidence that married couples are having less than two children on the average. However, various types of living arrangements outside of marriage and increased marital dissolutions are having a depressing effect on overall fertility rates. To the extent that Canadian rates of divorce are very much lower than in the United States, we may not have seen the end of the trend. A study of the perceptions, attitudes, and expectations of marriage may help in predicting future trends in nuptiality and its effect on childbearing. (By 'nuptiality' we mean the formation, characteristics, and dissolution of marriages or, more generally, of all sexual unions.)

Objectives of the study

The country's available data were obviously inadequate for an in-depth analysis of fertility at the national level and its consequences. Basic changes were occurring in nuptiality patterns, in the timing and spacing of family-building, and in the childbearing expectations of present and prospective mothers. Patterns of contraceptive use and of the incidence of abortion and sterilization were also undergoing drastic changes. In a situation of an aging population and of an increase in divorce rates and female labour-force participation, these nuptiality and fertility changes take on an additional dimension. A national survey such as this should provide the data to address some of the issues arising from these changes. Apart from the obvious strategic importance in the national scene, the survey will at least partly restore the already slipping position of Canada in the international scene as a country committed to significant research in the social sciences. During the last years, national fertility surveys have been conducted in forty-one developing and nineteen developed countries as part of the World Fertility Survey. Canada was the only country in the Western world of any significant size that has not taken part in the survey. While Canada has given considerable financial assistance for research on fertility at the international level through donor agencies, it was rather paradoxical that she had not surveyed her own situation.

To satisfy the above needs this study examines (1) Canadians' attitudes, aspirations, and motivations with regard to family size and timing of births and family planning; (2) expectations within marriage, value of children, satisfaction or utility from work outside the home, and in general family and life conditions as they affect childbearing and vice versa; (3) the relative importance of factors such as religion, ethnicity, education, income, place of residence, and female labour-force participation on fertility and marriage; (4) separation and divorce as factors in fertility behaviour; (5) trends and patterns of contraceptive use including sterilizations; (6) the implications of trends and differentials in reproductive behaviour for population aging and, more specifically, its possible impacts on the elderly through living arrangements and emotional and social support from one's own children.

Brief review of fertility research in Canada prior to 1984

Since the 1950s, fertility research in the developed countries has been abundant and greatly influenced by work done by American demographers who had the privilege of collecting data through major national surveys. Various fertility surveys, starting with the Indianapolis study in 1941, the Growth of American Family Studies based on surveys of 1955 and 1960, and the National Fertility Study of 1965 and 1970, followed by surveys taken by the National Center for Health Statistics, constitute for the United States a solid body of data on the reproductive behaviour of American couples. Many European countries have also conducted such surveys, and reports emanating from the World Fertility

Survey organization provide information for many countries, both developed and developing. These surveys in general contained questions that allowed measurements of fertility and fertility aspirations, contraceptive behaviour, fecundity, marriage history, and socio-economic background.

In Canada, no national study has been undertaken until this one (Krótki 1989). Major regional surveys have been conducted: in Toronto in 1968 (Balakrishnan et al. 1975), in the province of Quebec in 1971 and 1976 (Henripin et al. 1974, 1981), and in Edmonton in 1974 (Krishnan and Krótki 1976). In 1980, a telephone survey was done in Quebec (Lapierre-Adamcyk 1982). Despite the fact that no national in-depth survey has been done until 1984, fertility research has not been neglected in Canada. Census and vital registration data have been analysed, and our knowledge of Canadian fertility behaviour is far from being limited.

Our review of Canadian fertility research prior to the availability of national surveys will follow Morsa's (1979) review of European fertility studies, arranged under three broad categories: the measurement of fertility differentials, psycho-sociological studies, and the micro-economic theory of fertility.

1. *Fertility differentials in Canada.* Three extensive analyses on fertility determinants and factors for the whole of Canada have been done. Based respectively on the 1941, 1961, and 1971 censuses, these studies by Enid Charles (1948), Jacques Henripin (1968), and Balakrishnan et al. (1979) have measured and described the impact of a variety of factors on the cumulative number of children. In addition, the 1981 census provided information on children ever born by selected socio-economic characteristics of women. From these studies one clearly sees the steady decline of the average number of children per ever-married Canadian woman from well over four for women born at the beginning of this century to just about two for those born around 1950. After Charles, Henripin, using mostly cross-tabulation analysis, shows that women who just completed their fertility in 1961 were still exhibiting substantial differences in behaviour: differences varying from 25 per cent to 40 per cent were noticeable between extreme categories of residence, schooling of wife or husband, religion, and income after other factors were controlled. Surprisingly, the mother-tongue differential was very weak, the traditionally high fertility of French-speaking Canadians being mainly due to their Catholic religious affiliation.

Ten years later, Balakrishnan and his colleagues, using multivariate analysis as well as detailed tabulations, showed that around 35 to 40 per cent of the variance in fertility could be explained by factors measured by census data; one of the most interesting findings of this study is the decreasing influence of sociocultural variables in the statistical explanation of fertility variations among younger women, leaving space for education and labour-force participation to play a more important role. Age at first marriage remained a major factor for all birth cohorts.

These results reveal the homogenization of fertility behaviour. Despite the presence of some differential, large families have almost completely disappeared and families of two or three children have become the norm for the majority of Canadian couples. Finally, just at the time the Canadian Fertility Survey (CFS) was conducted, Romaniuc showed, in a concise and synthetic study, that the low fertility regime was well in place, and examined some possible explanations and consequences (Romaniuc 1984a).

Morsa includes among fertility differential studies those that take into account various family-formation factors, such as length of birth intervals, age at marriage, and age at first birth as well as family planning behaviour. Knowledge about some of these factors is quite incomplete in Canada and we have to draw from U.S. studies and from regional surveys to get an idea of the situation. Census data give us some limited idea of family formation (Légaré 1974; Henripin 1968; Balakrishnan et al. 1979). What we have learned from these studies is that the accelerated tempo that followed the Second World War has been slowing down drastically with marriages occurring in the late 1960s and that, since 1975, not only are births postponed, but marriage itself is delayed, if not put off completely, by large numbers of young people.

What was missing from Canadian data was a complete picture of contraceptive behaviour. The regional studies (Balakrishnan et al. 1975; Henripin 1981; Krishnan and Krótki 1976) let us know that contraception is widely used, and that modern technology has been adopted almost impulsively; but cultural differences that appeared between Quebec and Toronto women in the choice of methods and the timing of use could not be fully studied owing to a lack of relevant data. On the basis of the Toronto and Edmonton surveys, one could conclude that English Canadians willingly followed Americans in contraceptive patterns, adopting contraception early in marriage, and preferring mechanical methods rather than relying on rhythm as Quebec women did. However, things seem to have changed in the last chapter of the 'contraceptive revolution.' Canadians seem to adopt tubal ligation in larger proportions than their southern neighbours (Marcil-Gratton and Lapierre-Adamcyk

1981). Their reliance on vasectomy is greater than in most Western societies, where relevant data are available, yet smaller than among their American neighbours (Bachrach 1984), to some, no doubt, a feature of some socio-psychological interest.

In terms of fertility differentials, Canada has not been lacking data or studies, except for two important aspects: tempo of family-building and contraceptive patterns. On the basis of census data, one has been able to associate the evolution of fertility with the fantastic structural transformation of our society under the social and economic pressures of urbanization, industrialization, education, and increasing female participation in the labour force. Lower fertility first associated with particular socio-economic categories became widely accepted when more profound changes took place and the new perspectives prevailed.

2. Studies in motivation for parenthood. What Morsa et al. (1979) call studies in motivation for parenthood are those works that try to measure satisfactions and costs related to having children, both well discussed by Fawcett (1972). In Canada, we can identify two studies that explored socio-psychological factors associated with fertility. Turner and Simmons (1977), analysing data from a survey of mothers and their teenage sons and daughters in Toronto in 1972, showed that the motivational system that favours the childbearing and home roles and plays down the employment roles exerts some influence on childbearing from marriage onwards. In 1980, Veevers, from data collected during in-depth interviews, produced an exploratory study of motivations of childless married persons and proposed a typology based on positive and negative motivations that lead individuals to remain childless (Veevers 1980). A third study devotes its efforts to measuring costs associated with having one more child; data were collected from that perspective in the follow-up survey in Quebec in 1976. With those data Henripin et al. (1981) showed that half of the respondents (women aged 20–40, married for at least five years) expressed no desire or interest whatsoever for one more child, even if all material barriers were removed. On the other hand, many women felt that one more child would create many problems, that is, relating to finances, health, and loss of freedom. In other words, the costs of one more child, after a certain number has been reached, were perceived as high.

The difficulties of getting at the motivations for parenthood encountered by these researchers are great, since respondents may not be conscious of their deeper reasons to have or not to have children. But given the fact that socio-economic variables provide less and less potential to explain fertility levels, the 'value of children' approach may still be a direction that can produce interesting results.

3. *Micro-economic theory of fertility.* Beyond studies of fertility differentials and motivation for parenthood, several attempts have been made to develop a more integrated framework based on the explicit hypothesis that family size depends more on individual choices, allowed to be rational by the availability of efficient contraceptive methods. The various micro-economic approaches to the study of fertility behaviour can be found in the writings of Becker (1981), Easterlin (1973), Butz and Ward (1979) and others (Willis 1973; Oppenheimer 1970).

The micro-economic theory of fertility has not inspired many original studies in Canada, mainly because data were unavailable. However, Kyriasis (1979, 1982) and Beaujot, Krótki, and Krishnan (1979) have made interesting contributions. Kyriasis, using census data, showed the relevance of introducing a sequential decision-making approach to make the theory more adequate; Beaujot et al., with data from Edmonton, demonstrated that in many sociocultural groups, 'the social context, with its associated normative constraints, is sufficiently strong to make the economic model largely inoperative' (p. 325). Although the economic models have not been able to account for the fertility behaviour in many instances, one cannot disregard the importance of economic variables, which should be included in any comprehensive study of reproductive behaviour.

This brief review of research directions and of Canadian research shows that: (1) Studies of fertility differentials do not produce any more new perspectives to a deeper understanding of fertility. The homogenization of behaviour lowers the impact of the socio-economic variables, although the sociocultural diversity of Canada forces us to keep these factors in our framework of analysis. (2) Few Canadian studies have been done on motivation for parenthood and based on micro-economic theories. (3) Data on contraceptive patterns at the national level are needed. In 1984, Canada needed new data and the CFS was welcome. At the same time, Statistics Canada also launched the Family History Survey, more limited in scope but getting information from a broader sample of both men and women (Catlin et al. 1989).

Theoretical approach and conceptual framework

Theories of fertility have largely concentrated on trying to explain the prevalence of high fertility in societies and the processes of change from a high- to low-fertility society. Given the preoccupation of students of population with the demographic transition theory it was only natural that theoretical approaches to fertility behaviour were also seen in this historical perspective. Thus, we see that the various theoretical investigations of fertility involve a large set of social and economic variables that affect childbearing and change over time as societies go from an underdeveloped to a modern industrial stage. For societies that have already completed the transition, we need theories not only to explain why overall levels of fertility are low, but to explain the cyclical fluctuations or any other patterns that may emerge.

Given the need to explain fertility declines, heavier emphasis had been put in the past on variables such as religion, education, economic benefits of children, urbanization, family and kinship systems, and intergenerational flow of assets. In modern societies such as Canada and the United States, the lesser importance of these factors is clear in the converging fertility differentials. However, noticeable fertility differentials do exist by labour-force status, ethnicity, and social class, and both period and cohort rates show some cyclical fluctuations. The need for a different conceptual framework and theoretical approach has lately been recognized. Economists have tried to apply the theory of relative income to explain fertility differentials (Easterlin 1973). Sociologists have underscored the large number of changes occurring in the social institutions, such as marriage, and in the social norms regarding sex roles, abortion, and equality for women as the main determinants of reproductive behaviour in contemporary Western societies. It is this latter approach that this study takes and tests the underlying hypotheses of changes in social institutions and norms being related to fertility declines.

1. *New facts and questions raised.* Some empirical facts related to marriage and the number of children that couples have raise several questions. In the last two decades, fertility rates have decreased to a point well below replacement levels. Following the Second World War nuptiality rates remained high and age at marriage low until about the early 1970s, when an abrupt reversal occurred. Nuptiality rates started to fall rapidly, and have reached a point that, if current rates are maintained, celibacy will go up substantially. Simultaneously, cohabiting has become more prevalent. Divorce rates are stabilizing at high levels, indicating that as many as 30 per cent of couples married since 1965 may get a divorce (Dumas 1985). Contraceptive use is widespread and the methods used are efficient. Abortions are numerous and couples who do not want any more children are getting a tubal ligation or vasectomy at a young age.

These factors are a clear indication that investigations about fertility and its determinants should take different directions than they did in the 1960s, when women married young, had at least two or three children, and stayed married.

The fundamental question for a demographer is the following: Are these new facts indicating that replacement of the generation is not assured any more? In order to answer this basic question, several others have to be raised. Do men and women still find it essential to live in a permanent union for most of their life? Does forming a marital union imply having one or more children? If this is not true for a growing number of young people, will we see childlessness raised to levels higher than those observed at the beginning of the century, when extensive childlessness of some women was societally compensated for by large families elsewhere? How does divorce affect the fertility behaviour of couples for whom having children was one of the main justifications for marriage? Will resistance to the so-called only child vanish? And, finally, will the fragility of marriage itself incite young couples to have fewer children than the two they think they want today? To address these questions, we will call upon the reflections by Roussel (1975, 1978, 1989a, 1989b, 1989c) and by Roussel and Festy (1979) on their study of European populations. Roussel first studied the evolution of the institution of marriage, showing its transformation since the French Revolution. From a rigid institution, marriage has slowly evolved to an individual engagement based only on 'affective solidarity.' The decline in fertility has accompanied this change in the matrimonial institution, and this transformation has been such that in the most advanced countries of Europe marriage is no longer the only exclusively accepted milieu to raise children.

2. *New basis for marriage and the significance of children for a couple.* Traditionally, the family has been an institution founded on the mutual commitment of the spouses and oriented towards social and biological reproduction. The commitment of the spouses was sanctioned by legal marriage, a public and almost irrevocable contract. Love and affection certainly existed: the choice of the spouse often, even mostly, was based on them, within obvious social constraints. But once married, the spouses had rights and duties that were rather well-defined and their union did not depend on the continuation of the affection and love. Sexual relations usually began with marriage and they were considered an expression of, and way to reinforce, love. Feelings were well integrated in the institution.

In recent years, a shift in the equilibrium seems to have taken place: the stability of a union is no more ensured by the strength of the institution, but by the continued intensity of love and affection. When love does not exist any more, or even when it becomes less exciting, the union is questioned and divorce is envisaged, and often occurs.

The importance given to love as a basis for marriage has also changed the attitudes towards sexual relations before marriage: when love exists, sexual relations are justified, even when marriage is not considered; more and more young people have sexual relations before marriage. And slowly the need for legal marriage becomes less and less evident, at least up to the point where the couple wants a child. Cohabitation has become more popular and probably explains why nuptiality rates are falling.

From the importance given to love follows the new type of relationship between man and woman, based on more independence and autonomy for each spouse. In that context, what is the place of the child? In the past, widely accepted values made children a justification for marriage, and the absence of very efficient contraceptive methods and the prohibition of abortion made the coming of children an almost ineluctable result of marriage. For a young couple of today, the situation is different: they have to decide if they want a child or not, and when to have it. The value attached to children is questioned. They are not an economic asset any more. The decision to have a child *is now tied to the need of reaching a better emotional balance*. The presence of children is seen as a means to *complete the fulfilment* of what is expected from the couple's relationship. The problem has become: how many children should we have in order to be happier?

Our main concern here is then to understand how reproductive goals, which under the influences of and in association with social and economic changes have reached low levels, are going to evolve from now on. We are making the hypothesis that the evolution of the the institution of family, determined to a large extent by the post-industrial society, will have an impact on the reproductive aspirations of individuals. Today, in our society, different sets of attitudes on marriage and family coexist simultaneously. There is no more a single model, one 'social norm,' acceptable to most people. There are a variety of patterns that seem to be parts of a continuum between a traditional model that is losing ground and an emerging pattern that is still not precisely defined. At the traditional end of the continuum, reproduction, biological and social, constituted the ultimate justification of the family institution; at the other end, the institution is shaky and reproduction goals are tied to the fulfilment of an individual's emotional needs. We will first try to assess the strength of the family as a social institution by looking at aspects such as (a) legal marriage perceived as a necessity, (b) acceptance of premarital sexual relations, (c) resistance to divorce, (d) the nature of the role of the spouses, and (e) the strength of the link between marriage and reproduction. This analysis will allow us to identify the different types of unions that individuals perceive as acceptable. The relationship of these types to actual fertility behaviour and aspirations should make it possible to answer some of the questions asked earlier about the direction of reproductive goals in our society.

3. *Factors in the emergence of the new basis of the family.* The new basis for marriage and the significance of having children have not emerged suddenly. They resulted from broader social transformations and were influenced by the changes in many factors. Some of the forces that brought about the conditions favouring the emergence of the new basis for the family are more immediate and directly related to the phenomenon, while the impact of others is more indirect and harder to understand.

The factors directly related to the change in the basis for the family are the availability of modern contraceptive technology, the new independence of women, and the new economic situation of young people. Until recently, contraceptive methods, even where practised regularly and widely accepted, did not present for the individual couple a real guarantee against an unwelcome conception. In societies where abortion was not tolerated, sexual relations had to be limited to a context where children could be raised and taken care of. The sexual revolution, along with the increase in cohabitation, probably could not have occurred as fast as it did, if new technology had not been developed.

The attenuation of the institutional aspects of marriage could not have occurred if women had not become more and more economically independent. The integration of women in the labour force is a complex phenomenon that results not only from the needs of the economy itself, which has developed in areas where physical strength is no longer necessary, but also from the will and need of women to earn their living. The new type of commitment to marriage, theoretically easy to revoke, could not have become widespread if women were not able to take care of themselves.

The improvement of the standard of living in general has meant that the earnings of young people are no longer necessary for their family of origin. As soon as young men and women get a job, they become financially independent from their parents. They can easily move out and live by themselves or with friends. But soon they need to develop deeper emotional relationships and cohabitation can start easily, without the formality and long-term commitment attached to marriage.

Deeper factors underlying the change in the basis for the family include the new collective attitudes and the type of society itself. The improvement in the standard of living, the greater independence of women, and modern contraceptive technology have gradually resulted in a set of new collective attitudes. Slowly small numbers of individuals, whose life is influenced by new circumstances, develop new needs and aspirations, adopt different patterns of behaviour. For example, until the 1950s, marriage was seen as a permanent, irrevocable union by most people and divorce had remained quite low. Slowly, more and more individuals felt that their marriage was not satisfying and wanted to terminate it. Divorce laws were changed and now marriage, although it may still be the only way of life for a majority of people, is no longer the unbreakable engagement it was. Fundamentally, one has to look at the relationship between society and the type of attitudes it favours to find an explanation for these recent demographic changes. Roussel argues that there is a necessary correspondence between social relationship and the new family. In his reflective mood, he suggests that no society is known to have survived where there was no clear differentiation between gender roles. Low fertility can then be viewed as merely a facilitator of such a more profound development.

While the main hypothesis of this study is that the change in the institution of the family is the primary determinant of recent reproductive behaviour, we do not underestimate the various socio-economic factors that affect fertility such as labour-force participation, education, minority and linguistic status, and ethnic background. Much is still to be learned about these fertility differentials in Canada.

Methodology[1]

1. Target population and sample selection. The Canadian Fertility Survey collected information through interviews from women in the reproductive years of 18 to 49 irrespective of their marital status. Since the survey was planned for January/February 1984, it was considered advisable to have the target population aged 18–49 as of 1 January 1984. Unfortu-

1 Much of this section is adapted from Tremblay and Trudell, *Canadian Fertility Survey: A Methodological Report.* University of Montreal, Centre de Sandage, 1984.

nately, the fieldwork for CFS was delayed a few months and was done during April/May 1984, meaning that the target population at the time of the survey was three to four months older. Therefore, we have no women younger than 18 years and 3 months at the time of the survey and a few women who are older than 50 by one to three months. Tabulations in this report are, however, made on the age at interview, rather than at age as of 1 January 1984, primarily because we did not want to ignore the experience of the women between 1 January 1984 and the survey date. Therefore, our sample slightly underestimates women in the 18–19 age category and slightly overestimates women in the 45 and over age category.

Since the sampling plan was based on a sample of telephone numbers and not on addresses or individuals, only households that could be reached by direct dialling were retained. Thus, our target population excludes those who are not in households and, further, in households without telephones. According to Statistics Canada only about 2.1 per cent of the private households in Canada do not have a telephone.

All the ten provinces were covered, but not the Yukon or the North-west Territories for reasons of cost and efficiency. The effect of this omission is minimal as only 0.2 per cent of Canadian women over the age of 18 were in these provinces according to the 1981 census of Canada. Finally, for practical reasons we were compelled to exclude people living in institutions who did not have their own telephone and those who were unable to speak either English or French.

The telephone sample was established by means of a computerized generation of random telephone numbers. Random dialling makes it possible to bypass the main obstacle encountered when selecting telephone numbers directly from the telephone book, that is, the insufficient coverage of the population with telephones.

The bank of telephone numbers created for all the ten provinces contained a total of 14,239,721 numbers. A total of 22,169 random numbers were used, which resulted in 5315 completed interviews. Further details on the breakdown of the numbers can be found in appendix B.

Where there was more than one eligible respondent in a selected household, one of them was randomly selected and interviewed. In 89.9 per cent of the households there was only one eligible respondent.

2. *Questionnaire.* The survey questionnaire (included as appendix A to this book) is an outgrowth not only of the World Fertility Survey questionnaire, but of other surveys done in Canada and of surveys done

recently in Europe and in the United States. In addition, the CFS questionnaire contained a substantial number of questions on attitudes towards marriage and the family not usually asked in fertility surveys.

The questionnaire consisted of nine sections. The first section, Respondent's Background, included socio-demographic questions on the respondent's origins, schooling, mother tongue, and so on. This section not only provided some essential information but also allowed the interviewer to build up a rapport with the respondent by getting the respondent to answer some factual questions. Section 2, Opinions and Attitudes on the Family, included a battery of fifty questions on the life of the couple, marriage, divorce, abortion, sharing of household chores, and so forth. This section took about half the time of the interview. Sections 3 and 4 covered marriage and pregnancy history in detail. Sections 5 and 6 collected information on past and current contraceptive use. Section 7 dealt with detailed work history and its interface with fertility behaviour. Section 8 covered certain economic aspects of the family, such as financial success, savings, and lodgings, in relation to the respondent's status. Section 9 collected information on the respondent's partner or husband, if applicable. The four last questions in the questionnaire were designed to obtain the respondent's general impression of the interview.

3. *Fieldwork.* During the period September 1983 to February 1984, four pre-tests were done, mainly to fine-tune the draft questionnaire and to make sure that the translated versions in English and French were strictly comparable in question wording and meaning conveyed, and that their average length was close to 45 minutes, since a considerable part of the cost of the survey would depend on the interview time on the telephone.

The interviews were conducted from five cities: Montreal, Toronto, Regina, Edmonton, and Vancouver. Using five centres meant a reduction in the proportion of long-distance calls, resulting in increased savings without too much loss of control in quality and supervision because of decentralization. More than 125 interviewers participated in the survey across Canada, all of them female. Almost all the interviews were completed in April and May of 1984, with a handful done in the first week of June.

The interviewer introduced the survey by reading a brief introduction and asked how many men and women aged 18 and over lived regularly at that telephone number. This represented an important screening, because the telephone numbers of potentially eligible private homes were distinguished from commercial or institutional numbers. The interviewer would then proceed with the selection of an eligible person and go on with the interview.

As already mentioned, a total of 22,169 telephone numbers through-out the ten provinces were generated for the Canadian Fertility Survey. These numbers can be divided into four general categories: (a) non-residential numbers, (b) residential numbers of households with no el-igible respondent, (c) residential numbers where no interviews were conducted for various reasons (refusal, absence, etc.), and (d) numbers that resulted in completed questionnaires.

4. *Response rates.* The overall response rate was 70.2 per cent, including loss at the household contact (80.5 per cent response) and the eligible respondent (87.2 per cent response) levels, a rate that is average or better than those obtained in similar telephone surveys and only slightly lower than those in face-to-face interviews. As is usual, the rates were lowest in the large cities, though Montreal fared quite well with a percentage of 70.1 compared to 62.5 in Toronto and 58.2 in Vancouver. Response rates were significantly higher in the prairie provinces of Manitoba, Saskatchewan, and Alberta as well as in Newfoundland.

5. *Other methodological aspects.* One of the important features of the Canadian Fertility Survey was that it proved that it is feasible to conduct lengthy telephone interviews with a non-specialized population of di-verse backgrounds. The average length of the interview was 36 minutes. This average time is, however, somewhat misleading since the actual time spent, excluding the screening questionnaire, varied between 13 and 115 minutes.

The weighting system for the data file consists of three components: (a) a basic weighting factor, or the inverse of the selection probability of each respondent; (b) a factor compensating for the non-responses, or the inverse of the response rate at an appropriate regional level; and (c) an age/province factor allowing us to adjust the estimate of the number of women in a province and an age group to reflect an independent estimate.

After these calculations are made, the sum of the weights for the respondents in the data file corresponds to the independent estimate of the number of Canadian women the sampling was intended to represent, 6,046,884. In order to make the statistical tests and the sampling error values produced by the SPSS (Statistical Package for the Social Sciences) or other computer software more realistic, all the weights were multi-plied by a constant K, making the sum of the final weights equal to the total number of respondents, namely 5315.

The SPSS computer program used in this study rounds the number of weighted observations in the various cells of the tables produced. This can often create situations where the marginal row or column totals do not exactly add up and are off by one. Instead of arbitrarily trying to correct this result we have left the numbers as they are. They are not of any consequence for the percentages estimated or for the conclusions arrived at.

Since the data were collected from a sample and not the whole target population, they will contain a certain margin of so-called sampling error related to the random process used to select the respondents. In our case, though the sample is a random sample of telephone numbers, it departs in a number of ways from simple random sampling owing to such factors as differences in sampling fractions, response rates, and the existence of more than one eligible respondent in some households. Therefore, a slight adjustment is necessary. This adjustment, which de-pends on the individual weights of the questionnaires, is found to be only 1.066 for the sample as a whole. This means that when a common programme for a simple random sample in an SPSS software establishes a 2 per cent sampling error (95 per cent confidence level) associated with an estimation, the real error would in fact be in the order of 2.13 per cent. It is clear that the corrective factor has little impact and is only worthwhile implementing when a high degree of accuracy is required. It should be noted that all proportion-type measurements (the dicho-tomous variables estimated at the national level using the whole sample) have a sampling error of 1.4 per cent at most at a confidence level of 95 per cent.

Initial apprehensions about doing an in-depth fertility survey using the telephone were found to be largely unfounded. Apart from the dis-tinct advantages of reduced cost and increased speed in fieldwork, there were other unexpected advantages. Better quality control could be main-tained through greater centralization of field operations. Random sam-pling of telephone numbers also meant that the sampling error is likely to be much smaller than in face-to-face interviews owing to lack of clustering. This does not mean that there are no negative aspects to the telephone. Non-response rates may be higher than face to face. Certain important questions, such as frequency of sexual relations (essential to calculating good exposure to risk rates), cannot be asked because of their sensitive nature. The somewhat higher than usual non-response on certain questions such as income may be attributable to use of the telephone, though we do not know if it would have been higher otherwise. On the whole it was felt that the merits of the telephone outweighed its demerits.

2

Current and expected fertility

The Canadian Fertility Survey ascertained through in-depth interviews detailed pregnancy, birth, marriage, and work histories, as well as information about fertility expectations, family-planning practices, and attitudes towards marriage, family, childbearing, and abortion. It also collected information on many other life-cycle events and socio-economic characteristics, not only of the women interviewed but also of their husbands or partners, to enable detailed investigation of reproductive behaviour. This chapter will focus on the current and expected fertility patterns as derived from these data. Table 2.1 presents the mean number of children ever born for ever-married women in the sample with comparisons from the earlier censuses. For older women, past the age of 35, who have largely completed their childbearing, the downward decline is clear. The mean number of children ever born for the 35–39 age group was 2.12 in the 1984 CFS, compared to 2.33 in the 1981 census, with similar declines evident for the 40–44 and 45–49 age groups. The declines in the 1971–81 decade seem to have continued in the period 1981–4. For the younger age cohorts, because their fertility is not completed, it is hazardous to draw valid conclusions. The slightly higher fertility noticeable in the 20–24 and 25–29 age groups of CFS respondents need not necessarily mean that they will have a higher completed fertility than the older cohorts. Apart from the fact that they need not behave like their older sisters, their calculated rates must have been influenced by childless women, seldom at home, among the 30 per cent of non-respondents.

Trends in expectations

Expectations data come from two questions asked of all women, depending on their pregnancy status at the time of the survey. Women

TABLE 2.1
Mean number of children ever born per ever-married woman, 1961, 1971, 1981, and 1984

Age of woman	Mean number of children ever born per ever-married woman			
	1961 census	1971 census	1981 census	1984 survey
15–19	0.74	0.63	0.43	
18–19				0.48
20–24	1.33	0.91	0.69	0.82
25–29	2.18	1.71	1.29	1.35
30–34	2.78	2.62	1.88	1.82
35–39	3.10	3.16	2.33	2.12
40–44	3.23	3.35	2.84	2.59
45–49	3.11	3.32	3.26	3.17
Total	2.66	2.47	1.98	2.02

SOURCE: 1961 and 1971 – Cat 92-718 (Statistics Canada); 1981 – Cat 92-906

who were not pregnant were asked, 'Do you expect to have a child in the future?' and those who answered yes were asked, 'How many children do you expect to have (not counting the children that you already have)?' For pregnant women, the questions were, 'Would you like to have other children, in addition to the one you are expecting now?' followed by, 'How many children in addition to your present pregnancy, do you expect to have?' The total expected children were calculated by adding the actual children ever born and additional ones expected, including current pregnancy if any. The mean number of children ever born and total expected for the various age cohorts are presented in table 2.2 and figure 2.1. A number of cautions should be stressed in interpreting expectations data obtained from a single survey such as this one. Expectations are a function of not only one's desires, but also the subjective perceptions of getting married, having the time to have the children, and the extent of sterility or subfecundity. For example, among the never-married women, the total expected number of children decreases rapidly with age. Even for the very young in the 18–24 age group, for whom most of their reproductive life lies ahead of them, the expected number may not be achieved because of the above-mentioned factors. Similarly for the currently married group, inter-cohort comparisons are fraught with problems. The older cohorts have had a choice of marrying at later ages, compared to the younger cohorts. Those who marry early not only have a longer duration for childbearing, but may be different in socio-eonomic characteristics related to fertility behaviour (Ryder and Westoff 1971). Even with these caveats, one may venture

TABLE 2.2
Actual and total expected number of children by age at interview and marital status

Age at interview	All women			Never-married			Currently married			Separated, divorced, widowed		
	Number	Children ever born	Total expected children	Number	Children ever born	Total expected children	Number	Children ever born	Total expected children	Number	Children ever born	Total expected children
18–19	313	0.06	2.30	287	0.02	2.28	23	0.45	2.54	3	0.67	1.97
20–24	1006	0.36	2.25	670	0.14	2.19	303	0.78	2.41	34	1.12	2.06
25–29	990	1.08	2.17	253	0.31	1.76	645	1.38	2.36	92	1.13	1.93
30–34	924	1.62	2.01	120	0.27	1.05	680	1.87	2.20	125	1.58	1.90
35–39	847	2.03	2.15	51	0.57	0.98	663	2.19	2.29	132	1.79	1.90
40–44	643	2.50	2.53	27	0.26	0.38	513	2.55	2.58	104	2.78	2.80
45–49	592	3.04	3.05	23	0.08	0.08	457	3.23	3.23	111	2.92	2.95
Total	5315	1.52	2.30	1430	0.17	1.93	3283	2.02	2.47	601	1.98	2.26

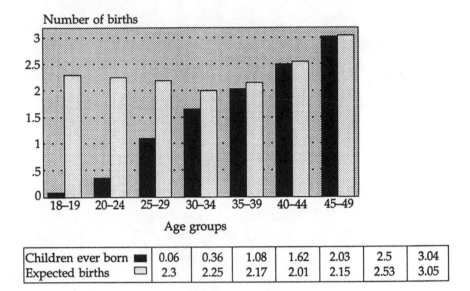

Children ever born ■	0.06	0.36	1.08	1.62	2.03	2.5	3.04
Expected births ▨	2.3	2.25	2.17	2.01	2.15	2.53	3.05

Figure 2.1 Actual and expected number of births

to comment on the noticeable increase in expectations among the younger cohorts of women in our sample. Total expected number of children among currently married women aged 30–34 was 2.20, while in the younger age groups of 25–29 and 20–24 they were 2.36 and 2.41 respectively. (Those still younger, aged 18–19, have still higher expectations – 2.54 children.) This is a trend not observed in the recent U.S. surveys, where the expectations are remarkably stable across these age groups (U.S. Bureau of the Census 1984). Until another survey is done in a few years and comparisons are made across corresponding age cohorts over time, too much should not be read into the expectations figures presented here.

Though national surveys on fertility have not been done in Canada in the past, we do have extensive surveys done in Toronto in 1968 and in Quebec in the years 1971, 1976, and 1980, in which future expectations on childbearing were explored. The 1976 Quebec survey was a re-interview of a selected number of women who had been interviewed in 1971 and could still be found; hence this accidental group is not representative of the entire population in the reproductive years in 1976. Therefore, the comparisons with the present Canadian Fertility Survey is limited to 1971 and 1980 Quebec surveys. Toronto women and Quebec women in our sample who are comparable in age with the women

TABLE 2.3
Mean total number of children expected by married women* in Metropolitan Toronto,
1968 and 1984

| | Age | | Mean total expected children | |
Year of birth	1968	1984	1968	1984
1960–6		18–24		2.30
1955–9		25–29		2.30
1950–4		30–34		2.11
1944–50	18–24	34–40	2.78	1.98
1939–43	25–29	41–45	2.76	2.40
1934–8	30–34	46–50	2.87	2.44

SOURCE (1968 data): T.R. Balakrishnan et al., *Fertility and Family Planning in a Canadian Metropolis* (Montreal: McGill-Queen's University Press 1975)

*1968 figures refer to once-married, currently married; 1984 figures refer to ever-
married.

interviewed earlier were selected and their expectations in 1984 compared with the expectations they held previously. Of course, they are
not the same women, but only belong to the same birth cohorts. Tables
2.3 and 2.4 show the fertility expectations in these surveys. The expectations revealed by young women in 1968 in Toronto were substantially
higher than the figures reported in 1984. Currently married women in
Toronto in 1968 who were then aged 18–24 expected a total of 2.78
children. However, ever-married women in Toronto aged 34–40 in 1984
who belong to the same birth cohort expect only 1.98 children on average. Even given the smaller sample size in this age group in 1984 this
is a significant difference. The differences over the time period decrease
for the older age groups, mostly because they have had some children
by 1968. For example, women born in 1939–43 who were aged 25–29
expected a total of 2.76 children in 1968, but only 2.40 in 1984, and
those born in 1934–8, who were 30–34 in 1968 expected 2.87 children
in 1968 but only 2.44 in 1984.

Similar patterns are observable when the 1971 and 1984 Quebec
women are compared. The 1971 Quebec survey presented expectations
not only by age cohorts but also marriage cohorts. In 1971 there were
very few differences among the cohorts in their expectations. Women
born in 1951–5 who were very young in 1971 gave a mean expectation
of 2.9 children, but in the 1984 survey the same cohort of women aged
29–33 expected only 2.0 children. Just as in the case of Toronto, the
older women already had a number of children by 1971 and hence the

TABLE 2.4
Mean total number of children expected by ever-married women in Quebec, 1971, 1980, and 1984

	1971	1980	1984
Year of birth			
1936–40	3.2		2.8
1941–5	2.9		2.4
1946–50	2.8		2.1
1951–5	2.9		2.0
1956–60			2.4
1961+			2.5
Year of marriage			
1951–5	3.4	3.6	3.3
1956–60	3.0	3.1	3.1
1961–5	2.9	2.6	2.5
1966–70	2.8	2.1	2.2
1971–5		2.2	2.0
1976–80		2.2	2.2
1981–4			2.2

SOURCES
- 1971 data: J. Henripin and E. Lapierre-Adamcyk, *La fin de la revanche des berceaux: Qu'en pensent des Québécois?* (Montreal: Les Presses de l'Université de Montréal 1974)
- 1980 data: E. Lapierre-Adamcyk, 'Les aspirations des Québécois en matière de fécondité,' *Cahiers Québécois de demographie* (Montreal), August 1981

changes in the expectations are not so drastic. What is striking in the Quebec case is the remarkable stability of expectations since 1980. Unfortunately, the Quebec report on the 1980 survey did not present expectations by age cohorts, but only by marriage cohorts (Lapierre-Adamcyk 1981).

Comparisons by marriage cohorts show that the differences occurred during 1971–80; since then there are hardly any noticeable changes. The youngest marriage cohort of 1966–70, most of whom would be in their early twenties in 1971, expected a total of 2.8 children in 1971. By 1980 their expectations have declined to 2.1, and remain about the same since then. There are very little differences among the cohorts married after 1966, either in the 1980 survey or in the present 1984 survey. The older cohorts, married before 1960, also show stability, but primarily because they have already had most of their children by 1971. The above comparisons do show that expectations data vary widely over time, especially in a period of rapidly changing fertility. Ryder's caution on U.S. surveys, that too much emphasis should not be placed on expectations, is supported by our data (Ryder and Westoff 1971). Our data also seem to document the hypothesis that there is a tendency to overstate the childbearing expectations during a period of declining fertility (Lee 1980).

Parity distribution

Parity distribution for ever-married women on children ever born and total expected are shown by age at interview in table 2.5. For the young women, because of the short marriage duration, current parity distribution is not too revealing. Forty-six per cent of women aged 18–24, 26 per cent of women 25–29, and 13 per cent of women aged 30–34 were childless at the time of the survey. The 1981 census figures show that 30 per cent of ever-married women in the age group 25–29 and 14 per cent in the 30–34 group were childless (Statistics Canada 1983a). Given the short duration of three years since the census, it is not surprising that there is little difference. In 1971, the figures were 21 per cent and 9 per cent respectively for the two age groups (Statistics Canada 1973). What is striking in table 2.5 is the expectations data on childlessness. Among the 18–24 and 25–29 age groups, only 3.0 per cent and 3.7 per cent of the ever-married women expect to be childless, which is close to natural sterility levels. A higher proportion of these will undoubtedly end up childless for various reasons, one of the most important being marital disruption. Even among the 45–49 age cohort who married early, had high fertility, and were in their prime reproductive years at the height of the baby boom of 1955–60, childlessness is still 4.3 per cent. Childlessness and having only one child continue to be unacceptable norms of behaviour for most married women. More than half the women in our sample expect to have two children, and more expect to have three than one, during their lifetime. Another salient trend is the decrease in the number of women who expect large families of five or more children. As many as 17 per cent of women in the oldest age group of 45–49 had five or more children. But among women who are younger than 35 years of age only about 2 per cent expect to have families of such size.

Future expectations of childbearing are largely a function of the children already had by a woman. If we take only women who can be considered definitely exposed to risk, such as currently married women, and examine their expectations by current parity, it can be seen that very few women expect to have any children once they have had two (table 2.6). Among women with two children, only 11.1 per cent expect to have children in the future, and at parities of three or higher this

TABLE 2.5

Percentage distribution of ever-married women by age at interview and children ever born and total expected

Age at interview	Number of children						Mean	Number of women
	0	1	2	3	4	5+		
	Ever born by time of survey							
18–24	45.9	32.9	17.4	3.3	0.6	–	0.80	362
25–29	25.6	27.9	34.5	10.4	1.1	0.5	1.35	736
30–34	12.6	19.8	46.3	16.0	4.8	0.5	1.82	805
35–39	11.2	13.0	42.0	23.5	8.4	2.0	2.12	795
40–44	6.8	11.8	31.5	29.5	13.0	7.4	2.59	617
45–49	4.3	8.7	23.7	28.7	17.7	17.0	3.16	569
Total	15.7	18.3	34.8	19.3	7.6	4.3	2.02	3884
	Total expected children							
18–24	3.0	6.1	53.0	27.9	7.7	2.2	2.39	362
25–29	3.7	9.2	52.2	26.3	6.2	2.4	2.30	733
30–34	6.3	13.0	50.4	21.8	7.2	1.4	2.15	799
35–39	8.6	12.4	43.4	23.7	8.9	2.9	2.22	792
40–44	6.4	11.7	31.4	29.7	12.9	7.9	2.62	614
45–49	4.3	8.7	23.7	28.7	17.5	17.2	3.17	569
Total	5.7	10.7	42.6	25.9	9.8	5.3	2.44	3869

percentage is less than 5 per cent. Practically nobody with five or more children expects to have any more. Among those who were childless at the time of the survey, 38.3 per cent expect to have no more children. However, these women formed only 13.3 per cent of the total of currently married women and are probably having problems of sterility or sub-fecundity. About half of those who had one child also expect to have no more children.

Childlessness

Because of the clear increase in childlessness, at least among younger women, there has been considerable interest in knowing how many will eventually remain childless by the time they complete their reproductive life. Expectations data are poor indicators, especially of final childlessness. Apart from fertility within marriage, they are affected by nuptiality factors, such as proportion marrying, marriage dissolution, and age at marriage. Our data at least enable us to look at expectations by marital status. Table 2.7 presents data on the percentage childless at time of the

TABLE 2.6
Percentage of currently married women 18–49 expecting no more children by parity

Children ever born plus present pregnancy if any	Total number of women	% expect no more children
0	436	38.3
1	586	45.5
2	1197	88.9
3	663	95.6
4	254	96.4
5 or more	134	99.2
Total	3270	76.7

survey and the percentage who expect to be childless in the future. Among all women, 35.2 per cent were childless at the time of the survey and 9.6 per cent expect to remain childless. There is little difference between ever-married and currently married women in their expectations, mostly because the latter group form about 85 per cent of the former. But among the never-married women 20.4 per cent expect to be childless. It is not surprising that after the age of 30 many single women expect no children in the future because of their uncertainty about getting married and having enough time to bear children. But it is significant that among the young single women in the age group 18–24, the proportion who expect to remain childless is rather high. Among single women, the proportion who expect to have no children was 16.0 per cent for those aged 18–19 and 11.9 per cent for those 20–24. Since we saw earlier in table 2.5 that only 3.0 per cent of the ever-married women in the age group 18–24 expect to be childless, it seems that women who do not marry early include a higher proportion of those who accept the norm of childlessness. The factors of later age at marriage and increasing proportion not marrying by age 50 should increase overall childlessness, other conditions being the same.

Regional differences

Actual and expected fertility by the geographical regions are shown in table 2.8. Sample sizes do not permit provincial estimates for the small provinces. The traditional differences found in fertility for many years are also present in our data. Current fertility is highest in the Maritimes, at 2.46 children ever born at the time of the survey, and lowest in Quebec, at 1.92 children. Ontario and British Columbia are very close

TABLE 2.7
Percentage of women childless at time of interview and expecting to remain childless by marital status

Age at interview	All women		Ever-married		Currently married		Never-married
	Childless at survey	Expect to be childless	Childless at survey	Expect to be childless	Childless at survey	Expect to be childless	Expect to be childless
18–19	94.3	15.0	56.2	4.0	59.4	4.5	16.0
20–24	74.5	9.0	45.2	3.1	47.2	2.9	11.9
25–29	39.9	7.9	25.6	3.7	23.9	3.1	20.6
30–34	21.6	10.5	12.6	6.3	11.0	5.2	39.8
35–39	14.5	10.9	11.2	8.6	10.0	7.4	47.1
40–44	10.1	9.3	6.8	6.4	6.6	6.2	77.1
45–49	7.9	7.9	4.3	4.3	4.5	4.5	92.1
Total	35.2	9.6	15.7	5.7	15.4	5.1	20.4
Number of women	5315		3884		3283		1431

TABLE 2.8
Mean number of children ever born and total expected per ever-married women by age and region of residence

Region	Age of women 18–24 Children ever born	Total expected	25–34 Children ever born	Total expected	35–49 Children ever born	Total expected	All ages Children ever born	Total expected	Number of women
Maritimes	1.03	2.29	1.80	2.44	3.37	3.41	2.46	2.89	356
Quebec	0.66	2.50	1.54	2.13	2.41	2.46	1.92	2.34	1005
Ontario	0.84	2.34	1.56	2.21	2.44	2.50	1.97	2.37	1398
Manitoba, Saskatchewan	0.88	2.46	1.80	2.46	2.71	2.78	2.13	2.62	302
Alberta	0.80	2.49	1.60	2.28	2.69	2.71	2.01	2.50	370
British Columbia	0.68	2.23	1.53	2.08	2.56	2.61	1.95	2.37	453
Total	0.79	2.39	1.60	2.22	2.57	2.62	2.02	2.44	3884

to Quebec in their levels of fertility. The prairie provinces are in between, with Manitoba and Saskatchewan having a mean of 2.13, and Alberta 2.01, children on an average per ever-married woman. The total expected number of children closely follows the actual fertility trends. In the maritime provinces the mean number expected was 2.89, while in Quebec it was only 2.34 per ever-married woman. It should be recognized that it is not region per se that creates differences in fertility levels and expectations, but the characteristics of the population, such as rural/urban residence, education, religion, and labour-force participation, and the general economic climate. Some of the effects of these factors on fertility will be investigated in the next chapter.

Cohort fertility

Because the survey collected complete reproductive histories of all the women interviewed, it is possible to calculate cumulative fertility data at various points of time for the different cohorts of women. This will give a picture of change in the levels and timing of childbearing as a woman goes through her reproductive period. Table 2.9 presents the cumulative number of children ever born by exact ages for the various age groups. For example, those women who were 45–49 at the time of the survey had 1.35 children by the time they were 25, 2.33 children on average by age 30, 2.84 children by age 35, and so on. When we compare the women in the different age cohorts, we find that cumulative fertility at exact ages has been steadily going down. Thus, while women 45–49 years old had 1.35 children by age 25, those who were 30–34 had only 0.73 children by the same age. Similarly, while the older women in the 45–49 age group had 2.33 children by age 30, those aged 35–39 had only 1.58 and those aged 30–34 even fewer, at 1.43 children on average. Similar declines can also be noticed at other exact age points for the various cohorts. The patterns for ever-married women and currently married women are basically the same as for all women, primarily because they form a large part of the total.

An interesting relation shown in table 2.9 is the number of children born to younger cohorts compared with older cohorts. The number of children born to women aged 25–29 by the time they were 25 years old is about the same that the 30–34 cohort had when they were 25 years old. For ever-married women, there is actually an increase from 0.81 children on average to 0.90 children. Further, if we assume that women in the age group 25–29 are uniformly distributed in that age range and fertility is unlikely to change in the immediate future, they probably

TABLE 2.9
Mean number of children ever born by selected exact ages for all women, ever-married women, and currently married women

Age at interview	Cumulative number of children ever born by exact age						Number of women
	25	30	35	40	45	50	
All women							
18–24	0.29*						1319
25–29	0.73	1.08*					990
30–34	0.73	1.43	1.62*				924
35–39	0.87	1.58	1.96	2.01*			847
40–44	1.20	2.00	2.38	2.48	2.48*		643
45–49	1.35	2.33	2.84	3.00	3.03	3.03*	592
							5315
Ever-married women							
18–24	0.79*						362
25–29	0.90	1.35*					736
30–34	0.81	1.60	1.82*				805
35–39	1.12	1.65	2.05	2.11*			795
40–44	1.25	2.08	2.48	2.57	2.58*		617
45–49	1.41	2.42	2.96	3.12	3.15	3.15*	569
							3884
Currently married women**							
18–24	0.76*						326
25–29	0.89	1.38*					645
30–34	0.76	1.61	1.86*				680
35–39	0.89	1.66	2.11	2.18*			663
40–44	1.16	2.01	2.42	2.53	2.54*		513
45–49	1.38	2.41	2.99	3.18	3.21	3.21*	457
							3283

* Fertility incomplete in these cells.
** Includes 234 women married more than once.

will have at least as many if not more children by age 30 than the present 30–34 cohort had by that age. Ever-married women aged 18–24 have some more time left before they reach age 25, and most likely exceed the fertility of the 25–29 age cohort. It seems not unreasonable to conclude that the declining levels of fertility, at least at the young ages of 18–29, show a trend of levelling off. Of course, one has to realize that a considerable portion of this group's reproductive life is ahead of them, with the future's inherent unpredictability.

Age at marriage, marriage duration, and fertility

Mean age at first marriage for all ever-married women in the sample was 21.22 years (table 2.10). Those in the younger age groups of 18–19 and 20–24 have to be married early to be considered in the calculations, while women in the older groups (over age 30) could have married later. Therefore, we cannot comment on the mean ages at marriage shown in the table for the younger cohorts, many of whom are not married by the survey date. Because of this censoring effect the mean ages at marriage for the younger cohorts in table 2.10 are underestimates, as they are based only on women who are married by the survey date.[1] What is surprising is the fairly constant figure around 21.5 for the cohorts over age 30. Increase in age at marriage and censoring operate in opposite directions to give a constant mean age at marriage for the 30-and-over cohorts.

Mean marital duration in table 2.10 is calculated by subtracting the date of first marriage from the date of interview. Thus, it is the same as the census definition of marriage duration. It should not be confused with the actual marriage duration, which takes into account date of marriage dissolution, if any. Later, we will construct actual marriage duration and investigate its relation to fertility. It can be seen from table 2.10 that increase in fertility is largely a function of marriage duration, at least until the age of 35. The very close figures for actual and expected fertility after 35 reveal that couples plan to have very few children after 35.

Marriage cohorts reveal basically the same trends as age cohorts, which is not surprising as marriages are contracted in a short age span by the various marriage cohorts. The age at first marriage for those who married before 1955 or even in 1956–60 is strongly influenced by censoring, as they have to be married early to be included in the sample with its cut-off at age 49. Thus, they are too biased downwards and do not represent the true age at first marriage of those marriage cohorts. This due-to-censoring bias is much less for the later cohorts, and their ages at first marriages are comparable. The later marriage cohorts show

1 Censoring is a serious problem in fertility surveys where women are interviewed over a long range of ages, in our case, 18 to 49. Means based on those who experience an event such as marriage or birth by the survey date are not representative of all those who will eventually experience the event. As censoring affects different age cohorts to varying degrees, it is essential that adjustments be made before arriving at conclusions. Life-table techniques are necessary to unravel the underlying trends in age at first marriage.

TABLE 2.10

Mean age at first marriage, marital duration, and children ever born and expected by age and marriage cohorts

	Number of women	Mean age at first marriage	Mean marital duration	Children ever born	Total expected
Age cohort					
18–19	26	17.72	1.22	0.48	2.47
20–24	336	19.81	2.89	0.82	2.38
25–29	735	20.98	6.16	1.35	2.30
30–34	802	21.47	10.45	1.82	2.15
35–39	794	21.57	15.28	2.12	2.22
40–44	616	21.36	20.58	2.59	2.62
45–49	567	21.52	25.66	3.17	3.17
Total	3875	21.22	13.73	2.02	2.44
Marriage cohort					
1955 or earlier	146	18.02	30.18	3.75	3.80
1956–60	466	19.84	25.62	3.25	3.26
1961–5	554	20.76	20.69	2.51	2.54
1966–70	747	21.25	15.69	2.22	2.29
1971–5	812	21.38	10.73	1.85	2.12
1976–80	753	22.04	5.79	1.34	2.21
1981–4	398	22.73	1.72	0.51	2.26
Total	3875	21.22	13.73	2.02	2.44

a trend to increasing age at first marriage. Age at first marriage was 20.76 among those who married in 1961–5, gradually increasing to 22.04 for the 1976–80 marriage cohort, and even higher, to 22.73, for those who married recently, after 1980. The mean expected number of children decreased steadily to 2.12 for the 1971–5 cohort, and since then has shown a slight increase to 2.26 for the 1981–4 marriage cohort. One must note, in line with our earlier discussion, that the declining expectations of the oldest five marriage cohorts are supported by the declining numbers of children ever born. The increasing expectations of the two most recent marriage cohorts are not yet supported by increasing numbers of children ever born. For all we know, such support may be forthcoming, but then it may not. The next survey will show.

The younger the age at first marriage, the more the number of children, an association that is clear throughout the age groups (table 2.11). The earlier age at marriage implies not only a longer marriage duration and hence greater exposure time, but also is selective of women in an education and social class who are more pronatalist than those who

TABLE 2.11

Mean number of children ever born by age at interview and by age at first marriage (ever-married women)

| Age at interview | Age at first marriage | | | | | | | Mean no. of children |
	Less than 20	20–21	22–24	25–26	27–29	30–34	35+	
18–19	.48							.48
20–24	1.17	0.73	0.21					.82
25–29	1.89	1.41	1.00	0.63	0.36			1.35
30–34	2.26	1.90	1.67	1.33	1.15	0.55	–	1.82
35–39	2.49	2.13	2.04	1.73	1.89	1.03	–	2.12
40–44	3.18	2.52	2.43	2.05	1.82	1.39	0.74	2.59
45–49	3.79	3.13	2.94	2.57	2.13	2.61	0.60	3.16
	2.45	1.98	1.80	1.58	1.48	1.44	0.60	2.02
Total no. of women	1236	1112	988	277	165	81	16	3875

marry later in life. For example, those aged 45–49 who married before the age of 20 had 3.79 children on an average, compared to 3.13 for those who married at ages 20–21. Similarly among women 40–44, fertility of women who married in their teens was 3.18 as against 2.52 for those who married at 20–21, and 2.05 for those who married at 25–26. Since most marriages take place before the age of 27, shifts in the distribution of marriages in the age group 18–26 can have substantial impact on overall fertility. Though some recent studies show that there is a slight increase in fertility beyond age 30, it is hardly likely to compensate. for any decrease that might take place owing to delayed age at first marriage. In other words, if women marry late, they are unlikely to catch up on their fertility with women who marry early and have a longer duration of exposure.

Fertility levels in various durations after marriage are presented for ever-married women and once-married, currently married women in table 2.12. 'Ever married' includes those who are separated, divorced, or widowed. Some of these women may not have been exposed to the risk of pregnancy in the durations shown. As marriage duration was calculated ignoring marital dissolution if any, separate figures are shown for once-married, currently married women, for whom marriage duration is correct. A comparison of the two panels shows that fertility levels are practically the same for ever-married and once-married, currently married women. It is possible that marital dissolution takes place usually

TABLE 2.12

Mean number of children ever born by age and marital duration for ever-married and once-married, currently married women

Age at inter-view	Marriage duration (years)						Mean no. of children ever born	Number of women
	< 0 Premarital births	0–4	5–9	10–14	15–19	20+		
	Ever-married							
18–19	0.08	0.38	–	–	–	–	0.46	26
20–24	0.12	0.66	0.03	–	–	–	0.81	336
25–29	0.12	0.96	0.26	0.01	–	–	1.35	736
30–34	0.08	1.08	0.58	0.08	–	–	1.82	805
35–39	0.09	1.20	0.63	0.18	0.02	–	2.12	795
40–44	0.07	1.51	0.75	0.21	0.04	0.01	2.59	617
45–49	0.08	1.72	0.96	0.29	0.10	0.01	3.16	569
							2.02*	3884
	Once-married, currently married							
18–19	0.09	0.35	–	–	–	–	0.43	23
20–24	0.10	0.66	0.02	–	–	–	0.78	299
25–29	0.10	0.99	0.28	0.01	–	–	1.37	613
30–34	0.05	1.13	0.63	0.06	–	–	1.88	632
35–39	0.06	1.28	0.68	0.19	0.01	–	2.21	594
40–44	0.05	1.52	0.76	0.20	0.03	0.01	2.55	469
45–49	0.09	1.76	0.98	0.31	0.11	0.01	3.26	418
							2.02*	3048

* The same figure for mean number of children ever born for ever-married and once-married, currently married is one of coincidence and not an error.

after the children are born. Though these data roughly imply that marital dissolution does not have much effect on fertility, more careful analysis is necessary to evaluate the impact of marital disruption on fertility.

Premarital births among ever-married women show some increase for the younger cohorts of women. Women aged 20–29 had an average of about 0.12 births before marriage, while women aged 30 and over had an average of 0.08 births. This is consistent with the general increase in the proportion of illegitimate births found in the vital-statistics data for recent years. Some of the births in the marriage duration 0–4 years are premaritally conceived. The extent of premarital conception is presented later in this chapter. Fertility declines can be observed in all the marital-duration categories. Fertility is incomplete in some of the cells in table 2.12, which should be kept in mind when interpreting the data.

For women aged 30 and over, the duration 0–4 years is largely complete. Mean number of children ever born in this duration has steadily decreased from 1.72 for the 45–49 age cohort to 1.08 for the 30–34 cohort. The extent of decline in the 5–9 years duration and 10–14 years duration seems to be as much as in the 0–4 years duration, indicating that there has not been a shift in the timing of births to any significant degree.

Premarital births and premarital conceptions

One of the significant phenomena of recent years is the increasing proportion of women cohabiting before a legal marriage. This has obvious implications for fertility trends, especially marital fertility. If children are born in the cohabitation period, then the fertility in any subsequent marriage will be decreased. When a woman gets pregnant while cohabiting, is she likely to get married before the birth of the baby or likely to have the baby without getting married? We still do not know the answers to this question. The data in this survey are analysed to see how many women had a premarital birth before their legal marriage, and how many had a premarital conception (table 2.13). The number of women who had a premarital birth had been going up with the most recent age cohorts. Among women aged 45–49 years at the time of the interview, 5.1 per cent had a birth before their marriage. This proportion was fairly steady down to the 30–34 age cohort, at 5.5 per cent. But in the age group 25–29, the proportion with a premarital birth was 10.2 per cent and in the 18–24 age group 10.1 per cent. Premarital conceptions, however, show a smaller change. The proportion of women who had a premarital conception as indicated by a birth in the first seven months of marriage was 10.6 per cent among women aged 45–49 and 13.0 per cent among the younger women aged 18–24, with the figures for the other age groups falling in between. The proportion of women who neither were premaritally pregnant nor had a premarital birth decreased from 84.3 per cent for the 45–49 cohort to 76.9 for the 18–24 age cohort of women.

Age at first birth and lifetime fertility[2]

It is clear from the previous sections that childbearing in the teens and early twenties has been going down in Canada. This is largely due to

2 This section draws heavily on T.R. Balakrishnan et al., 'Age at first birth and lifetime fertility,' *Journal of Biosocial Science* 20, 1988, 167–74.

TABLE 2.13
Percentage distribution of ever-married women by pregnancy status at marriage and age at interview

Age at interview	Ever-married women			
	No. of women	Premarital birth	Premarital conception	Neither
18–24	362	10.1	13.0	76.9
25–29	736	10.2	12.2	77.6
30–34	805	5.5	13.9	80.6
35–39	795	6.7	11.2	82.2
40–44	617	5.0	12.4	82.6
45–49	569	5.1	10.6	84.3
Total	3884	269	474	3141

the increasing age at first marriage. Corresponding to this trend the mean age of women at first birth has also been going up, as most fertility in Canada occurs within marriage. One is naturally interested to see whether the delay in starting childbearing will have a result in the total lifetime fertility of Canadian women, or whether women will just have their children later in their life compared to the past.

The strong inverse relationship between age at first birth and lifetime fertility of women, long taken for granted, has come under closer scrutiny in recent years. Analysing U.S. data it has been found that the relationship, while it is still significant, has weakened among the younger women (Trussell and Menken 1978, Millman and Hendershot 1980). There seems to be a new trend among those who had a first birth early to have fewer children in their later reproductive years, and these therefore may complete their fertility at a level not much higher than those who start their childbearing somewhat later in life. If this is generally true, then some of the concerns about the bad consequences of early childbearing among women for their subsequent life chances may be exaggerated.

The negative consequences of early childbearing, especially if followed by high subsequent fertility, have been well documented in past research. For example, early childbearing has been found to interrupt education and most often terminate it altogether (Moore and Waite 1977, Hendershot and Eckard 1978), partly because early childbearing was followed by higher fertility later, so that the woman was not able to complete raising young children early enough to re-enter the educational system. Moreover, early fertility, if followed by higher subsequent fertility, puts economic strains on the family that last throughout their lives (Freedman and Coombs 1966, Card and Wise 1978, Trussell 1976, Furstenberg 1976). If women who start their childbearing earlier also end their fertility earlier and do not proceed to have a larger family, then they will be young enough to return to an educational institution or in other ways train themselves for a career. Early childbearing will also have an important impact on future fertility trends: it does not result in a higher lifetime fertility it should depress overall fertility rates.

The higher completed fertility of women who start their childbearing early is supported by research over almost three decades, as well as by common logic. Where most of the fertility takes place within marriage, early childbearing indicates a young age at marriage and therefore a long potential exposure to pregnancy. Lower probabilities of marriage dissolution would also ensure continuous exposure. Besides, where contraceptive use is not too efficient the chance for unwanted births increases with duration. Those who marry early are also exposed to pregnancy during the high-fecundity years of the late teens and early twenties, in contrast to those who marry late and thus avoid exposure in these highly fertile years. Moreover, women who marry early and start a family soon thereafter may also have the characteristics usually found to be correlated with a higher family size, such as low education, low income, and a strong religious background.

If there is an emerging trend in recent years for early first birth to lose some of its significance for subsequent high fertility, what are the possible reasons? First, at present a larger proportion of births to women under twenty years of age occur outside of marriage than in the past. This is not only due to the fact that age at marriage has increased, but also because an illegitimate birth is more acceptable in the society. An early first birth to a single woman in present times need not lead to a marriage and a rapid second birth as well, as might have happened in the past. Second, use of effective contraception even at younger ages has increased greatly in Canada (Balakrishnan et al. 1985). Thus unwanted births can be avoided for long periods of exposure. Canadian women, especially, adopt sterilization in large numbers at an early age. As many as 39 per cent of all women in the age group 30–49 are sterilized, and another 13 per cent are protected by their partners having had a vasectomy (ibid.). Thus, the probability of a woman who had an early first birth having a sterilization if she does not want a large family is likely to be high. Third, the probability of a marriage dissolution is higher when there has been an early first birth, premarital or not (Balakrishnan et al. 1987, Teachman 1982, Menken et al. 1981). The mean marriage duration at time of separation has decreased substantially among the younger cohorts, to around seven years, making it highly likely that the separation takes place before the desired number of children are born. Thus, the lifetime fertility of these women may be reduced unless they have children later in a second marriage or otherwise. Fourth, the general convergence of fertility rates in Canada by religious and socio-economic characteristics means that those who have an early first birth, need not experience a higher fertility because they belong to a particular religious or socio-economic group.

The present analysis investigates the number of children ever born to women by various exact ages, classified by their age at first birth. This is done separately for the different birth cohorts of women in the sample. Since the women may not have completed their fertility, their future expected births are added to their fertility at the time of the survey to ascertain the expected lifetime fertility.

We restrict our analysis to women born 1935–59 (aged 25–49 in 1984) who had married or had a first birth prior to age 25. The cut-off at age 25 was necessary as women who neither married nor had a birth until later years will be included in the older cohorts but not in the younger cohorts, creating a bias (see Millman and Hendershot 1980). Cumulative fertility by exact ages 20, 25, 30, 35, 40, and 45 were calculated. Additional expected births including any current pregnancy were added to current fertility at the time of the survey to arrive at total expected lifetime fertility. Women were classified into five cohorts, born 1935–9, 1940–4, 1945–9, 1950–4, and 1955–9. Women younger than 25 were not included so that a minimum of a few years of exposure is possible for the younger cohorts. The ages at first birth were classified as younger than 18, 18–19, 20–21, 22–24, and 25 or after. The last category included the childless women in the sample.

Table 2.14 presents the cumulative births by specified age, survey date, additional births expected, and total expected over the lifetime. The five separate panels are for the different birth cohorts. Among the oldest group of women, who were 45–49 at the time of the survey, the relation of age at first birth to subsequent fertility is apparent. These women also have completed their fertility by the time of the survey. Those who had a first birth as a teenager, less than 18 years old, had a total lifetime fertility of 4.71 births, while women who did not have a birth before 25 had only 2.01 births. Women who did not start their childbearing before 25 did compensate somewhat by having more children after age 30, compared with other women. By age 30 these women had only an average of 0.89 births, but had 1.12 births afterwards.

TABLE 2.14

Cumulative mean number of births by selected ages, number of additional expected births, and expected completed births per woman by age at first birth for various birth cohorts of Canadian women

Age at interview (birth cohort) / Age at first birth	Cumulative births by age						Mean no. of births by survey date	Additional expected from survey date	Total expected mean no. (no. of women)
	20	25	30	35	40	45			
45–49 (1935–39)	0.23	1.41	2.42	2.95	3.12	3.14	3.14	.01	3.15 (568)
≤ 17	1.86	3.33	4.24	4.57	4.71	4.71	4.71	.00	4.71 (21)
18–19	1.17	2.90	3.78	4.35	4.44	4.44	4.44	.00	4.44 (79)
20–21	–	2.27	3.29	3.64	3.74	3.76	3.76	.01	3.77 (125)
22–24	–	1.35	2.57	2.96	3.11	3.14	3.14	.00	3.14 (167)
No birth < 25	–	–	0.89	1.70	1.96	2.01	2.01	.00	2.01 (176)
40–44 (1940–44)	0.26	1.27	2.09	2.49	2.58	–	2.59	.03	2.62 (615)
≤ 17	2.13	3.53	4.03	4.37	4.45	–	4.45	.03	4.48 (38)
18–19	1.10	2.54	3.14	3.33	3.36	–	3.36	.00	3.36 (70)
20–21	–	1.96	2.76	2.99	3.02	–	3.04	.02	3.07 (122)
22–24	–	1.32	2.26	2.58	2.63	–	2.63	.00	2.63 (172)
No birth < 25	–	–	0.89	1.54	1.72	–	1.73	.05	1.78 (213)
35–39 (1945–9)	0.20	0.92	1.66	2.06	–	–	2.11	0.10	2.22 (800)
≤ 17	1.94	2.76	3.09	3.24	–	–	3.30	0.05	3.35 (33)
18–19	1.11	2.11	2.57	2.69	–	–	2.70	0.04	2.74 (89)
20–21	–	1.75	2.27	2.54	–	–	2.57	0.03	2.60 (125)
22–24	–	1.22	2.05	2.33	–	–	2.37	0.07	2.44 (201)
No birth < 25	–	–	0.87	1.48	–	–	1.57	0.17	1.74 (352)

Age at interview (birth cohort) / Age at first birth	Cumulative births by age						Mean no. of births by survey date	Additional expected from survey date	Total expected mean no. (no. of women)
	20	25	30	35	40	45			
30–34 (1950–4)	0.19	0.83	1.61	–	–	–	1.82	0.33	2.15 (814)
≤ 17	1.41	2.41	2.69	–	–	–	2.74	0.10	2.85 (39)
18–19	1.06	1.86	2.34	–	–	–	2.45	0.12	2.56 (96)
20–21	–	1.70	2.26	–	–	–	2.36	0.11	2.47 (107)
22–24	–	1.17	2.04	–	–	–	2.17	0.13	2.29 (186)
No brith < 25	–	–	0.92	–	–	–	1.25	0.56	1.81 (386)
25–29 (1955–9)	0.22	0.94	–	–	–	–	1.37	0.95	2.32 (767)
≤ 17	1.40	2.09	–	–	–	–	2.28	0.22	2.51 (53)
18–19	1.05	1.97	–	–	–	–	2.26	0.35	2.61 (92)
20–21	–	1.82	–	–	–	–	2.13	0.43	2.57 (105)
22–24	–	1.18	–	–	–	–	1.66	0.71	2.37 (199)
No birth < 25	–	–	–	–	–	–	0.52	1.56	2.08 (318)

However, this delayed childbearing is not apparent in the other age-at-first-birth categories. Irrespective of their start, the other women had about 0.6 children after age 30. For example, those who had a first birth at a very young age, before 18, had 4.24 births by age 30, and 0.47 births after. Those who had a first birth during ages 22–24 had 2.57 births by age 30, but had an additional fertility of only 0.57 births. In other words, there was no catching up among those who started later. For this birth cohort, the lifetime fertility differences are largely determined by their reproductive behaviour before age 30.

It is interesting to observe that, for this oldest age cohort, the range in the total number of births by age at first birth is substantial, 2.70 children (4.71 to 2.01 births). This is to some extent due to the period effects that can be attributed to the peak of the baby-boom period. Those women who had their first birth before age 20 did so during the period 1955–60. They probably also wanted a larger family given the norms that existed at that time. In contrast, the sixties were a time of rapidly changing norms on family size, and of the appearance and adoption of highly effective contraceptives such as oral pills and the IUD, not to mention improved sterilization techniques. Those who had a first birth later had more of their fertility after the mid-sixties.

The second panel for the next younger age group, 40–44 (born 1940–4) shows a narrowing in the total expected number of children. Even though those who had a first birth before age 18 expected a total of 4.48 children, women who had a first birth at ages 18–19 expected to have only 3.36 births. In fact, these women had 3.14 births by age 30, and had only an additional 0.22 births since then. Here again, as in the older cohort, most of the fertility has been completed by age 30 among those who had a first birth before 25. Thus, the differences in their final expected fertility are largely a function of early fertility behaviour. Delayed childbearing is evident only among those who had a first birth at age 25 or after.

The third and fourth panels display the cumulative number of children for the next two younger cohorts of women, those aged 35–39 and 30–34 at the time of the survey. Unlike the earlier older cohorts, these women have not completed their fertility and have many years of reproductive life left. However, they expect very few children in the future, an average of 0.10 and 0.33 births respectively. The differences in the total expected births by age at first birth have systematically decreased. Among women aged 30–34, those who had a first birth at ages less than 18 expected a total of 2.85 births during their lifetime, compared with 2.29 births for those who had their first child at ages 22–24, a difference of only 0.56 births on the average.

The last panel is for the youngest cohort of women, aged 25–29 at the time of the survey, who were born 1955–9. The mean number of births by age 25 show substantial differences by age at first birth. Naturally, duration of exposure has a strong effect on the cumulative fertility by age 25. Those who had a first birth at age 17 or younger had an average of 2.09 births by age 25, compared with 1.18 births among those who had a first birth at ages 22–24. This is to be expected, since the latter women have not had enough time for a second birth. The most significant point to be noticed, however, is that those who had a first birth before age 18 expect to have very few births in the future, even though they are still young at the time of the survey. Their total expected mean number of children is only 2.51, not too different from the 2.37 births expected by those who had a first birth much later at ages 22–24. Thus, the differences in the total expected number of children by age at first birth have all but disappeared among the younger women. Of course there is a large element of uncertainty about the stability of future intentions and the likely avoidance of unwanted births given the long period of future exposure. Nevertheless, the weakening effect of early childbearing on potential lifetime fertility is nothing short of remarkable.

Sterilization by age at first birth

Expectation data on future fertility collected from young women will naturally contain a large element of uncertainty because of at least two factors. First, their expectations may change for various personal reasons. The instability of expectation data and the perils of placing too much confidence in them have been eloquently stated by Ryder and Westoff (1971). Second, young women will have a long period of exposure in the future, increasing their chances for unwanted births.

In the Canadian Fertility Survey a good deal of information was collected on contraceptive use in general and sterilization in particular. If those who had children early are more likely to get sterilized, and at an early age, then the uncertainty about future fertility is reduced and their expectation will be closer to true lifetime fertility. Table 2.15 displays the percentage of cases where the women or their husbands have gotten a sterilization or vasectomy, for the three younger cohorts. Among women aged 25–29, those who had a first birth at a very young age (before 18), a surprising 49 per cent are protected by sterilization (38 per cent tubal ligation and 11 per cent vasectomy). Similarly, among those who had a first birth in the ages 18–19 and 20–21, a high proportion of 43 per cent had sterilization. In contrast, among those who had a first birth at ages 22–24, only 15 per cent are sterilized, and among those who did

TABLE 2.15
Percentage of women protected by sterilization* of self or husband/partner by age at first birth

Age at first birth	25–29		30–34		35–39	
	No.	% sterilized	No.	% sterilized	No.	% sterilized
≤ 17	53	49	39	79	33	79
18–19	92	43	96	70	89	65
20–21	105	43	107	61	125	70
22–24	199	15	186	57	201	65
No birth < 25	318	3	386	22	352	48
Total	767	20	814	43	800	59

* Where both are sterilized only the female sterilization is included, to avoid double counting.

not have first birth before age 25, only 3 per cent are sterilized. This would mean that the figures for the total expected children may not be unreasonable for the young women who had a first birth early, as a teenager.

In the age group 30–34, 79 per cent of the women who had a first birth before 18 years of age had a tubal ligation, or their husbands had a vasectomy. The figure was 70 per cent for women with a first birth at ages 18–19 and decreasing for later age-at-first birth categories. It is clear that when women had a first birth early, they were careful to avoid unwanted pregnancies later in life and were prepared to resort to an extreme contraceptive measure such as sterilization at an early age.

In summary, among the national sample of Canadian women studied here, the excess cumulative fertility of early starters over others has steadily decreased. What used to be a difference of the order of two births between early and late starters among older women is likely to be of the order of half a child among the younger women. Since women have not completed their fertility we had to add additional expected fertility to actual fertility to arrive at lifetime fertility. Except for those who start childbearing after age 25, there is little evidence of women trying to catch up after age 30, irrespective of the starting age.

It is not surprising that the effect of early childbearing on lifetime fertility is declining. The norm of two children is widespread in Canadian society across all socio-deconomic groups, as is knowledge and use of effective contraception. Tubal ligation is especially popular among the less-educated, the group traditionally prone to earlier childbearing and a higher lifetime fertility (Balakrishnan et al. 1985). Women who have an early first birth may compensate by having a lower fertility in later years or avoiding it altogether by getting a sterilization. This is not to say that early childbearing will not continue to have its costs in foregone education for the mother, higher chances for marital dissolution, and negative economic consequences for the couple.

Birth spacing

Birth-interval analysis of survey data where the sample of respondents is representative of all women in the reproductive years 18–49 has a number of methodological problems (Ryder and Westoff 1971). First is the effect of censoring. Women in the younger ages have not had all the children they are eventually going to have. For example, among women 18–24 years of age, who are ever-married in our sample, only 54 per cent have had a first birth. Naturally many of the others will have a first birth later on in their lives. The mean birth interval between age at marriage and first birth calculated on the basis of those who had a first birth will be shorter than the true interval if we could observe the other women until they complete their reproductive life. Older women are likely to have a longer interval as they have had a longer time to have a first birth. Thus, in table 2.16, it can be noticed that, while among women 18–24 54 per cent had a first birth on an average of 22.4 months after their marriage date, among the 30–34-year-old women 87 per cent had a first birth at an average duration of 38 months after marriage. Censoring biases various intervals differently and makes the comparisons tenuous in the absence of controls or life-table analysis. A second methodological problem arises owing to negative intervals or very short intervals. If one is interested in investigating the period from first marriage to first birth, assuming exposure to pregnancy starts at marriage, it is only logical that premarital births and premarital conceptions resulting in births in the first seven months of marriage be excluded from the calculation of mean intervals.

Mean length of birth intervals and percentage having first, second, third, and fourth births by age at interview for ever-married women are presented in table 2.16. They should be interpreted keeping in mind the above cautions. Detailed life-table analysis is beyond the scope of this book, though some life-table measures will be introduced later, owing to the seriousness of the censoring for interval analysis. Mean first interval, from marriage to first birth, is calculated omitting premarital births and births in the first seven months of marriage. For second and higher-order intervals, premarital births were excluded, but not births in the first seven months of marriage.

Young women, who are less than 30 years old, are in the middle of

TABLE 2.16
Mean length of birth intervals and percentage having first, second, third, or fourth birth by age at interview (ever-married women)

Age at interview	Number of women	Mean number of months*				Percentage having**			
		Marriage to 1st birth	1st to 2nd	2nd to 3rd	3rd to 4th	1st	2nd	3rd	4th
18–24	362	22.4	30.1	22.6	†	54.0	21.1	3.7	0.5
25–29	736	33.1	32.4	34.4	30.7	74.4	46.5	12.0	1.6
30–34	805	38.4	36.3	37.7	34.9	87.4	67.6	21.3	5.3
35–39	795	35.4	37.3	43.0	40.3	88.8	75.8	33.8	10.4
40–44	617	30.3	32.9	41.2	36.7	93.2	81.4	49.9	20.4
45–49	569	28.3	32.0	37.0	36.5	95.7	87.0	63.3	34.6
Total	3884	32.8	34.4	39.1	36.8	84.3	66.0	31.2	11.9
Number of intervals		2510	2538	1184	450	3272	2563	1210	462

Mean length of birth intervals and percentage having first, second, third, or fourth birth by year of marriage (ever-married women)

Year of marriage	Number of women	Mean number of months*				Percentage having**			
		Marriage to 1st birth	1st to 2nd	2nd to 3rd	3rd to 4th	1st	2nd	3rd	4th
1955 or earlier	145	27.5	32.8	37.8	35.7	98.7	90.9	75.9	51.3
1956–60	466	28.8	30.6	36.8	39.0	97.1	89.5	66.9	35.9
1961–5	554	28.6	35.4	42.2	35.8	93.7	83.0	49.7	17.2
1966–70	747	36.7	43.0	39.0	39.0	92.6	79.9	34.7	11.1
1971–5	812	38.9	35.7	37.7	29.9	87.7	70.0	22.6	4.2
1976–80	753	32.0	29.9	29.0	17.7	78.0	45.9	8.7	1.0
1981–4	398	18.7	35.6	†	†	40.0	9.7	1.3	0.1
Total	3875	32.8	34.4	39.1	36.8	84.2	65.9	31.2	11.9
Number of intervals		2510	2532	1184	450	3265	2557	1211	462

* For marriage to 1st birth, negative intervals and intervals of 0–7 months are excluded. For subsequent intervals, those which involved multiple births are excluded.

** Includes all ever-married women, irrespective of premarital birth or births 0–7 months following marriage.

their childbearing and the figures are clearly affected. The intervals are biased downwards. Parity progression ratios are also underestimates of final ratios. Only 54.0 per cent of the 18–24 age group and 74.4 per cent of the 25–29 group have had a first birth. If we assume that by their early thirties most women who are going to have at least one child would have had one, the figure of 87.4 per cent having a first child among the 30–34 age group is close to the final figure. For this group and for the next group of 35–39-year-old women (88.8 per cent), the final percentage having a first child is unlikely to reach 90. Among the 45–49 age group, who were in their prime reproductive years in the baby-boom period of the late 1950s, the percentage who had at least one child was astonishingly high, at 95.7 per cent. Under the assumption that childbearing is by and large completed by age 35, only 34 per cent of the 35–39 age cohort went on to have a third child, in contrast to 63 per cent among the 45–49 age cohort who had most of their fertility in the baby-boom period.

Mean birth intervals and parity progression ratios for marriage cohorts show much the similar patterns, as they are closely related to age cohorts. One cannot but notice that those who married before 1955, though their numbers are small, show extremely high parity progression ratios. In the 1956–60 marriage cohort (the peak baby-boom years) 97 per cent had a first birth, 90 per cent a second birth, and 67 per cent a third birth. In contrast, among those who married in 1971–5, and are likely to have completed their childbearing by the 1984 survey date the percentages having first, second, and third births were only 88, 70, and 23 respectively. It is difficult to forecast the future childbearing patterns of those who married after 1976.

The effect on mean first birth interval of including or excluding the premarital births and premarital conceptions is apparent in the figures shown in table 2.17. The mean interval from marriage to first birth increases from 28.4 months for births excluding premarital births to 32.8 months for births excluding premarital births and births in the first seven months of marriage. Among young women below the age of 30, the differences are more pronounced than among the older women. This is because the proportion of intervals made up of premarital births or births in the first seven months of marriage is as high as 43 per cent among the 18–24 age group and 30 per cent among the 25–29 age group of ever-married women.

Life-table analysis of birth intervals helps one to calculate the probability of giving birth or delaying a birth at different durations (table 2.18). The probability of a woman giving birth in the two years of mar-

TABLE 2.17
Mean interval from first marriage to first birth for ever-married women by pregnancy status at marriage

	Total number of ever-married women	Number of women having a first birth	Excluding premarital births		Excluding premarital and 0–7 months	
			Number of women	Mean number of months	Number of women	Mean number of months
Age at interview						
18–24	362	196	159	17.0	110	22.4
25–29	736	547	471	27.5	379	33.1
30–34	805	700	656	32.7	544	38.4
35–39	795	699	649	31.2	561	35.4
40–44	617	569	540	26.7	464	30.3
45–49	569	541	512	25.3	452	28.3
Total	3884	3251	2987	28.4	2509	32.8
Year of marriage						
1955 or earlier	145	143	136	24.8	121	27.5
1956–1960	466	451	431	25.3	366	28.8
1961–1965	554	516	489	24.7	408	28.6
1966–1970	747	685	649	31.1	538	36.7
1971–1975	812	711	647	34.2	558	38.9
1976–1980	753	586	519	27.9	440	32.0
1981–1984	398	159	116	14.1	78	18.7
Total	3875	3251	2987	28.4	2509	32.8

riage, including premarital conceptions, is .48. The fairly high probability of .25 for the first year indicates considerable premarital conceptions. About 6.4 per cent are likely to remain childless even after 20 years of exposure, after which there is no probability of giving birth according to the experience of our sample women. If we include premarital births, this probability for being childless for those who marry reduces to 4.8 per cent (not shown in the table). Second and third births are delayed much longer than the first birth. Cumulative probability of having a birth reaches .55 only after three years. The proportion eventually likely not to proceed to have a second child after the first is about 9.7 per cent. Once two births have taken place, the probability of a third birth drastically decreases. Only 58.9 per cent are likely to proceed to have a third child, even after allowing for maximum exposure. Life-table anal-

TABLE 2.18
Cumulative probabilities of birth and birth delays for the first three births

Duration in months	First birth		Second birth		Third birth	
	Cumulative prob. of birth since marriage	Cumulative prob. of birth delay	Cumulative prob. of birth since first birth	Cumulative prob. of birth delay	Cumulative prob. of birth since second birth	Cumulative prob. of birth delay
1–5	.074	.926	.000	1.000	.000	1.000
6–11	.253	.747	.026	.974	.010	.990
12–23	.485	.515	.303	.697	.162	.838
24–35	.629	.371	.554	.445	.291	.709
36–47	.736	.264	.711	.289	.389	.611
48–59	.804	.196	.780	.220	.450	.550
60–71	.848	.152	.822	.178	.490	.510
72–83	.876	.124	.846	.154	.510	.490
84–119	.912	.088	.876	.124	.564	.436
120–239	.936	.064	.903	.097	.589	.411
240+	.936	.064	.903	.097	.589	.411

ysis provides a measure of interest in fertility research, namely 'parity progression ratio' – women who pass on from one parity to the next. Of course this measure is a synthetic one, based on the experience of all sample women, and does not represent the experience of any real cohort of women. In times of rapid fertility change, as experienced by the cohorts in our sample, the values of the parity progression ratios calculated from life tables are more limited than in situations of fairly constant fertility. They are, however, presented in table 2.19, with comparisons of similar measures constructed in a much earlier study done in Toronto in 1968. Taking the experience of all the ever-married women in our sample, the proportion who are likely to have a first child among those who did not have a premarital birth is 0.936. Inclusion of premarital births raises this proportion to 0.952 (not shown in the table). All the parity progression ratios in 1984 are lower than those found in Toronto in 1968, which is not surprising given the decline in fertility rates in the last 15 years. Relative declines in the ratios are greater for the later parities than for the first or second. One should be cautious in expecting these parity progression ratios in 1984 to operate for the very young women in our sample, 18–24 years of age, as with any other expectation figures for a relatively young cohort, because of the long duration they have in the future for their reproductive behaviour.

TABLE 2.19

Parity progression ratios for married women calculated
from life tables, Toronto 1968 and CFS 1984

	Toronto 1968	Canada 1984
Marriage to first	0.954	0.936
First to second	0.927	0.903
Second to third	0.702	0.589
Third to fourth	0.636	0.439
Fourth to fifth	0.572	0.382

3

Sociocultural factors in fertility

In the last chapter we examined fertility trends estimated from the Canadian Fertility Survey and tried to place them in the context of other studies and the censuses. The decline in fertility over the last two decades was confirmed by the family sizes of various age and marriage cohorts. Further, cumulative fertility by selected exact ages for the various age cohorts of women threw light on changes in the timing patterns of childbearing among Canadian women. An explanation of these changes, however, would require the investigation of the sociocultural factors associated with these reproductive behaviours. This chapter will look at some of these variables on which data were collected in the CFS.

Religion

Several studies done in the 1950s and 1960s in the United States and Canada emphasized the higher fertility of Catholics compared with Protestants and other religious groups (Freedman, Whelpton, and Campbell, 1959; Whelpton, Campbell and Patterson 1966; Ryder and Westoff 1971; Balakrishnan, Kantner, and Allingham 1975; Henripin and Lapierre-Adamcyk 1974; Westoff and Ryder 1977; Balakrishnan, Ebanks, and Grindstaff 1979). The higher fertility of Catholic women has been attributed to their adherence to the church doctrine on use of contraceptive methods and in general to the strong pronatalist position of the Catholic church. Religious differences persisted even when other socio-economic factors were controlled. In contrast, surveys done after 1970s and the Canadian census data which contain information on religion show that fertility differences by religion have been converging since the early 1970s. Analysing the 1976 U.S. National Survey of Family Growth, Jones and Westoff report that Catholic fertility has declined much faster than

Protestant fertility (Jones and Westoff 1979). Though accepting the overall convergence, some others have stressed that religious differences persist within specific categories, such as those who had sectarian education, or depending on when religion was measured: at the time of the survey or in early childhood (Johnson 1982; Janssen and Hauser 1981). In Canada, Catholic-Protestant fertility rates have converged to the point where by 1980 there is practically no difference among the younger cohorts of women (Statistics Canada 1983a).

In the CFS religion was ascertained at the time of the interview by asking the question 'What is your religion?' Though the responses were coded in great detail, for most of the analysis in this chapter we will resort to four categories: Catholics, Protestants, Other religion, and No religion. Table 3.1 and figure 3.1 present data of children ever born and total expected by broad religious groups for the various age and marriage cohorts. As found in other studies, there is a convergence of fertility by religion. Comparison of Catholic and Protestant women show that among the older cohort, aged 45–49 years of age, Catholic women had a mean of 3.22 children while Protestant women had only a mean of 2.82 children. But among women less than 35 years of age, there is practically no difference between Catholics and Protestants, either in actual fertility or in total expected fertility.

Since most fertility in Canada takes place within marriage, it is not surprising that the pattern by religion found among all women is also the same as among ever-married women; namely, Catholics have a higher fertility than Protestants if aged 35 or over, but about the same if younger than 35.

Because age-at-marriage distributions are similar between Catholics and Protestants, fertility by marriage cohorts also shows patterns that are not too different from that by age. For example, Catholic women who married before 1970 had a higher mean number of children than Protestant women who married before 1970. But among those who married after 1970, there were no noticeable differences.

In Canada, Catholics formed 47.3 per cent of the population in 1981, a proportion that increased from 41 per cent in 1931 to 47 per cent in 1961 and has remained fairly constant since then. Outside of Quebec, which has an 88 per cent Catholic population, Catholics formed about a third of the population in the other provinces except in Alberta and British Columbia, with a lower proportion of Catholics. That Catholics have no longer higher fertility than Protestants is a significant factor in the below-replacement fertility prevailing in Canada for more than a decade before the CFS was taken. Since the population of Quebec is

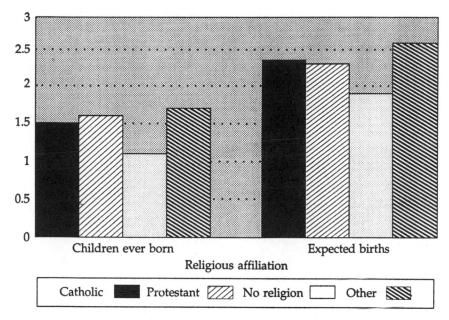

Figure 3.1 Actual and expected number of births by religions

predominantly Catholic and there has been an astonishing turnaround in Quebec fertility rates from being the highest to the lowest among all the provinces, one might be tempted to attribute the narrowing of Catholic-Protestant fertility differences to Quebec residence. The question to answer is 'Are Catholic-Protestant differences a function of Quebec residence?' Table 3.2 shows they are not. The patterns in Quebec and the rest of Canada are basically the same. Since there are very few Protestants in Quebec, the age breakdowns for Protestants in Quebec shown in table 3.2 are not reliable. All ages taken together, the mean number of children was 1.42 for the Catholic women in Quebec compared to 1.45 children for Protestants. In the rest of Canada, the mean number of births for Catholics was 1.61 as against 1.60 for Protestants. Thus, while the overall fertility was higher for both religions in the rest of Canada compared to Quebec, there were no differences by religion. We do not wish to take our data too seriously, but one cannot help noticing that the minorities (Protestants in Quebec and Catholics elsewhere) have a somewhat higher fertility in line with the minority-relations theory, which expects minorities to 'defend' themselves through higher fertility from the onslaughts of the majority. A breakdown by age for the rest of Canada shows that while in the older cohorts the Catholics had

TABLE 3.1
Children ever born and total expected by religious affiliations for age and marriage cohorts

	Catholic			Protestant			No religion			Other			Total		
	No. of women	CEB	Total expt.	No. of women	CEB	Total expt.	No. of women	CEB	Total expt.	No. of women	CEB	Total expt.	No. of women	CEB	Total expt.
Age at interview	All women														
18–24	661	0.26	2.30	426	0.34	2.19	115	0.28	2.19	119	0.26	2.31	1320	0.29	2.26
25–29	481	1.06	2.20	323	1.12	2.17	88	0.87	1.80	92	1.34	2.46	983	1.09	2.18
30–34	417	1.62	1.99	339	1.71	2.09	87	1.11	1.46	81	1.80	2.40	924	1.62	2.01
35–39	407	2.09	2.20	293	1.93	2.09	72	1.69	1.72	73	2.44	2.56	844	2.03	2.15
40–44	301	2.46	2.49	254	2.58	2.60	35	2.30	2.30	52	2.41	2.53	642	2.49	2.53
45–49	282	3.22	3.24	237	2.82	2.83	31	2.42	2.42	43	3.51	3.51	592	3.04	3.05
Total	2547	1.51	2.34	1871	1.59	2.29	428	1.13	1.91	459	1.64	2.53	5305	1.52	2.30
Age at interview	Ever-married women														
18–24	163	0.74	2.43	127	0.86	2.28	31	0.82	2.24	40	0.72	2.57	361	0.79	2.38
25–29	349	1.33	2.32	254	1.38	2.30	59	1.13	2.05	72	1.58	2.46	735	1.35	2.31
30–34	352	1.87	2.15	306	1.87	2.20	72	1.30	1.59	75	1.91	2.44	805	1.82	2.15
35–39	381	2.19	2.30	275	2.03	2.15	69	1.75	1.79	69	2.48	2.57	795	2.12	2.22
40–44	282	2.60	2.62	251	2.61	2.63	33	2.48	2.48	49	2.55	2.67	616	2.59	2.62
45–49	269	3.37	3.39	229	2.92	2.92	29	2.57	2.57	41	3.68	3.68	568	3.17	3.18
Total	1795	2.07	2.50	1443	2.02	2.40	294	1.58	2.00	346	2.12	2.67	3879	2.02	2.44

Age at interview / Marriage cohort	Catholic			Protestant			No religion			Other			Total		
	No. of women	CEB	Total expt.	No. of women	CEB	Total expt.	No. of women	CEB	Total expt.	No. of women	CEB	Total expt.	No. of women	CEB	Total expt.
All women															
Ever-married women															
< 55	62	4.00	4.06	62	3.71	3.74	12	3.20	3.20	8	3.30	3.30	145	3.77	3.80
56–60	210	3.51	3.54	194	2.97	2.98	23	2.63	2.63	33	3.67	3.67	459	3.25	3.26
61–65	258	2.54	2.54	223	2.42	2.45	35	2.35	2.40	35	3.24	3.24	551	2.52	2.54
66–70	342	2.31	2.37	279	2.15	2.30	55	1.67	1.68	69	2.51	2.65	746	2.22	2.29
71–75	375	1.86	2.12	292	1.88	2.12	66	1.46	1.74	75	2.02	2.45	808	1.85	2.12
76–80	356	1.39	2.21	242	1.34	2.26	71	1.01	1.88	88	1.46	2.32	757	1.34	2.21
81–84	191	0.47	2.36	149	0.60	2.18	29	0.64	2.00	37	0.43	2.35	406	0.53	2.26
Total	1793	2.07	2.50	1441	2.02	2.41	292	1.58	2.00	346	2.12	2.66	3871	2.02	2.44

CEB = Children ever born
Total expt. = Total expected

TABLE 3.2
Children ever born by religion and age for Quebec and rest of Canada

Age at interview	Religion	Quebec	Non-Quebec
18–24	Catholic	.24 (322)	.29 (337)
	Protestant	.34 (14)	.34 (410)
25–29	Catholic	0.98 (230)	1.13 (252)
	Protestant	0.84 (10)	1.13 (315)
30–34	Catholic	1.49 (233)	1.75 (183)
	Protestant	1.51 (10)	1.72 (329)
35–39	Catholic	1.99 (214)	2.20 (194)
	Protestant	1.84 (9)	1.93 (284)
40–44	Catholic	2.18 (155)	2.76 (146)
	Protestant	2.71 (13)	2.57 (241)
45–49	Catholic	2.92 (149)	3.57 (132)
	Protestant	1.67 (6)	2.87 (231)
All ages	Catholic	1.42 (1302)	1.61 (1244)
	Protestant	1.45 (62)	1.60 (1810)

slightly higher fertility, in the younger cohorts below the age of 30 this is no longer the case. The table also shows that Catholics in Quebec have lower fertility than Catholics elsewhere in all the age cohorts. Even older Catholic women past the age of 40 had an average of half a child less than their counterparts in the rest of Canada.

A trend in the reporting of religion is that the number of those who give the response of 'no religion' has been increasing. For example, in the 1961 census, less than 1 per cent of the population said they had no religious preference. By 1981, however, the percentage of Canadians with no religious preference had climbed to 7 per cent (Mori 1987). In the CFS, about 8 per cent reported 'no religion.' Another 8.4 per cent reported religions other than Catholic or Protestant. The CFS figures are not strictly comparable with the census since they are based on women in the reproductive years 18–49, while the census included the whole population. While the 'other religion' group had slightly higher fertility than the Protestants and Catholics, those who reported 'no religion' had much lower fertility. The actual mean number of children as well as total expected mean number of children were lower in each age cohort in the 'no religion' category compared with other religious categories. For example, in the 30–34 age cohort, ever-married women who report 'no religion' expect only a mean of 1.59 children compared with a mean of 2.15 children expected by Catholics and 2.20 by Protestants. This is also true in the 25–29 cohort. It seems that while Catholic-Protestant differences have ceased to exist among the young women, reporting 'no religion' makes a significant difference. However, since those who report 'no religion' are more educated, one wonders whether their lower fertility should not be attributed to their educational attainment status. Table 3.3 shows that this is not the case. In every educational category, the 'no religion' group have lower fertility than the Catholics or the Protestants.

Table 3.3 shows that among the less educated the Protestants have actually higher fertility than Catholics, and even in the other educational categories Catholics have no higher fertility than Protestants. Among ever-married Catholic women with less than 9 years of schooling, the mean number of children was 2.88, compared with 3.41 among Protestant women with the same education. One should, however, be careful of the effect of age distributions of mothers and their mean number of children ever-born. Catholics on the whole have lower educational attainment and older women are likely to be less educated. For example, 28 per cent of Catholics are in the highest educational group, and 35 per cent of the Protestants. A more reliable figure for comparisons is total expected number of children. Catholic ever-married women with the least education, less than 9 years of schooling, expect a total of 2.99 children on an average, compared with 3.61 for Protestants. The pattern is reversed among the most educated. Those who had 14 or more years of schooling expected 2.34 births if they were Catholic, but only 2.19 births if Protestant. This implies that while the inverse relationship of education to fertility is strong both among the Catholics and Protestants, it is stronger among the Protestants. Among Protestant ever married women, the mean number of children born ranges from 1.66 for those with 14 or more years of education to 3.41 for those with less than 9 years of education. The range for the Catholics is only from 1.62 to 2.88 children. Similarly, the range for the total expected is less for the Catholics (from 2.99 to 2.34) compared with Protestants (from 3.61 to 2.19). One could suggest that the unifying influence of religion among Catholics still remains stronger than among Protestants.

Religion and Religiosity

Religiosity or religious commitment, as distinct from reporting a religion, has received much attention in the last two decades in terms of conceptualization and measurement (Roof 1979). In fertility surveys, however, a simple variable such as frequency of church attendance has been quite effective as an unambiguous and differentiating measure of religiosity. It has been found that while fertility differences by religion have

TABLE 3.3
Children ever born and total expected by religion and education

	Catholic			Protestant			No religion			Other			Total		
Educational achievement	No. of women	CEB	Total expt.	No. of women	CEB	Total expt.	No. of women	CEB	Total expt.	No. of women	CEB	Total expt.	No. of women	CEB	Total expt.
All women															
≤ Gr. 8	291	2.62	2.81	72	3.23	3.50	9	1.94	2.51	36	3.48	3.66	408	2.79	3.00
Gr. 9–11	624	1.99	2.51	428	2.18	2.50	68	1.53	2.35	85	2.02	2.53	1205	2.03	2.50
Gr. 12–13	907	1.23	2.20	725	1.45	2.19	159	0.90	1.80	183	1.54	2.54	1974	1.31	2.20
Gr. 14+	724	1.01	2.18	646	1.17	2.12	192	1.15	1.81	155	1.11	2.26	1717	1.10	2.13
Total	2546	1.51	2.34	1871	1.59	2.29	428	1.13	1.91	459	1.64	2.53	5304	1.52	2.30
Ever-married women															
≤ Gr. 8	257	2.88	2.99	67	3.41	3.61	7	2.39	2.63	33	3.74	3.89	364	3.04	3.18
Gr. 9–11	495	2.38	2.65	385	2.36	2.58	50	1.92	2.41	71	2.33	2.76	1000	2.35	2.62
Gr. 12–13	602	1.80	2.29	543	1.90	2.31	96	1.39	1.83	138	2.00	2.63	1378	1.83	2.30
Gr. 14+	441	1.62	2.34	449	1.66	2.19	140	1.55	1.93	105	1.62	2.26	1135	1.63	2.22
Total	1794	2.07	2.50	1443	2.02	2.40	294	1.58	2.00	346	2.12	2.67	3878	2.02	2.44

CEB = Children ever born
Total expt. = Total expected

narrowed, those by religiosity have not (Mosher and Hendershot 1984). While religion is a fairly stable variable, religiosity is not. Most people see themselves as belonging to a religious denomination, which seldom changes during their lifetime. In contrast, religiosity, as indicated by their religious practices, church attendance, and other measures of religious commitment can vary substantially from time to time. It is necessary to differentiate between religion and religiosity in assessing their effect on demographic behaviour. Though overall church attendance may have declined in recent decades, variations by religiosity continue to be significant. Women who are very religious are expected to be traditional in their views, and hence have a larger family-size norm and accept the role of motherhood more readily than less religious women. Religiosity was determined by the question, 'How often do you attend religious services? Would you say ... every week, every month, a few times a year, rarely or never.' For our analysis here these five categories were collapsed into three: weekly (every week), sometimes (every month and a few times a year), and rarely or never (rarely and never).

Children ever born and total expected are shown by religion and religiosity in table 3.4 and figure 3.2. It can be seen that fertility differences by religiosity are more important than by religion. The pattern is consistent across religious categories. Those who go to church regularly have higher fertility than those who go only sometimes or rarely or never. Among Catholics, those who go to church at least once a week expect a total fertility of 2.67 children, compared with 2.28 for those who go sometimes and 2.03 for those who rarely or never go to church. The same level of variation can be noticed among the Protestant and other religious groups. Distribution by church attendance varies significantly by religion. Among Catholics, 32 per cent report going to religious services weekly, in contrast to 18 per cent among the Protestants. The most religious are the 'other religions,' with a regular attendance of 47 per cent. Correspondingly, the proportion who report rarely or never going to church amounted to 26 per cent among the Catholics, but among the Protestants it was as high as 40 per cent. One interesting observation to be made is that, though the Catholics who are least religious had higher fertility than those of their Protestant counterparts, at the time of the survey, their total fertility expectations were lower 2.03 children compared with 2.20 children.

Education and fertility

As briefly observed earlier, one of the strongest inverse relationships is between education and fertility. In fertility research this is one of the

TABLE 3.4
Children ever born and total expected by religion and religiosity

	Catholic			Protestant			No religion			Other			Total		
	No. of women	CEB	Total expt.	No. of women	CEB	Total expt.	No. of women	CEB	Total expt.	No. of women	CEB	Total expt.	No. of women	CEB	Total expt.
Age at interview	**All women**														
Attend Religious Services:															
Weekly	818	1.95	2.67	329	1.99	2.54	4	1.31	2.00	215	1.99	2.87	1365	1.97	2.66
Sometimes	1071	1.39	2.28	786	1.49	2.27	35	1.07	1.88	150	1.28	2.35	2042	1.42	2.27
Rarely, never	658	1.67	2.03	753	1.52	2.20	387	1.13	1.91	94	1.38	2.11	1892	1.31	2.08
Total	2547	1.51	2.34	1869	1.59	2.29	426	1.13	1.91	458	1.63	2.52	5300	1.52	2.30
Age at interview	**Ever-married women**														
Attend Religious Services:															
Weekly	646	2.45	2.80	291	2.24	2.64	4	1.31	2.00	174	2.44	2.99	1116	2.39	2.79
Sometimes	757	1.89	2.41	589	1.92	2.32	22	1.68	2.03	100	1.86	2.42	1468	1.90	2.37
Rarely, never	392	1.79	2.19	561	2.00	2.38	266	1.57	2.00	71	1.66	2.19	1291	1.83	2.23
Total	1795	2.07	2.50	1442	2.02	2.40	292	1.58	2.00	345	2.11	2.66	3875	2.02	2.44

CEB = Children ever born
Total expt. = Total expected

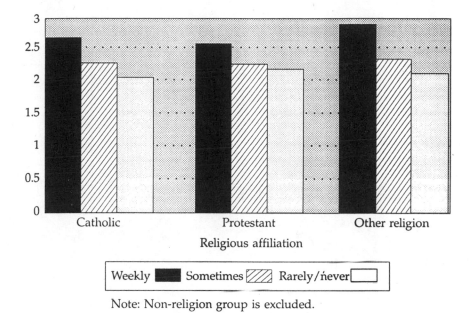

Note: Non-religion group is excluded.

Figure 3.2 Total expected number of children by religion and religiosity

universally proved relationships. Education delays entry into first marriage, increases the chances of women entering the labour force, and changes the attitudes towards gender roles, all of which have a negative effect on fertility. The data in table 3.5 and figure 3.3 confirm this association. The inverse relationship is evident in all the age cohorts. Among ever-married women of all ages, those with 14 or more years of schooling had only an average of 1.63 births, compared with 3.04 for those with less than 9 years. However, since older women are likely to be less educated, one needs to control for age. Yet even within age cohorts the relationship is consistent. In the age cohorts of 35 and above, who have by and large completed their fertility, there is a difference of almost one child between the extreme categories. For example, ever married women aged 45–49 with less than grade 9 education had an average of 3.69 children, compared with 2.61 for those who had 14 or more years of schooling. The corresponding figures for the 35–39 cohort were 2.72 and 1.84 respectively.

For women who are less than 35 years of age at the time of the survey, it is more appropriate to compare their total expected fertility rather than actual fertility. Women with less education are more likely to have started their childbearing earlier than the more educated, and by the same token

TABLE 3.5
Children ever born and total expected by age and education

All women

Age at interview	≤ Grade 8			Grade 9–11			Grade 12, 13			Grade 14+			Total		
	No. of women	CEB	Total expt.	No. of women	CEB	Total expt.	No. of women	CEB	Total expt.	No. of women	CEB	Total expt.	No. of women	CEB	Total expt.
18–24	41	0.83	1.84	239	0.73	2.28	617	0.22	2.19	426	0.09	2.38	1322	0.29	2.26
25–29	27	1.78	2.14	215	1.58	2.24	380	1.25	2.22	364	0.58	2.09	985	1.09	2.18
30–34	51	2.24	2.57	169	2.01	2.18	358	1.62	1.96	346	1.34	1.90	924	1.62	2.01
35–39	66	2.68	2.80	220	2.28	2.35	275	1.99	2.13	284	1.71	1.85	846	2.03	2.15
40–44	92	3.14	3.22	181	2.74	2.77	198	2.23	2.25	172	2.20	2.22	643	2.50	2.53
45–49	132	3.63	3.64	183	3.27	3.28	149	2.77	2.77	128	2.41	2.43	593	3.04	3.05
Total	408	2.79	3.00	1207	2.03	2.50	1977	1.31	2.20	1722	1.10	2.12	5314	1.52	2.30

Ever-married women

Age at interview	≤ Grade 8			Grade 9–11			Grade 12, 13			Grade 14+			Total		
	No. of women	CEB	Total expt.	No. of women	CEB	Total expt.	No. of women	CEB	Total expt.	No. of women	CEB	Total expt.	No. of women	CEB	Total expt.
18–24	16	1.42	2.09	103	1.31	2.60	164	0.65	2.27	79	0.29	2.41	362	0.79	2.39
25–29	19	1.99	2.21	178	1.75	2.29	301	1.47	2.32	239	0.86	2.31	736	1.35	2.31
30–34	48	2.28	2.62	155	2.11	2.27	320	1.78	2.08	282	1.63	2.08	805	1.82	2.15
35–39	64	2.72	2.84	211	2.31	2.37	261	2.10	2.21	259	1.84	1.96	795	2.12	2.22
40–44	87	3.26	3.35	175	2.82	2.85	194	2.27	2.29	160	2.36	2.37	617	2.59	2.62
45–49	130	3.69	3.70	180	3.32	3.33	140	2.95	2.95	119	2.61	2.63	569	3.17	3.17
Total	364	3.04	3.18	1001	2.35	2.62	1380	1.83	2.30	1138	1.63	2.22	3883	2.02	2.44

CEB = Children ever born
Total expt. = Total expected

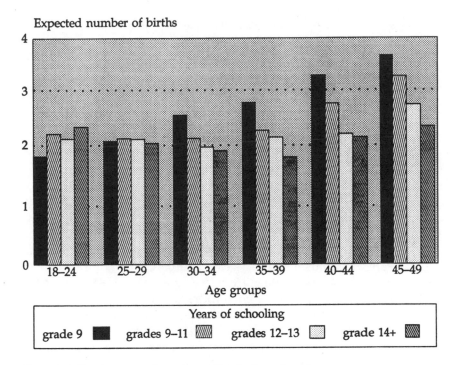

Figure 3.3 Total expected number of births by education

may end their childbearing earlier. Thus, the effect of censoring could be different for women in the different education categories. An important finding is that the differences in expected fertility by education are much less among the younger cohorts. Since very few women who are below 30 years of age have less than 9 years of schooling, this category is no more relevant for analysis. For the other three education categories there is no clear inverse pattern. For example, among ever-married women aged 25–29, the total expected number of children is practically the same at 2.3 irrespective of the educational category. Among the 18–24 group, there is a mild U-shaped relationship (the grades 12–13 dipping to 2.27), which is probably of no statistical significance. Their observed fertility at the time of the survey, which is largely incomplete of course, shows a strong inverse relationship. This must be due to the different entry ages into marriage. The important question is whether those who start childbearing early, such as the less educated, can contain their final family size to the expected number compared with the more educated who start their childbearing later in life. But at least their desires are no greater than those of the more educated, which is a departure from past trends.

Since education is likely to be highly correlated with age at first marriage and hence the age at first birth, it is worthwhile to examine the effect of education on final fertility in the context of these intermediate variables.[1] By age 35, Canadian women have by and large completed their fertility, as less than 5 per cent of births occur to women over the age of 35. If we limit ourselves to a study of women over 35 we can reduce some of the biases of incomplete observation. The higher the educational attainment the later the age at first marriage. Given that education delays marriage, and that in Canada most fertility takes place within marriage, we should expect to find a direct relationship between educational attainment and the start of childbearing. Table 3.6 presents the mean age at first birth by education for women aged 35–49 in the CFS. Those with some university education postpone their first birth substantially, by as much as 4 to 5 years, compared with those who had fewer than 9 years of schooling. Considering all ages 35–49, the mean age at first birth was 21.14 for women with 8 or fewer years of education, compared with 23.49 for women with 12–13 years of education and 25.55 for those with some university education. In the youngest cohort of 35–39 the range in the mean ages at first birth was even larger at 5 years, 20.55 to 25.71. Why this widening of the range with younger age? The proportions with lowest education decline drastically from 23 per cent at 45–49 to 8 per cent at 35–39; presumably, with most people moving into further educational years, those left behind with low education are the most difficult to modernize, the most reluctant to stay in school and learn more.

Because education is strongly related to age at first birth, which in turn influences final fertility, it will be instructive to see the relationship between age at first birth and fertility, controlling for education. Table 3.7 presents children ever born and additional expected by age at first birth within each educational category for women aged 35–49. Though the inverse relationship between age at first birth and cumulative fertility is evident in all the education categories and in each age cohort, certain differences can be noticed. The range of fertility by age at first birth is greater in the less educated groups compared with more-educated groups. For example, in the 40–44 cohort, women with less than 9 years of

1 Some of the analysis between education, age at first birth, and fertility is adapted from a more detailed report, T.R. Balakrishnan and C.F. Grindstaff, 'Early adulthood behaviour and later life-course paths'(1988).

TABLE 3.6

Mean age at first birth by educational attainment and present age – ever-married women

Education (no. of years of schooling)	Present age			
	35–39	40–44	45–49	35–49
≤ 8	20.55 (60)	20.63 (83)	21.76 (126)	21.14 (270)
9–11	21.78 (195)	22.18 (164)	22.50 (171)	22.14 (530)
12–13	23.74 (240)	23.58 (181)	22.94 (136)	23.49 (557)
≥ 14	25.71 (211)	24.86 (146)	26.15 (111)	25.55 (468)
Total	23.52 (706)	23.08 (574)	23.18 (544)	23.28 (1825)

Note: The numbers in parentheses denote the number of women.

education, if they had their first birth before the age of 20, had an average of 4.07 births, compared with 2.45 births if the first birth took place at 25 or after. The corresponding figures for the group with 12–13 years of education were 3.15 and 2.05 respectively. In other words, for the more educated, the timing of the first birth seems to be less consequential as far as final fertility is concerned. It is very likely that the more educated have small family size norms and, even though they had a first birth early, can control their timing more effectively and complete their child-bearing early or soon.

Place of residence and fertility

Place of residence in the Canadian Fertility Survey is given by the respondent. The question put to the respondent on the national telephone survey was 'Do you currently live in a city, a small town or on a farm?' Though the telephone numbers include the exchange codes that would enable us to identify the respondent residences by rural-urban classification fairly accurately, this elaborate procedure is not adopted here. The respondents' answers are considered sufficient to give an idea of the type of place. Probably those who live in a metropolitan area see themselves as living in a city. The frequencies in the responses in the CFS are close to the census distributions by metropolitan area, other urban, and rural categories: 64.5 per cent in a city, 28.7 per cent in a small town, and the remaining 6.7 per cent on a farm.

Within all age groups the relationship between place of residence and fertility is clear (table 3.8). Those who live on a farm have about 50 per cent higher fertility than those living in a city, with small-town residents

TABLE 3.7
Mean number of births and additional expected by age at first birth and education for the three age cohorts of women

Educa-tion/age at first birth	Present age								
	35–39			40–44			45–49		
	N	Mean births	Addi-tional expt.	N	Mean births	Addi-tional expt.	N	Mean births	Addi-tional expt.
≤ 8 years									
≤ 19	24	3.42	0.08	28	4.07	0.07	40	4.35	0.08
20–21	18	2.67	0.00	23	3.52	0.00	31	4.61	0.00
22–24	12	2.75	0.00	21	2.90	0.00	34	3.21	0.00
≥ 25	6	2.00	0.33	11	2.45	0.19	22	2.45	0.00
Childless	4	–	1.33	4	–	0.00	4	–	0.00
9–11 years									
≤ 19	58	2.83	0.00	41	4.05	0.00	41	5.10	0.00
20–21	49	2.57	0.02	44	3.28	0.14	40	3.53	0.05
22–24	42	2.43	0.00	41	2.63	0.00	51	3.04	0.00
≥ 25	46	2.05	0.10	37	2.00	0.00	39	2.31	0.00
Childless	16	–	0.31	11	–	0.00	9	–	0.00
12–13 years									
≤ 19	30	2.44	0.13	27	3.15	0.00	15	3.40	0.00
20–21	34	2.35	0.00	38	2.66	0.00	47	3.49	0.00
22–24	90	2.35	0.12	57	2.33	0.00	39	3.03	0.00
≥ 25	82	2.06	0.15	60	2.05	0.05	32	2.25	0.00
Childless	21	–	0.39	13	–	0.00	4	–	0.00
≥ 14 years									
≤ 19	9	2.67	0.11	11	3.36	0.00	4	3.75	0.00
20–21	19	2.84	0.16	17	2.65	0.00	7	2.43	0.00
22–24	53	2.38	0.02	54	2.79	0.00	43	3.30	0.00
≥ 25	131	2.10	0.06	63	2.24	0.03	58	2.34	0.00
Childless	48	–	0.36	14	–	0.00	8	–	0.00

falling in between. Among older ever-married women 45–49, the mean number of children for city residents was 2.81, compared with 3.67 for those in small towns and 4.15 for those living in farm areas. Among those aged 35–39 who would also have completed most of their fertility, the range was from 1.93 to 2.68 children.

TABLE 3.8
Children ever born and total expected by age and place of residence

	City			Small town			Farm/reserve			Total		
Age at interview	# of women	CEB	Total expt.	# of women	CEB	Total expt.	# of women	CEB	Total expt.	# of women	CEB	Total expt.
All women												
18–24	910	0.24	2.23	351	0.41	2.33	62	0.37	2.15	1322	0.29	2.26
25–29	642	0.86	2.03	272	1.47	2.35	70	1.72	2.78	985	1.09	2.18
30–34	598	1.43	1.87	267	1.97	2.26	57	1.91	2.26	922	1.62	2.01
35–39	508	1.82	1.96	266	2.25	2.34	72	2.61	2.73	846	2.02	2.15
40–44	388	2.29	2.32	203	2.77	2.80	52	3.01	3.01	643	2.50	2.53
45–49	380	2.65	2.66	167	3.63	3.64	43	4.15	4.15	591	3.04	3.05
Total	3426	1.30	2.15	1526	1.86	2.53	357	2.18	2.78	5309	1.52	2.30
Age at interview												
Ever-married women												
18–24	225	0.68	2.31	113	0.99	2.48	24	0.88	2.60	362	0.79	2.39
25–29	439	1.14	2.16	232	1.62	2.43	64	1.86	2.84	736	1.35	2.30
30–34	494	1.69	2.06	254	2.03	2.29	54	1.98	2.25	803	1.82	2.15
35–39	471	1.93	2.05	254	2.31	2.38	69	2.68	2.78	795	2.12	2.22
40–44	367	2.41	2.44	199	2.82	2.86	51	3.03	3.03	617	2.59	2.62
45–49	358	2.81	2.82	165	3.67	3.68	43	4.15	4.15	567	3.17	3.18
Total	2355	1.82	2.28	1218	2.27	2.64	305	2.50	2.92	3878	2.02	2.44

Nativity and fertility

Nativity is defined as foreign-born or native-born. Foreign-born women seem to have slightly lower fertility than native born women within each age cohort (table 3.9). Though foreign born women taken together have a mean of 1.67 children compared to 1.50 for native-born, this is a function of age composition. Foreign-born women are comparatively older. In the younger age groups, 18–24 and 25–29, foreign-born women had only 0.21 and 0.92 children respectively, compared with 0.30 and 1.11 children among the native-born. Similar trends can be noticed among the ever married younger women as well. Differences are less noticeable in the age range 30–44. In the oldest age cohort, foreign born women again have much lower fertility than the native-born, 2.48 children compared with 3.18 for native-born.

The foreign-born having the same or even lower fertility than the native-born is a phenomenon of post–Second World War fertility in Canada. Historically, around the turn of the century, the foreign-born women had higher fertility than the native born. The reversal of this trend is not hard to interpret. Immigration to Canada in the last few decades has been very selective. In the fifties and sixties, European immigrants brought with them the low-fertility norms and behaviours prevalent there. Though the trend has changed since 1970, to immigration from the Third World, recent immigrants, especially from Asia, who are selective of high socio-economic class and education have lower fertility than average. The question whether immigrants adjust to Canadian norms on arriving, so central to studies on ethnicity and immigration, did not arise. They started adjusting before they came to Canada and were selected thanks to the points system. To conclude whether nativity in itself has an effect on fertility one needs to control for some of these other correlates of fertility.

Ethnicity and fertility

The relationship between ethnic origin and fertility has been extensively studied in the past in Canada (Henripin 1972; Kalbach and McVey 1979; Balakrishnan et al. 1979). Analysing 1971 census data, Balakrishnan et al. conclude that among the younger women, ethnic differences in fertility are less noticeable. The reason may be, as others have stated, that with increasing modernization and urbanization, the ethnic-origin concept has little behavioural significance (Beaujot 1975; Sly 1970; Goldscheider and Uhlenberg 1969). However, as ethnicity continues to be a

TABLE 3.9
Children ever born and total expected by age and nativity

	Native-born			Foreign-born			Total		
	No. of women	CEB	Total expt.	No. of women	CEB	Total expt.	No. of women	CEB	Total expt.
Age at interview	All women								
18–24	1213	0.30	2.26	109	0.21	2.23	1322	0.29	2.26
25–29	884	1.11	2.20	102	0.92	1.96	985	1.09	2.18
30–34	789	1.62	1.99	135	1.60	2.12	924	1.62	2.01
35–39	684	2.03	2.15	163	2.00	2.14	847	2.03	2.15
40–44	532	2.49	2.52	112	2.53	2.58	643	2.50	2.53
45–49	476	3.18	3.19	117	2.48	2.50	593	3.04	3.05
Total	4576	1.50	2.31	739	1.67	2.25	5315	1.52	2.30
Age at interview	Ever-married women								
18–24	326	0.82	2.39	36	0.54	2.34	362	0.79	2.39
25–29	658	1.37	2.32	78	1.18	2.20	736	1.35	2.31
30–34	678	1.84	2.15	127	1.71	2.16	805	1.82	2.15
35–39	640	2.13	2.23	155	2.07	2.20	795	2.12	2.22
40–44	506	2.60	2.63	111	2.55	2.60	617	2.59	2.62
45–49	456	3.31	3.32	113	2.58	2.60	569	3.17	3.17
Total	3265	2.02	2.46	619	1.97	2.34	3884	2.02	2.44

variable of considerable interest in Canadian social science research, it was decided in this study to examine its relevance to fertility behaviour using the CFS data. Two problems arise in the measurement and use of ethnic data in the CFS. The question asked was 'To what ethnic or cultural group did you or your male ancestor belong on first coming to North America?' Thus, it measures ancestry only on the male side, as in the earlier Canadian censuses. Further, the small sample size in many ethnic-origin categories makes the CFS unsuitable for detailed analysis. Therefore, broad groupings had to be used. As a matter of fact, for most of the analysis we had to settle with British, French, and Other.

Table 3.10 presents the mean number of children ever born by broad ethnic categories. Subject to high sampling variability arising from a small sample size, one can make some cautious conclusions. Among the youngest cohort, 18–29, there is very little variation in fertility by ethnicity. Those with ethnic origins in Eastern or Southern Europe or Asia have actually lower fertility than the British or French charter groups or Western Europeans. In the next age group, 30–39, there is also no

TABLE 3.10
Mean number of children ever born by ethnic origin age at interview

Ethnic origin	Age at interview		
	18–29	30–39	40–49
British	.77 (753)	1.80 (727)	2.64 (440)
French	.73 (531)	1.70 (489)	2.58 (261)
German	.70 (152)	1.92 (114)	2.93 (87)
Western Europe	.73 (127)	1.96 (99)	2.79 (62)
Eastern Europe	.49 (158)	1.73 (125)	2.31 (64)
Southern Europe	.56 (136)	1.94 (68)	2.49 (43)
Asian	.45 (65)	1.64 (59)	3.14 (28)
Native Indian	1.08 (39)	2.45 (22)	3.63 (8)
Other	.66 (47)	1.74 (38)	2.45 (22)

evidence that those whose ethnic origin is Eastern Europe or Asia have any higher fertility than the lowest-fertility group, namely the French. This result is to some extent due to the fact that these people are more likely to be immigrants who are selective of low fertility. Native Indians have the highest fertility, but their numbers are too small for reliability. Since the CFS did not cover Yukon and the Northwest Territories, where a large portion of the native peoples live, it is important to keep in mind that the figures are only representative of native peoples off reserves in the ten provinces.

Because the sample sizes were too small and large differences by ethnicity were not found in table 3.10, the categories were regrouped into just three categories – British, French, and Other – for more detailed analysis. Table 3.11 shows the mean number of children and total expected for each of the age cohorts. Though the French and Other seem to have a lower fertility than the British, on closer analysis it becomes apparent that this is largely a function of age distribution. Within each age group, there is no significant difference in actual or expected fertility. Clearly, ethnic differences in fertility are no longer important in Canada.

Work status and fertility[2]

One of the most significant changes in women's lives in the last two decades in Canada is their increasing participation in the labour force. The impact of this change on marriage and fertility has been extensively

2 This section on work status and fertility is adapted from Balakrishnan and Grindstaff 1988.

TABLE 3.11
Children ever born and total expected by age and ethnicity

All women

Age at interview	British			French			Other			Total		
	No. of women	CEB	Total expt.	No. of women	CEB	Total expt.	No. of women	CEB	Total expt.	No. of women	CEB	Total expt.
18–24	418	0.31	2.22	290	0.29	2.30	610	0.28	2.26	1322	0.29	2.26
25–29	333	1.15	2.17	230	1.05	2.16	422	1.06	2.20	985	1.09	2.18
30–34	370	1.66	2.01	226	1.49	1.83	328	1.66	2.13	924	1.62	2.01
35–39	313	1.94	2.07	193	1.95	2.06	342	2.15	2.27	847	2.03	2.15
40–44	271	2.51	2.52	145	2.29	2.34	227	2.62	2.66	643	2.50	2.53
45–49	229	2.97	2.97	139	3.09	3.11	225	3.08	3.09	593	3.04	3.05
Total	1935	1.60	2.28	1227	1.47	2.24	2153	1.48	2.36	5315	1.52	2.30

Ever-married women

Age at interview	British			French			Other			Total		
	No. of women	CEB	Total expt.	No. of women	CEB	Total expt.	No. of women	CEB	Total expt.	No. of women	CEB	Total expt.
18–24	115	0.87	2.31	76	0.78	2.55	171	0.75	2.36	362	0.79	2.39
25–29	259	1.41	2.29	162	1.36	2.29	316	1.30	2.33	736	1.35	2.31
30–34	330	1.82	2.14	183	1.79	2.03	292	1.84	2.24	805	1.82	2.15
35–39	292	2.04	2.15	182	2.04	2.13	322	2.23	2.35	795	2.12	2.22
40–44	262	2.59	2.61	130	2.50	2.55	224	2.64	2.68	617	2.59	2.62
45–49	223	3.05	3.06	130	2.30	3.31	216	3.21	3.22	569	3.17	3.17
Total	1481	2.04	2.40	863	2.01	2.42	1540	2.00	2.50	3884	2.02	2.44

researched (Weller 1977; Oppenheimer 1970; Balakrishnan et al. 1979). In the developed industrialized societies, such as Canada and the United States, these studies show an inverse relationship between female employment and fertility. Explanations for this result have centered around arguments about the basic incompatibility between the roles of motherhood and child care and work outside the home (McDaniel 1988). The association itself is more complex, because work is correlated with other factors, such as education and age at first marriage, that also affect fertility levels, thus creating the possibility of a spurious relationship.

In the CFS, much data were collected on the work history of women, enabling one to look at this relationship more closely. For our analysis here, however, we will restrict ourselves to two variables that could be constructed from the work history data, namely current work status and past work experience. Current work status indicates whether the woman was working at the time of the survey. Though it is measured only at one point of time, it is often found to be a powerful variable in differentiating fertility behaviour. This is because present work is related not only to other variables such as education, but also to past work, and denotes a commitment, all of which influence fertility behaviour. Table 3.12 presents data on children ever born by present work status. Women working at the time of the survey had fewer births than those who were not working, 1.33 children on an average compared to 1.75 children. The pattern persists within each of the three broad age groups. Among women over the age of 30, the difference is more than half a child. For example, in the cohort 30–39, those who were working at the time of the survey had only 1.52 children, compared with 2.21 for those who were not working. The corresponding figures were 2.52 and 3.07 for the 40–49 cohort. Of course the data do not tell us whether it is the number of children that prevents women from working or being in the labour force that reduces their fertility. To determine this would require a sequential analysis of the events involved. But the fact remains that work status is clearly related to fertility. Though the relevant table is not presented here, our analysis showed that the association persists even when other factors such as religion, religiosity, and place of residence are controlled.

Since work and fertility are so intertwined, an investigation of their relationship may become simpler if we restrict ourselves to those women who have largely completed their fertility, namely those over the age of 35. For these women, a second variable, past work experience, was created. It has three categories: continuous work, interrupted work, and never worked. Continuous work means that once a woman started to

TABLE 3.12
Children ever born and total expected by age and work status

Age at interview	Currently not working			Currently working		
	Number of women	CEB	Total expected	Number of Women	CEB	Total expected
18–29	1119	0.83	2.32	1189	.45	2.13
30–39	746	2.21	2.44	1025	1.52	1.81
40–49	525	3.07	3.09	711	2.52	2.55
All women	2390	1.75	2.53	2925	1.33	2.12
Age at interview	Ever-married woman					
18–29	534	1.50	2.44	564	.85	2.24
30–39	708	2.29	2.50	891	1.71	1.94
40–49	515	3.12	3.14	670	2.67	2.69
All ever-married women	1757	2.29	2.67	2125	1.78	2.26

work for the first time she had not stopped and was working at the time of the survey. Where the woman had stopped for less than six months, this stop was ignored and she was assumed to have worked continuously. Thus, it can include women who have stopped work for childbearing, but have returned to the labour force after an interruption of no more than six months. The interrupted-work category includes women who have worked with one or more stops of at least six months each or longer. They may or may not be working at the time of the survey. The third category covers women who have never worked.

Children ever born to women aged 35–49 in the Canadian Fertility Survey, by their work status and education, are presented in table 3.13. Women working at the time of the survey had fewer births than those who were not working, 2.36 children on an average compared with 2.87 children. These differences by current work status persist even when controlled for education. Those women with the least education, less than 12 years of schooling, had 2.74 children if they are in labour force, as against 3.21 if not working. Similarly, those who had some university education had only 2.04 births if they were working, in contrast to 2.43 if not working.

There is also a parallel association between lifetime work status and fertility. Women who have never worked had the highest fertility, 3.40 children, compared with those who have worked continuously until the

TABLE 3.13

Children ever born by current and past work status and education for ever-married women aged 35–49

Education	Mean number of children ever born		
	Current work status		
	Yes	No	
≤ 11 years	2.74 (429)	3.21 (418)	
12–13 years	2.24 (385)	2.55 (211)	
≥ 14 years	2.04 (368)	2.43 (169)	
Total	2.36 (1182)	2.87 (798)	
	Lifetime work status		
	Never worked	Interrupted work	Continuous work
≤ 11 years	3.73 (112)	2.85 (511)	2.84 (221)
12–13 years	2.66 (34)	2.41 (403)	2.14 (159)
≥ 14 years	2.82 (21)	2.26 (367)	1.83 (149)
Total	3.40 (167)	2.55 (1281)	2.34 (529)

Note: The numbers in parentheses denote the number of women.

time of the survey, 2.34 children on average. Those who have worked with one or more stops had 2.55 children. These differences are in the expected direction. Again, the patterns persist when controlling for education. Thus, among women with the highest education, 14 or more years of schooling, those who have never worked had 2.82 births, while those who have worked continuously had only 1.83, a full birth less.

In the investigation of the relationship between lifetime work status and fertility, it is important to consider age at the first work experience. Thus, women who have continuously worked might have begun early in life before starting their childbearing and kept on working throughout their life, or might have started to work after completing their fertility. These two groups of women can be substantially different, and grouping them together as having continuously worked can mask these differences. The effect of age at first work on fertility is examined in table 3.14 for all ever married women in the Canadian Fertility Survey who have ever worked. Among those who have continuously worked without interruption, there is a noticeable association between age at first work and fertility. When all the women aged 35–49 are considered, which provides a reasonable sample size, it can be noticed that where women start work when they are 20–22 years of age and work continuously, the family size is lowest. They have on an average only 1.69 children

TABLE 3.14
Births to ever-married women who have worked by work experience and age at first work

	Continuous work				Interrupted work			
Age at first work	N	Mean births	Addi-tional expt.	Total expt.	N	Mean births	Addi-tional expt.	Total expt.
	35–39							
≤ 17	38	1.55	0.08	1.63	156	2.14	0.08	2.22
18–19	42	1.51	0.06	1.57	162	2.29	0.14	2.43
20–22	53	1.48	0.23	1.71	122	2.17	0.05	2.22
23–29	54	1.95	0.13	2.08	51	2.13	0.20	2.33
≥ 30	37	2.44	0.00	2.44	18	2.12	0.00	2.12
	40–44							
≤ 17	20	2.01	0.00	2.01	180	2.71	0.01	2.72
18–19	23	2.27	0.09	2.36	95	2.53	0.00	2.53
20–22	17	1.65	0.05	1.70	73	2.10	0.03	2.13
23–29	38	2.71	0.08	2.79	28	2.34	0.10	2.44
≥ 30	65	2.88	0.00	2.88	25	3.15	0.00	3.15
	45–49							
≤ 17	25	2.61	0.06	2.67	171	2.86	0.00	2.86
18–19	10	3.29	0.00	3.29	61	3.40	0.00	3.40
20–22	14	2.50	0.00	2.50	65	2.78	0.00	2.78
23–29	15	2.84	0.00	2.84	29	3.12	0.00	3.12
≥ 30	77	3.37	0.02	3.39	31	3.38	0.00	3.38
	35–49							
≤ 17	82	1.99	0.05	2.04	508	2.59	0.02	2.61
18–19	75	1.97	0.06	2.03	318	2.58	0.07	2.65
20–22	84	1.69	0.14	1.83	259	2.30	0.03	2.33
23–29	107	2.34	0.10	2.44	109	2.45	0.12	2.57
≥ 30	179	3.00	0.01	3.01	74	3.00	0.00	3.00

at the time of the survey and expect to have a completed family size of only 1.83 births. Those who started to work even earlier and worked uninterruptedly had also less than two births, though the actual number was somewhat higher, at 1.98 births. The slightly higher fertility among them is probably due to the fact that these women who start work very early may also be less educated, have higher fertility desires and practise poor family planning methods. Women who begin work later in life have much higher fertility even though they have worked without interruption. Those who started to work in the age range 23–29 had an average of 2.34 births, and those who started after the age of 30, a mean of 3.00 children. It is clear that in the case of these latter women, their entrance into the labour force is after they have substantially completed their childbearing. The patterns observed for the group as a whole also hold in the three age cohorts, but the small sample sizes make them somewhat unstable. Still, small as the differences are, the pattern is firm for all four groups: U-shaped with the bottom at 20–22, those joining earlier combine the few children they had with work; those joining later do so after having had more births.

Among women who have worked with stops, the association between age at first work and fertility is unclear except where the age at first work is very late, after the age of 30. For the youngest age cohort, 35–39, there is practically no relationship between age at first work and fertility if there have been stops. Obviously, the lack of association has to do with the two-way relationship between work stops and having births, something that cannot be unravelled without a sequential study of the timing of events.

The influence of the timing of first work on fertility is further analysed by examining the fertility before and after the start of first work for those ever-married women 35–49 years old in the CFS sample who have continuously worked (table 3.15). Those who started work before the age of 22 had almost all their births after the start of work and had a low fertility of less than two births. Early entrance into the labour force and continuous commitment to work seem to depress fertility. In comparison, women who started work after the age of 30 not only had all their births before starting to work, but had a higher fertility of 2.91 births before work. They had an average of only 0.09 births after beginning to work. One may conclude that those women who are more committed to a larger family are likely to wait until their childbearing is completed before entering the labour force. However, though our sample is restricted to women 35–49 years of age only, we should be aware of the effect of age differences within this range on fertility. Though all women have by and large completed their fertility by age 30, those in the group who started to work after age 30 are likely to have been drawn more from the older cohort of 45–49, a group who had a large part of their fertility during the baby-boom years – a period of high-fertility norms and behaviour. The oldest, aged 49 in 1984, were born in 1935, joined motherhood at, say, 20 in 1955, and had 10 years of fertility in the most reproductive years until the end of the baby boom in 1966. The somewhat younger women aged 40 in 1984 were born in 1944 and joined motherhood at, say, 20 in 1964, right on the edge of the baby bust.

TABLE 3.15
Mean number of births before and after start of first work by women 35–49 who have continuously worked

Age at first work	Number of women	Mean number of births before first work	Mean number of births after start of first work	Total number of births
≤ 17	82	0.01	1.98	1.99
18–19	75	0.11	1.86	1.97
20–22	84	0.10	1.59	1.69
23–29	107	1.58	0.76	2.34
30 or later	179	2.91	0.09	3.00

Thus, we say that only the ones aged 45–49 were exposed to the influence of the norms of the baby boom.

Combinational analysis

The purpose of the combinational analysis applied in this section is to identify the combination of characteristics that maximize variation in fertility for any age cohort of women. The approach is no more than a parsimonious use of extensive cross-tabulations (see T.R. Balakrishnan et al. 1979 for a similar application to 1971 Canadian census data). It is an analysis of data using the program AID (Automatic Interaction Detector) developed by the University of Michigan. The program starts with the whole sample and successively splits into two groups at a time through a stepwise application of one-way analysis of variance techniques. The splits are so made as to maximize the sum of squares explained by the two groups. For our analysis, we have selected four independent variables found to be most highly related to fertility: work status, education, place of residence, and religiosity. For each age cohort, AID provides groups of 50 or more cases that can be ordered in terms of their fertility rates. The branching process also identifies the sequential importance of the variables.

Tables 3.16, 3.17, and 3.18 present, for the three broad age cohorts, the mean number of children for the various groups of women with the combination of characteristics indicated in the tables. For the 18–29 age cohort the range in the average number of children is from 0.53 for women working at the time of the survey who had 14 or more years of schooling to 1.87 for women who were not currently working, had less than or equal to 13 years of education, and lived in a small town or on a farm. For this age cohort, religiosity as measured by church

TABLE 3.16

Mean number of children per ever-married women aged 18–29 by selected combinations of characteristics

Combination of characteristics				No. of women	Mean no. of children
Work status	Education	Place of residence	Religiosity		
Working	14+ yrs	All	All	220	0.53
Working	12–13 yrs	All	All	299	0.87
Not currently working	14+ yrs	All	All	148	1.01
Working	≤ 11 years	All	All	131	1.37
Not currently working	≤ 13 years	Large city	All	224	1.52
Not currently working	≤ 13 years	Small town or farm	All	231	1.87

attendance was not a significant factor on fertility and place of residence was of minor importance. The most important factors were work status and education. Figure 3.4 shows the actual splitting process of the data presented in table 3.16.

Table 3.17 and figure 3.5 present the data for the middle age cohort, 30–39. For this group also the first split takes place on work status, though the remaining branching process does not have a set pattern. The mean number of children was lowest at 1.03 for women who were working at the time of the survey, had 14 or more years of education, lived in a large city, and rarely or never went to church. In contrast, women who were not currently working though they might or might not have worked in the past, lived in a small town or on a farm, and went to church weekly had a mean number of 2.71 children. The other groups of women fell in between these two extremes in their fertility. While in the younger cohort only work and education seem to be important, for the 30–39 cohort all the four variables seem to be relevant.

Table 3.18 and figure 3.6 present the data for the last cohort, aged 40–49. For this group, the first split takes place on education, and work status at the time of the survey seems to be the least relevant. Women with 14 or more years of schooling who went to church sometimes, rarely, or never had an average of 2.25 children. At the other extreme, women who had less than or equal to 11 years of education, lived in a small town, or on a farm and went to church regularly had an average

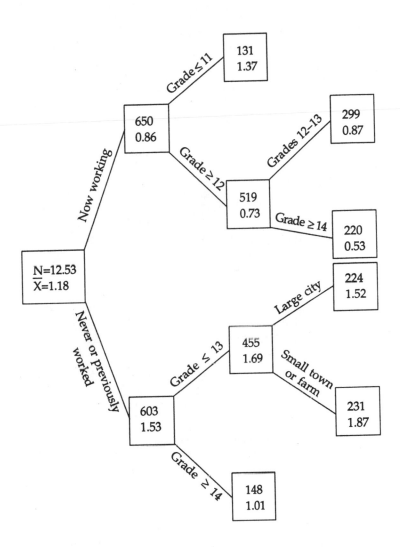

Figure 3.4 Stepwise split of 18–29 age cohort of ever-married women on selected characteristics, showing number of women and children ever born

TABLE 3.17
Mean number of children per ever-married women aged 30–39 by selected combinations of characteristics

	Combination of characteristics			No. of women	Mean no. of children
Work status	Education	Place of residence	Religiosity		
Working	14+ yrs	Large city	Rarely or never	108	1.03
Working	14+ yrs	Small town or farm	Sometimes, rarely, or never	84	1.50
Working	≤ 13 yrs	Large city	Rarely or never	133	1.52
Working	≥ 12 yrs	Large city	Weekly or sometimes	283	1.62
Working	≤ 13 yrs	Small town or farm	Sometimes, rarely, or never	173	1.68
Working	≤ 11 yrs	Large city	Weekly or sometimes	82	1.88
Not currently working	14+ yrs	All	Sometimes, rarely, or never	136	1.93
Not currently working	≤ 13 yrs	All	Sometimes, rarely, or never	194	2.00
Not currently working	≤ 11 yrs	Large city	Sometimes, rarely, or never	109	2.28
Working	All	Small town or farm	Weekly	119	2.32
Not currently working	All	Large city	Weekly	129	2.40
Not currently working	≤ 11 yrs	Small town of farm	Sometimes, rarely, or never	84	2.70
Not currently working	All	Small town or farm	Weekly	123	2.71

of 3.86 children. For this oldest cohort, work status does not seem to be important, while the other three factors are relevant in their fertility behaviour.

Multivariate analysis

We found that fertility differentials are to be found by many factors such as religion, education, religiosity, place of residence, province of resi-

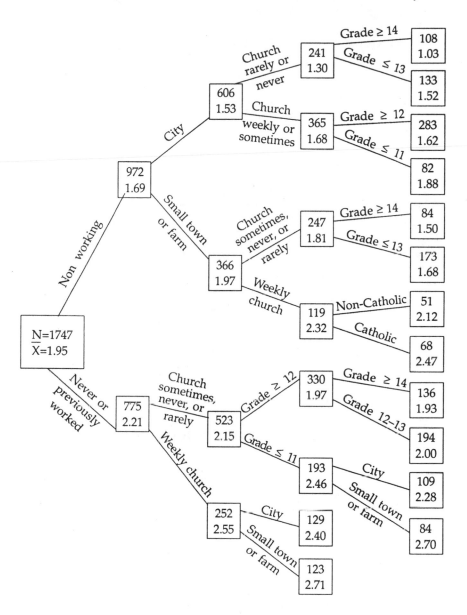

Figure 3.5 Stepwise split of 30–39 age cohort of ever-married women on selected characteristics, showing number of women and children ever born

TABLE 3.18
Mean number of children per ever-married women aged 40–49 by selected combinations of characteristics

	Combination of characteristics			No. of women	Mean no. of children
Work status	Education	Place of residence	Religiosity		
All	14+ yrs	All	Sometimes, rarely, or never	164	2.25
All	≤ 13 yrs	All	Sometimes, rarely, or never	203	2.38
All	≥ 12 yrs	Large city	Weekly	117	2.59
Working	≤ 11 yrs	Large city	All	149	2.59
Not currently working	≤ 11 yrs	Large city	All	139	2.89
All	≥ 12 yrs	Small town or farm	Weekly	71	3.03
All	≤ 11 yrs	Small town or farm	Sometimes, rarely, or never	128	3.37
All	≤ 11 yrs	Small town or farm	Weekly	85	3.86

dence, ethnicity, labour-force participation, and nativity. Interpretations of these differences are difficult because many of these factors are interrelated. Thus ethnic differences in fertility may be due to other factors such as education, religious affiliation, and religiosity rather than just ethnicity itself. To assess the relative importance of each of the factors on fertility we will employ a technique called Multiple Classification Analysis (MCA). Basically, this is an extension of Multiple Regression Analysis to situations where the independent variables can be either subclasses or discontinuous variables (Sonquist 1970). The technique provides adjusted mean values on the dependent variable for each subclass of an independent variable after controlling for all other independent variables. In addition, as in regression analysis, it provides standardized beta coefficients and multiple correlation coefficients.

Table 3.19 presents the results of the MCA performed on the CFS data on fertility and the covariates. Since age at first marriage is an important demographic variable affecting fertility we have introduced it as a covariate to be controlled in addition to the other socio-economic factors. The table provides, for each age cohort, the unadjusted mean number

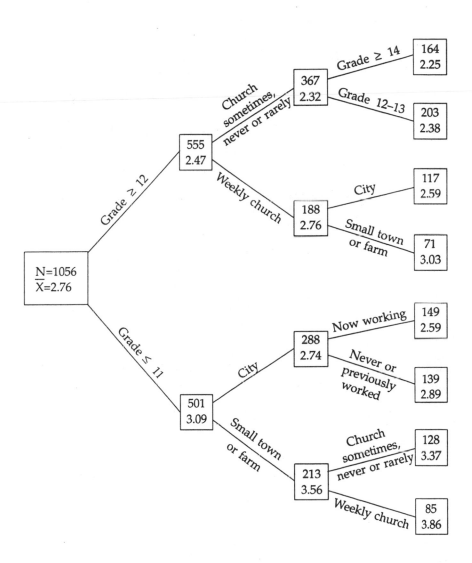

Figure 3.6 Stepwise split of 40–49 age cohort of ever-married women on selected characteristics, showing number of women and children ever born

TABLE 3.19

Multiple classification analysis of children ever born for ever-married women on selected socio-economic variables

| | Age at interview | | | | | |
| | 18–29 | | 30–39 | | 40–49 | |
	No. of women	Adjusted† deviation from mean	No. of women	Adjusted† deviation from mean	No. of women	Adjusted† deviation from mean
Mean no. of children	1092	1.16	1580	1.97	1174	2.87
Place of residence						
City	660	−.10	956	−.11	719	−.19
Small town	344	.13	502	.11	363	.24
Farm	88	.24	122	.36	93	.56
beta		.12*		.13*		.15*
Religion						
Catholic	511	−.01	723	.06	549	.11
Protestant	379	.03	576	−.06	475	−.14
Other religion	111	.05	143	.18	89	.23
No religion	91	−.14	138	−.27	61	−.17
beta		.05		.10*		.08*
Religiosity						
Weekly	253	.08	446	.22	409	.27
Sometimes	455	−.01	615	−.01	388	−.18
Rarely, never	384	−.04	520	−.18	377	−.11
beta		.05		.14*		.12*
Ethnicity						
British	374	.02	610	−.03	485	.02
French	237	.05	364	−.09	258	−.24
Other	481	−.03	606	.08	432	.11
beta		.03		.06*		.08*
Education						
≤ 8 years	35	.30	111	.20	215	.41
9–11 years	279	.21	360	.10	352	.15
12–13 years	461	−.01	575	−.07	330	−.33
14+years	317	−.21	533	−.03	277	−.12
beta		.16*		.08*		.16*

TABLE 3.19 — *continued*

| | Age at interview | | | | | |
| | 18–29 | | 30–39 | | 40–49 | |
	No. of women	Adjusted† deviation from mean	No. of women	Adjusted† deviation from mean	No. of women	Adjusted† deviation from mean
Work status						
Never worked	116	.00	108	.40	111	.59
Worked with stops	433	.38	947	.15	761	−.05
Always worked	542	−.31	525	−.36	303	−.09
beta		.32*		.23*		.11*
Nativity						
Native-born	981	.01	1305	.00	955	.03
Foreign-born	111	−.08	275	.00	219	−.15
beta		.03		.00		.04*
R squared		29.6%		23.2%		21.0%

† Adjusted for other factors and age at first marriage
* Significant at 5 per cent

of children by categories of the independent variables and means adjusted for all the other independent variables including age at first marriage. Comparisons will be made primarily across age cohorts for each independent variable.

Education is one of the most important variables determining fertility in all the age cohorts, with beta values that are significant at the .05 level. The strength of the inverse relationship between education and fertility is evident even when other factors are controlled. Among young women below 30 years of age, education makes more of a difference than among the older women. Thus, in the age cohort 18–29 women who had less than 9 years of schooling had an average of 1.46 (1.16 + 0.30) children compared to only 0.95 (1.16 − 0.21) children among those who had some university education, even when all the other socioeconomic factors as well as age at first marriage were controlled. The differences were smaller in the cohorts over 30 years of age. For example, among the age cohort 30–39, the clear inverse relationship that existed before controls was no longer present when other variables were controlled. The adjusted means were 2.17, 2.07, 1.90, and 1.94 births in the four education categories.

Equally important as education is the labour-force participation of women. Though the variable used here leaves a lot to be desired, it is quite differentiating as far as fertility is concerned. Except in the youngest age group, 18–29, there is a strong negative relationship of work status to fertility. Those who have always worked had the lowest fertility even when all the factors, such as education, place of residence, and age at first marriage, are controlled. For example, in the 30–39 age cohort, even after controlling for all other factors, those who had always worked had only 1.61 children, compared with 2.12 children among those who have worked with interruptions and 2.37 children among those who have never worked. In the oldest age cohort, 40–49, the range was from 3.46 children to 2.78 children. In the youngest age group (18–29) also, the women who have always worked had the lowest fertility, 0.85 children. However, those who have worked with stops had the highest fertility, 1.54 births, obviously because those who stopped may have done so specifically because they became pregnant (hence inflating the fertility rates). Stopping work for childbearing is more likely to occur among the younger women than among the old.

The other variable that is significantly related to fertility across all the age cohorts is place of residence. Urban women have a smaller family size compared to small-town or farm women. The difference between city and farm residence is of the order of 0.75 children in the 40–49 age cohort, 0.47 in the 30–39 cohort, and 0.34 in the 18–29 age cohort.

Among the rest of the variables considered here, religiosity is probably the most important. When we consider women 30 or older, the more religious have more children, even when other factors are controlled. Those who go to church weekly have an average of 0.40 and 0.38 births more than those who rarely or never go to church among women aged 30–39 and 40–49 respectively. However, for the youngest cohort, 18–29 years of age, religiosity seems to be less important (0.12 births) and not statistically significant.

When other factors are controlled, such factors as religion, ethnicity and nativity lose much of their impact on fertility.

Table 3.20 presents the multiple classification analysis performed on the total expected number of children. Since the actual number is part of the total expected, the patterns are not very different from those found in table 3.19. This is especially true for women aged 30 or over, as children already born are a larger part of the total expected. For the youngest cohort, since most of their fertility is still to occur, we are less

TABLE 3.20

Multiple classification analysis of total expected number of children for ever-married women on selected socio-economic variables

	Age at interview					
	18–29		30–39		40–49	
	No. of women	Adjusted† deviation from mean	No. of women	Adjusted† deviation from mean	No. of women	Adjusted† deviation from mean
Mean expected no. of children	1090	2.33	1574	2.18	1174	2.88
Place of residence						
City	660	−.09	953	−.09	720	−.19
Small town	343	.07	502	.08	361	.24
Farm	87	.40	119	.34	93	.54
beta		.14*		.11*		.15*
Religion						
Catholic	510	.01	719	.05	547	.10
Protestant	380	−.02	577	−.03	476	−.14
Other religion	110	.07	141	.22	89	.26
No religion	90	−.04	137	−.35	61	−.18
beta		.03		.12*		.08
Religiosity						
Weekly	251	.32	439	.19	408	.27
Sometimes	455	−.03	615	.00	388	−.17
Rarely, never	385	−.18	520	−.16	377	−.12
beta		.19*		.12*		.12*
Ethnicity						
British	373	−.04	609	−.03	485	.02
French	237	.03	365	−.13	256	−.24
Other	480	.02	600	.11	433	.11
beta		.03		.08*		.08*
Education						
< 8 years	35	−.31	110	.25	214	.42
9–11 years	279	.03	358	.02	351	.15
12–13 years	462	−.05	577	−.07	331	−.33
14+ years	317	.08	529	−.00	277	−.12
beta		.08		.07*		.16*

TABLE 3.20 — *continued*

	Age at interview					
	18–29		30–39		40–49	
	No. of women	Adjusted† deviation from mean	No. of women	Adjusted† deviation from mean	No. of women	Adjusted† deviation from mean
Work status						
Never worked	117	−.04	106	.42	109	.61
Worked with stops	433	.09	945	.11	762	−.06
Always worked	540	−.06	522	−.28	303	−.08
beta		.08*		.20*		.12*
Nativity						
Native-born	979	.01	1302	.00	954	.03
Foreign-born	112	−.12	272	.02	219	−.15
beta		.04		.01		.04*
R squared		8.7%		16.0%		21.0%

† Adjusted for other factors and age at first marriage
* Significant at 5 per cent

able to predict expected fertility. A noticeable point is that work status has little relationship to final expected fertility.

It is worth noting that while we can explain a greater variance in children ever born for the younger cohorts compared to the older age cohorts, the opposite is true in the case of total expected fertility. For example, the variance explained in children ever born was 29.6 per cent, 23.2 per cent, and 21.0 per cent respectively in the age cohorts 18–29, 30–39, and 40–49. The corresponding figures were 8.7 per cent, 16.0 per cent, and 21.0 per cent for total expected fertility.

Summary and conclusions

The study of fertility by sociocultural factors shows that the relative importance of these factors has changed in the last two decades. Religion seems to make much less difference in reproductive behaviour. The remarkable convergence of Catholic and Protestant fertility behaviour is not restricted to Quebec. Religiosity, however, continues to be an important determinant of fertility. In general, the traditional ascribed have lost their impact on childbearing. What emerges as more significant are such achieved factors as education, place of residence, and work. The overwhelming importance of labour-force participation and its complex interrelationship with fertility is underscored in our analysis. As both the educational attainment and labour-force participation of women are increasing in Canada, we can expect their impact on decreasing fertility to continue unless other ameliorating factors come into play. To the extent that education and work also profoundly influence values and norms about childbearing, attitudes towards sex roles, and decision-making in every area, the future of fertility in Canada is likely to be in a state of considerable uncertainty.

4

Economic factors in fertility

In the previous chapter we slipped from sociocultural factors, without quite noticing it, into the use of economic factors, particularly those concerned with labour-force participation. In this chapter we will investigate the relationship of the few other economic variables in the Canadian Fertility Survey to fertility behaviour. Basically there are two theoretical approaches. The first, developed by Becker and subsequently modified by others, sees the demand and supply of children as no different from that of other durable goods and contends that standard economic principles can be applied to reproductive behaviour (Becker 1960). Therefore, income should be positively related to fertility, when other factors are controlled and quality (better educated, well cared for, and so on) as well as quantity of children are taken into account. The second interesting economic approach to the explanation of fertility trends has been that of Easterlin (1978; Easterlin and Crimmins 1985). One of his propositions concerns relative income and fertility. Couples whose relative economic position improves compared with those born before them will have a larger fertility, and conversely those whose relative economic situation deteriorates will have fewer children. Those who belong to a baby-boom cohort when they enter the labour market will face greater competition than the pre-baby-boom cohort and hence will experience a smaller growth in wages, higher unemployment, and so on. These factors will result in a relative income deterioration and will motivate them to have fewer children. The reverse is true for baby-bust cohorts, whose relative income position should improve owing to their smaller size. They can then be expected to have higher fertility. While we cannot test this hypothesis directly owing to a lack of longitudinal data in the CFS, we intend to test the hypothesis that a person's perception of his relative income compared to others in the same age group may influence his desire to have a higher- or lower-than-average fertility. In the CFS, questions were asked of women as to their perceived relative economic position both at the time of marriage or cohabitation as well as at the time of the survey. Here again, our analysis will be brief because of the limited information.

Family income and fertility

The construction of family income variables in the CFS was somewhat complicated. For those living with a husband/partner, the basic question was, 'In all, what is the gross annual income of your family before taxes and deductions including yourself, your husband/partner and your children?' In the case of never married women or previously married women, family income was calculated by adding any employment income and other incomes such as family allowance, alimony, and investment income. In instances where the family income was not reported, but that of the wife and of the husband/partner was available, the family income was calculated from the reported component parts. In cases where the sum of individual incomes was different (usually higher) from the reported family income, a new family income was calculated. It should be remembered that the CFS universe was very different from that of the whole country covered by Statistics Canada. The CFS universe consisted only of households clustered around a telephone with at least one woman aged 18–49. Thus, the income was different and the composition and size of the family depending on the income was different. The average size of the CFS family was 3.5 persons, while that of the national family was variously reported for 1984 as 2.8 and 2.9 persons (Romaniuc 1984:92, Statistics Canada 13–207 1985a:21); the CFS did not intend to include the mainly male 'unattached individuals.' The total number of cases where family income was available was 4636 or 84 per cent of the total survey group. The breakdown of response rates for income by marital status was 89 per cent for those currently in a union, 89 per cent for those previously married, and 81 per cent for those never married. The mean family income was $32,635, not too far from $35,853 reported by Statistics Canada (Statistics Canada 13–208 1985b:6). It should be remembered that the universes are not the same, and it should not be expected that their incomes should be the same. Subsequent analysis is subject to the limitations of measurement and response rates mentioned above and should be interpreted with them in mind.

Table 4.1 presents the mean number of children by age and family income. Since age is strongly correlated to income it is necessary to

TABLE 4.1
Mean number of children by age and family income (all women)

Age at interview	Annual family income			
	< $25,000	$25,000–34,900	$35,000–49,900	$50,000 or more
18–29	0.63	0.85	0.68	0.38
	(949)	(420)	(339)	(264)
30–39	1.82	1.83	1.88	1.60
	(483)	(337)	(391)	(342)
40–49	2.89	2.64	2.58	2.61
	(385)	(193)	(238)	(252)
Total	1.43	1.56	1.63	1.52
	(1817)	(949)	(968)	(858)

Note: The numbers in parentheses denote number of women.

control for age before one can examine the relationships between income and fertility. Though those in the highest income category, $50,000 or more, seem to have the lowest fertility in each age group, the overall relationship between income and fertility is weak, if not non-existent. In the oldest age group, 40–49, women who have by and large completed their childbearing, the average number of children was 2.89 among those with incomes less than $25,000 compared with 2.61 among those with incomes over $50,000. The difference is also apparent among women aged 30–39 who have had most of their children, varying from 1.82 to 1.60. The pattern is blurred in the middle income groups, but the apparent conclusion remains: the fundamental bivariate message is the inverse relation between fertility and income, contrary to economic theory.

Family income is influenced by not only age but marital status. Married and cohabiting people are likely to have a higher family income because there may be more than one wage earner in the family. Furthermore, married people might be selected for their marital status because of their income-earning capacity, as much as they are for health reasons and life expectancy. Previously married women are likely to have small children living with them, affecting their income. Apart from these demographic factors, other sociocultural variables can affect the relationship between income and fertility such as education, religion, religiosity, nativity, and place of residence. Therefore, a multiple classification analysis was done and the summary results are shown in table 4.2. When age and marital status are controlled, the inverse association between income and fertility becomes significant. Mean number of chil-

TABLE 4.2
Unadjusted and adjusted mean number of actual and expected number of children by age and family income (all women)

Family income	No. of women	Mean number of children		
		Unadjusted	Adjusted for age and marital status	Adjusted for age, marital status, religion, religiosity, education, nativity, urban/rural res.
Actual				
<=$25,000	1816	1.43	1.70	1.58
$25,000–34,900	949	1.57	1.50	1.51
$35,000–49,900	968	1.64	1.39	1.48
$50,000 or more	858	1.53	1.29	1.45
Expected				
<=25,000	1802	2.33	2.41	2.34
$25,000–34,900	944	2.27	2.23	2.24
$35,000–49,900	962	2.26	2.19	2.24
$50,000 or more	855	2.21	2.15	2.25

dren steadily decreases from 1.70 to 1.29 as income increases. Not surprisingly, the same pattern can be noticed in the total expected number of children as well, declining from 2.41 in the lowest income category to 2.15 in the highest income category. The relationship, however, becomes much weaker when we control for five other sociocultural variables as well. One might say that the pure effect of income, if any, is small and slightly negative. It does not support the stated hypothesis of a positive relationship.

Home ownership and fertility

The limited information in the Canadian Fertility Survey does not enable us to examine the relationship between wealth accumulation and fertility in depth. In the literature there is evidence that early childbearing has negative effects on wealth accumulation (Freedman and Coombs 1966). What data are available on the economic variables in the CFS refer to the situation at the time of the survey, which prevents a careful sequencing of events to establish cause effect relationships. However, we will still make some use of the information to see whether the earlier association found between income and fertility also holds when other economic factors such as home ownership and value of home are ex-

TABLE 4.3
Mean number of children by home tenure and age (all women)

Age at interview	Home tenure	
	Owned	Rented
18–29	0.82 (935)	0.55 (1028)
30–39	1.94 (1200)	1.36 (449)
40–49	2.81 (891)	2.49 (226)
Total	1.85 (3027)	1.02 (1702)

Note: The numbers in parentheses denote number of women.

amined in relation to fertility. Table 4.3 presents the mean number of children by home ownership. Taken as a whole, the average number of children born to those who own their home is 1.85 compared to 1.02 for those who rent. However, this finding is heavily biased, because those who are likely to own a home are also likely to be older and have a larger number of children. But even within each of the age cohorts, home owners have more children than those who rent. For example, among those aged 30–39, home owners had 1.94 children on average, compared with 1.36 children among the renters. The same level of differences persist in the other two age cohorts as well. Of course, higher fertility in itself will be a causal factor in home ownership.

Is the value of a home associated with fertility? Table 4.4 presents the mean number of children by value of the home at the time of the survey. Since the young (18–29) are unlikely to have the resources to own more expensive homes compared to the older women (30 and over), they are overrepresented in the lowest value category. Therefore, it is necessary to control for age, when comparing the relationship between value of home and fertility. A clear pattern is evident in each age cohort. Fertility decreases with the value of the home. Among women 18–29 who own homes worth less than $40,000, the mean number of children was 1.07, compared with 0.41 among those with homes valued at more than $100,000. In the oldest cohort, 40–49 years old, the range was from 3.45 to 2.65 children. There are two possible explanations for this trend that could coexist. Those who live in more expensive homes need higher incomes and the association between income and fertility, though weak, is negative. The other argument may be that those who have a larger number of children, though they need a house with more space, have not been able to accumulate the assets to own a more expensive home.

TABLE 4.4
Mean number of children by age and value of house

Age at interview	Value of house			
	<=$40,000	$41,000–60,000	$61,000–100,000	$101,000 or more
18–29	1.07	0.94	0.77	0.41
	(234)	(213)	(315)	(173)
30–39	2.05	1.98	1.93	1.82
	(192)	(308)	(486)	(214)
40–49	3.45	2.83	2.67	2.65
	(118)	(226)	(370)	(177)
Total	1.93	1.94	1.85	1.65
	(544)	(747)	(1172)	(565)

Note: The numbers in parentheses denote number of women.

Relative economic position and fertility

Two questions were asked in the CFS to assess the relative economic position of the respondents with others of their same age group. The questions were, 'When you got married or when you started living together, was your standard of living better than, the same as, or worse than that of people you knew in your age group?', followed by, 'And now, is your standard of living better than, the same as, or worse than that of people you know in your age group?' Our first hypothesis was that those who saw their position to be better than others at the time of the union would be more confident of their future and will plan to have a relatively larger family than others. Table 4.5 shows the mean number of children by age and perception of relative standard of living at the time of marriage or cohabitation. There is a significant trend, but in the opposite direction than the one hypothesized. Those who stated that their standard of living was better at the time of the union had a lower fertility than those who stated that they were the same as others or worse in their standard of living. For example, women aged 18–29 whose relative position was better had only 0.89 children, compared with 1.26 children among those who reported that their position was worse in comparison to others. The differences were present in the older cohorts as well. In the oldest cohort, 40–49, the corresponding figures are 2.64 and 3.14 respectively. Clearly, those whose relative living standards are better can afford to have a larger family. However, because

TABLE 4.5

Mean number of children by age and perception of relative standard of living at time of marriage or cohabitation (currently married or cohabiting)

Age at interview	Relative standard of living at time of survey		
	Better	Same	Worse
	Actual number of children		
18–29	0.89 (428)	1.03 (735)	1.26 (76)
30–39	1.89 (355)	1.97 (1004)	2.01 (91)
40–49	2.64 (196)	2.92 (732)	3.14 (95)
Total	1.60 (979)	1.97 (2471)	2.20 (262)
	Total expected number of children		
18–29	2.29 (428)	2.28 (733)	2.48 (76)
30–39	2.20 (353)	2.18 (999)	2.22 (90)
40–49	2.71 (195)	2.93 (731)	3.14 (95)
Total	2.34 (976)	2.43 (2463)	2.63 (262)
Income at time of survey	$36,385	$35,230	$35,395

Q914: When you got married or when you started living together, was your standard of living better than, the same as, or worse than that of people you knew in your age group?

Note: The numbers in parentheses denote number of women.

of other factors such as education and occupation, they may hold smaller family-size norms.

The lower panel in Table 4.5 shows total expected number of children. The small range in the expected number of children by relative living standards at the time of the union is significant. In the youngest cohort, the mean number of children expected was 2.29, 2.28, and 2.48 respectively in the three relative-living standards categories. In the middle age groups there was practically no difference. There was a noticeable pattern only in the oldest age group, the mean number increasing from 2.71 to 3.14 as the relative living standard worsened. One has to conclude that for most women below the age of 39, their perception of relative living standard at the time of the union had little to do with their expected family size. An analysis of the present family income shows that the differences among the three groups were quite small, the mean annual incomes being $36,385, $35,230, and $35,395 respectively. This implies that though they started their married lives at different levels in their perceptions, by the time of the survey their economic positions had become more equal.

What is worth noting in table 4.5 is that two-thirds said that their living standards were the same as others in their age group, and only 7 per cent stated that they were worse off than others, while 26.4 per cent felt better off, a logical impossibility if perceptions were to reflect reality.

The same optimism is evident in table 4.6, which shows the economic situation at the time of the survey. About a third (34.4 per cent) stated that their standard of living was better than others in their age group, and only a surprisingly low (4.6 per cent) of women said that their position was worse in comparison to others in their age group. The relationship to fertility remains the same at the time of the survey as at the beginning of the union. Those who stated that they were better off had the lowest fertility and those whose positions were worse had the highest fertility in all the age cohorts. The strong pattern evident in the youngest cohort, ranging from 0.90 children among the better off to 1.40 among the worse off, may be deceptive, because those who are better off may have started their childbearing later, because of higher education, later age at marriage, and so on. For example, the total expected number of children in the youngest cohort does not reflect such a pattern. As a matter of fact, it is slightly in the opposite direction. The differences are smaller in the older age cohorts. Among these women, the actual and expected numbers of children are somewhat higher in the worse-off category.

Our analysis of relative economic position seems to indicate that Canadian women have an exaggerated assessment of their own standards of living compared to others. They are also not influenced by their perceptions as far as their childbearing is concerned to any significant degree. Income differences among the three groups as defined at the time of the survey were more substantial and in the right direction, $38,000, $34,880, and $24,660, in comparison with the three groups as defined at the time of the marriage/union. But we should remember that only 4.6 per cent put themselves in the third (worse-off) category.

Perceived social mobility and fertility

Since we have the information on perceived relative standards of living at the time of the start of the union and at the time of the survey, we can compare the two and identify those who feel that their relative position has improved, remained the same, or deteriorated. For example,

TABLE 4.6

Mean number of children by age and perception of relative standard of living at time of survey (currently married or cohabiting)

Age at interview	Relative standard of living at time of union		
	Better	Same	Worse
	Actual number of children		
18–29	0.90 (471)	1.04 (713)	1.40 (58)
30–39	1.94 (500)	1.96 (887)	2.05 (62)
40–49	2.81 (306)	2.89 (659)	3.32 (54)
Total	1.76 (1277)	1.94 (2259)	2.23 (175)
	Total expected number of children		
18–29	2.34 (471)	2.28 (710)	2.23 (58)
30–39	2.17 (496)	2.19 (884)	2.32 (62)
40–49	2.84 (306)	2.90 (657)	3.35 (54)
Total	2.39 (1273)	2.43 (2251)	2.61 (175)
Income at time of survey	$38,000	$34,880	$24,660

Q915: And now, is your living standard better than, the same as, or worse than that of people you know in your age group?

Note: The numbers in parentheses denote number of women.

women who said that their standard of living was the same as others in the same age group at the time of the union, but said that they were better off at the time of the survey, see themselves as upwardly mobile. Table 4.7 presents the percentage distribution of women by perceived relative standards at the two points in time. Using the figures in table 4.7 we can construct the percentage of women who perceived their relative standards as having improved, remained the same, or worsened. For about two-thirds of the women, 62.7 per cent (those in the diagonal of table 4.7), there has been no change. There is improvement in 23.4 per cent of the couples (those below the diagonal) and worsening in 13.9 per cent (those above the diagonal). It should be kept in mind that the interval between the date of union and date of survey will vary a great deal, as the women at the time of the survey are representative of women in the wide age range 18–49. As one would expect social mobility to be related to elapsed time, we should be careful in interpreting the social-mobility rates.

Our interest, however, is not so much in estimating perceived social mobility, but rather to see whether such mobility is related to fertility

TABLE 4.7
Percentage distribution of women by relative standard of living at time of union and at time of survey (currently married or cohabiting)

Relative standard of living at time of union	Relative standard of living at time of survey			
	Better	Same	Worse	Total
Better	14.8%	10.3%	1.3%	26.4%
Same	17.4	46.9	2.3	66.6
Worse	2.2	3.8	1.0	7.0
Total	34.4	61.0	4.6	100.0 (N=3699)
Income at time of survey	$38,000	$34,880	$24,660	

behaviour. Table 4.8 presents the actual and expected numbers of children by perceived social mobility in the three age cohorts. There are no significant differences between the various categories of social mobility. Those whose perceived relative position improved expected 2.48 children in total, compared with 2.40 for those whose position remained the same and 2.42 for those whose position deteriorated. Even within the three age cohorts, there were no significant differences.

Perceived financial success and fertility

We saw above that women's perception of their relative position compared with others in their age cohort did not have much influence on their reproductive behaviour. Does their perception of their own financial success have any impact on the number of children they are likely to have? The question 'From a financial standpoint, do you feel you have been very successful, reasonably successful, or not successful?' was asked of all respondents. The actual and expected fertility by age and perception of financial success are presented in table 4.9. Again, only 9 per cent felt that they were financially not successful, and they were concentrated in the youngest cohort, 18–29. Thirteen per cent in this young cohort said that they felt not successful, compared with 5 per cent in the 40–49 age cohort. Income among the young will naturally be low and they probably interpret this as being not-successful. The mean family income of the not successful group was $18,740, compared with $31,450 for the reasonably successful and $38,250 for the very successful. Because of the age effect on incomes and fertility, it is more meaningful to control for age in arriving at conclusions on the association between perceived financial success and fertility. The figures in table

TABLE 4.8
Mean number of children by age and perception of relative living standards between date of marriage and time of survey (currently married or cohabiting)

Age at interview	Relative standard of living		
	Improved	Same	Worsened
	Actual number of children		
18–29	1.06 (236)	0.95 (818)	1.12 (183)
30–39	2.03 (359)	1.91 (892)	2.03 (194)
40–49	2.96 (272)	2.87 (608)	2.81 (137)
Total	2.06 (867)	1.82 (2318)	1.91 (514)
	Total expected number of children		
18–29	2.36 (236)	2.28 (816)	2.27 (181)
30–39	2.19 (358)	2.17 (887)	2.26 (192)
40–49	2.97 (272)	2.89 (607)	2.85 (136)
Total	2.48 (866)	2.40 (2310)	2.42 (509)

Note: The numbers in parentheses denote number of women.

4.9 again show that there is no clear pattern. The small number who report as being not successful have a higher fertility in the oldest age cohort, but not in the two younger cohorts. Differences are minimal between the very successful and reasonably successful groups in all the three age groups. One will have to conclude again that perceived financial success is not too relevant in the reproductive behaviour of Canadian women.

Planning for the future and fertility

One would expect that those who are generally planning oriented are likely also to plan the number and timing of their children. It may not be unreasonable to expect them to use birth control more efficiently and have fewer unwanted pregnancies. In the Canadian Fertility Survey, the following question was asked of all respondents: 'Some couples make very precise plans for the future. In general would you say that you/ you (*as a couple*) plan things most of the time, occasionally, rarely or never?' Table 4.10 presents actual and expected fertility by the planning status of the respondent families. By and large, Canadians are committed planners. Fifty-three per cent said that they make plans most of the time and another 34 per cent plan occasionally. Only 3 per cent said that they never plan. A relationship between planning status and fertility

TABLE 4.9

Mean number of children by age and perception of success from financial standpoint (all women)

	Perception of success from financial standpoint		
Age at interview	Very successful	Reasonably successful	Not successful
	Actual number of children		
18–29	0.67 (443)	0.66 (1554)	0.43 (307)
30–39	1.80 (426)	1.84 (1238)	1.59 (101)
40–49	2.70 (326)	2.73 (839)	3.35 (68)
Total	1.63 (1195)	1.54 (3631)	1.09 (476)
	Total expected number of children		
18–29	2.33 (440)	2.22 (1538)	2.07 (302)
30–39	2.08 (423)	2.09 (1230)	1.91 (99)
40–49	2.72 (325)	2.75 (839)	3.39 (67)
Total	2.35 (1188)	2.30 (3607)	2.22 (468)
Income at time of survey	$38,250	$31,450	$18,740

Q800: From a financial standpoint, do you feel you have been ...?

Note: The numbers in parentheses denote number of women.

can be noticed only in the oldest age cohort. These women have mostly completed their fertility. Therefore their actual and expected fertility are practically the same. Women who said that they plan most of the time had a mean number of 2.61 children. In contrast, those who plan occasionally had 2.82 children on an average and those who plan rarely and never had 3.03 and 3.21 children respectively. In the middle age cohort the pattern was present but weaker. In the youngest cohort no pattern was evident. But for these women, most of their fertility is in the future and one does not know whether the poor planners among them will have a higher fertility because of unplanned pregnancies. But the fact that their expected fertility is not higher is an indication that those who do not plan for the future also have low family size desires.

Conclusion

Our brief exploration of the relationship of some economic factors to the reproductive behaviour of Canadian women showed that they have far less impact compared to the sociocultural variables considered in the

TABLE 4.10
Mean number of children by age and planning for the future

Age at interview	Plans for the future			
	Most of the time	Occasionally	Rarely	Never
	Actual number of children			
18–29	0.63 (1223)	0.60 (813)	0.66 (213)	0.84 (58)
30–39	1.77 (957)	1.87 (591)	1.82 (173)	2.03 (48)
40–49	2.61 (640)	2.82 (386)	3.03 (143)	3.21 (66)
Total	1.47 (2820)	1.49 (1790)	1.68 (529)	2.09 (172)
	Total expected number of children			
18–29	2.28 (1210)	2.23 (806)	1.89 (211)	2.09 (56)
30–39	2.04 (951)	2.12 (586)	2.07 (172)	2.20 (47)
40–49	2.63 (639)	2.84 (385)	3.05 (142)	3.21 (66)
Total	2.28 (2800)	2.33 (1777)	2.26 (525)	2.56 (169)

Q801: Some people (couples) make very precise plans for the future. In general would you say that you (as a couple) plan things ...?

Note: The numbers in parentheses denote number of women.

previous chapter. When controlled for other factors, the effect of income on fertility was weak. We also see that very few Canadian women see themselves as disadvantaged in relation to others, and their fertility behaviour is not affected by such perceptions. One is tempted to conclude that having a small family of one to three children is well within the means of most Canadian couples and, therefore, economic means by themselves are no more an important determinant of family size, as they were in the past. Other variables such as education, urban residence, and labour-force participation seem to be relatively more important in childbearing.

5

Nuptiality

To understand the recent fertility decline and its possible future trends one needs to look at its proximate determinants. Of these one of the most important is nuptiality, since the major part of the fertility in Canada occurs within marriage.[1] However, to the extent there is a significant and increasing amount of childbearing outside of legal marriage, it is also necessary to investigate the fertility outside of marriage in the study of the relationship of nuptiality to fertility.

Apart from its impact on fertility, our primary area of concern, the transformation taking place in the Canadian family is of enormous social and economic significance. In 1961, 90.1 per cent of all families in Canada were husband wife families; in the 1986 census this percentage has declined to 80.1 per cent (Statistics Canada 1963, 1982, 1987). What is clearly happening is that more and more women are marrying later in life or not marrying at all. Between 1971 and 1986, the mean age of brides at first marriage has increased from 22.2 to 24.6. During the same period, the proportion of women married in the age group 20–24 decreased from .592 to .391 (Statistics Canada 1973–87). Proportions married in the younger age groups in 1986 indicate that the final proportion ever marrying will be much less than .900 for the recent birth cohorts.

Not only has the tempo of marriage slowed down, but the rates of marital dissolution have gone up. The divorce rate of 169 per 100,000 existing marriages during 1960–2 steadily increased to 1129 by 1982. Since then there has been a slight decline to 1062 for 100,000 marriages by 1984. The ratio of divorces to marriages taking place in the same year increased from 5 per cent to 36 per cent during the same interval

---

1 Some of the materials in this chapter have appeared in two publications and a report: Balakrishnan et al. 1987, and 1989a and 1989b.

(Romaniuc 1984a; Dumas 1985). Because overall period rates of divorce are crude indicators, influenced by timing effects and age distributions, attempts have been made to construct more meaningful cohort rates of divorce. Using duration-specific divorce statistics, Dumas (1985) estimates that the probability of being divorced 5 years after marriage has increased from 4.4 per cent for the 1968–9 marriage cohort to 8.3 per cent for the 1976–7 marriage cohort. Adding the duration-specific divorce rates of various cohorts, Dumas also constructed a total divorce rate (comparable to the total fertility rate) for different calendar years. This total index for a 25-year marriage duration has increased from 1370 per 10,000 marriages in 1969 to 3655 for 10,000 marriages in 1982. Extrapolating past trends, McKie, Prentice and Reed (1983) estimated a total divorce rate of 4100 for 10,000 marriages in 1985. It may not be too unrealistic to predict that these trends may mean that one in two marriages entered into by young women now may end in divorce, a trend already evident south of the border (Martin and Bumpass 1989).

Another trend in family formation in Canada as in other industrialized countries is the increase in cohabitation. By cohabitation, we refer to persons of opposite sex living together as a married couple without having gone through a legal marriage process. In the CFS, 12.1 per cent of females aged 18–49 in all unions were in common law unions. This figure is very close to the 11.5 per cent found in the Family History Survey done in the same year for the corresponding age group (Balakrishnan 1989). In the 1981 and 1986 Canadian censuses, 8.5 per cent and 11.1 per cent of females aged 15–49 in all unions were in common-law unions (Statistics Canada 1983a, 1987). Whether cohabitation is a prelude to marriage or an alternative living arrangement is a much debated point now. Cohabitation and common-law union are terms used interchangeably in this chapter.

Complete marriage histories were collected in the Canadian Fertility Survey. These included dates of marriage and dates of separation and divorce if any. In addition, considerable information on cohabitation was collected.

Formation of first unions

Starting from a single state a woman can enter into a union by cohabitation or a legal marriage. Table 5.1 and figure 5.1 present cumulative probabilities of entry into a marriage or a common law union by a specified age for the three different age cohorts in the CFS. These figures are derived from a double-decrement survival table, in which marriage

TABLE 5.1

Cumulative probabilities of entry of females into first union (marriage or common-law) by specified age, by age cohort

Age	Marriage	Common-law union	Total
	18–29 (N = 2308)		
15	.00	.00	.00
20	.14	.22	.36
25	.37	.40	.77
	30–39 (N = 1771)		
15	.00	.00	.00
20	.23	.06	.29
25	.66	.16	.82
30	.74	.20	.94
35	.75	.21	.96
	40–49 (N = 1236)		
15	.01	.00	.01
20	.31	.01	.32
25	.79	.02	.81
30	.89	.02	.91
35	.92	.04	.96
40	.93	.04	.97
45	.93	.04	.97

N = sample size

and cohabitation are considered as competing risks, two mutually exclusive ways of leaving the single state (never being in a union). The table is restricted to first unions. The cumulative probabilities of entering first union through marriage by specific ages have been going down when we compare the different age cohorts of women. In the oldest age cohort, 40–49, the probability of moving to the married state directly from the single state by age 25 was 0.79. These were the women who got married during the baby-boom years of late 1950s and early 1960s. Marriage was more universal and early in that period. In the 30–39 cohort this probability was down to 0.66, and in the 18–29 cohort it was only 0.37. One should not confuse these figures with being ever married by these ages, which is likely to be greater, as some women who cohabit may have entered marriage by then.

Substantial changes have occurred in the probabilities of entering a common law union, as a comparison of figures by various age cohorts

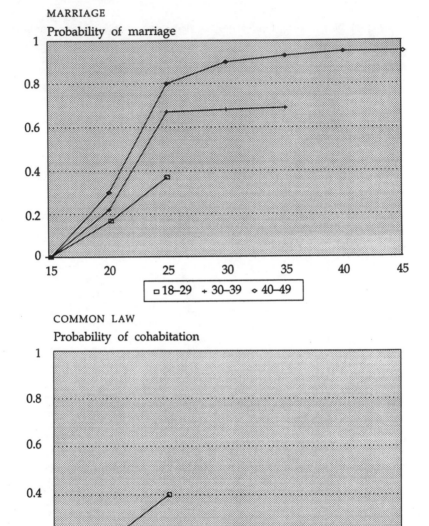

Figure 5.1 Cumulative probabilities of entry into first union

TABLE 5.2
Percentage of women in types of current union by age

Age at interview	Currently cohabiting			Currently married	Total in a union
	Never married	Previously married	Both		
18–19	10.7	0.0	10.7	7.2	17.9
20–24	13.0	0.3	13.3	30.1	43.4
25–29	7.9	3.2	11.1	65.2	76.3
30–34	3.5	4.5	8.0	73.6	81.6
35–39	1.0	4.0	4.9	78.3	83.2
40–44	0.8	4.5	5.3	79.7	85.0
45–49	0.1	3.8	4.0	77.2	81.2
Total	5.4	3.0	8.5	61.8	70.3
Number	289	162	451	3283	3734

shows. In the 40–49 age cohort, the probability of entering a cohabitation as a first union was very small, .02 by age 25 and only reaching an eventual value of .04 by age 35. The probability of entry by age 25 increased to .16 for the 30–39 age cohort, and for the 18–29 cohort was very high at .40. As a matter of fact the probability of entering a common-law union as a first union was actually higher than the probability of entering a legal marriage as a first union for this youngest group of women.

Cohabitation by marital status

Cohabitation is prevalent not only among the single never married, but also among the previously married. In the 1984 CFS, 36 per cent of the cohabiting females were previously married, not an insignificant proportion (table 5.2). After the age of 30, their numbers were more than never-married women cohabiting. The percentage of women never married and cohabiting was 10.7 per cent of all women in the 18–19 age group, increasing to 13.0 in the 20–24 age cohort, and then decreasing rapidly to 1.0 per cent of women 35–39 years old. In contrast, the percentage of women previously married and cohabiting increased from 0.3 per cent in the 20–24 age group to 3.2 per cent in the 25–29 age group. After age 30, their proportion was fairly constant, at 4 per cent of the total in the age groups. The recent increase in cohabitation is therefore due partly to two trends, increasing age at legal marriage and a higher and earlier marital dissolution, both creating an increased population exposed to risk of cohabitation.

TABLE 5.3
Females in common-law unions as a percentage of females in all types of unions by geographical regions

Region	Percentage
Atlantic (Nfld., PEI, NS, and NB)	8.1
Quebec	16.3
Ontario	11.2
Manitoba and Saskatchewan	8.7
Alberta	9.9
British Columbia	11.9
All Canada (except Yukon and NWT)	12.1
Age range: 18–49	

Characteristics of cohabiting women

Considerable geographic variation exists in the prevalence of cohabitation in Canada. Table 5.3 presents females in common-law unions as a percentage of females in all types of unions by regions. Beause of small sample sizes, sampling errors will be high and the figures should be taken only as broad indicators of regional differences in the incidence of cohabitation. The highest rates of common law unions are to be found in Quebec, 16.3 per cent of all unions. The lowest rates are in the Atlantic provinces. Ontario and British Columbia have rates somewhat in the middle range. Such wide regional differences are probably only partially explained by the socio-economic variations among the populations.

In the CFS, data were gathered on many socio-economic characteristics of the respondents, women in the age group 18–49. It should be interesting to identify factors correlated with cohabitation. Table 5.4 and figure 5.2 present the percentage of cohabiting women as well as currently married women by selected background variables. In the absence of control for age, one should be cautious in the interpretation of the figures in table 5.4. Age is correlated not only with union status (cohabitation or marriage), but also with other variables. The following comments will therefore acknowledge the possible impact of age wherever it is felt necessary.

Educational differences in cohabitation do not seem to be significant. The proportion who have ever cohabited is practically the same in the three education groups, and the differences in the percentages currently cohabiting are small.

Cohabitation is strongly related to place of residence. Thirty-one per

TABLE 5.4
Percentage of women cohabiting or currently married by selected socio-economic characteristics

Characteristic	Number of women	Ever cohabited	Currently cohabiting	Currently married
Years of education				
11 or fewer years	1615	29.3	8.6	68.5
12 or 13 years	1977	28.9	9.6	59.4
14 or more years	1722	30.0	7.0	58.2
Place of residence				
City	3426	31.0	9.2	55.9
Small town	1526	27.3	7.8	70.4
Farm	357	21.8	4.3	81.2
Nativity				
Canadian-born	4575	30.3	9.1	60.2
Foreign-born	736	23.2	4.3	72.0
Religion				
Catholic	2547	27.4	9.6	60.6
Protestant	1871	29.4	7.3	65.4
Other religions	459	17.5	1.2	63.7
No religion	428	53.3	14.7	51.0
Church attendance				
Every week	1368	12.9	2.6	74.4
Every month	665	19.8	4.3	70.6
Few times a year	1383	30.8	9.9	58.4
Rarely or never	1893	43.7	13.2	52.0
Language most often spoken at home				
English	3665	30.4	7.7	62.6
French	1380	30.9	12.0	59.0
Others	270	7.5	0.7	64.2

Notes: Ever cohabited includes currently cohabiting women. Percentages are calculated on the number of women shown. Since the three categories are not mutually exclusive, they are not additive.

cent of the women residing in a city have cohabited, compared with 21.8 per cent living on a farm. The differences are even more noticeable in current cohabitation, the prevalence being more than double in the city compared to the farm, 9.2 per cent versus 4.3 per cent. One should also note that the proportion currently married is much higher on the farm, 81.2 per cent in contrast to only 55.9 per cent in the city. Cohabitation in small urban places is somewhere in between the large-city and farm levels.

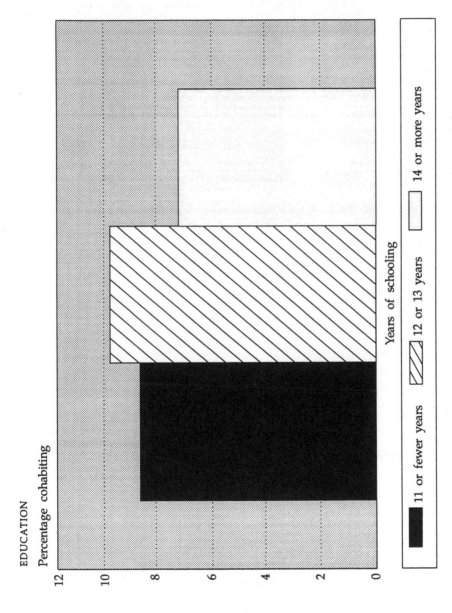

EDUCATION
Percentage cohabiting

Years of schooling

■ 11 or fewer years   ▨ 12 or 13 years   ☐ 14 or more years

Figure 5.2 Percentage of women currently cohabiting by socio-economic characteristics

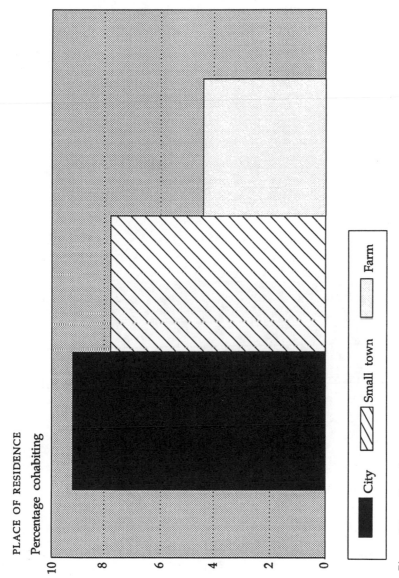

PLACE OF RESIDENCE
Percentage cohabiting

City   Small town   Farm

Figure 5.2 continued

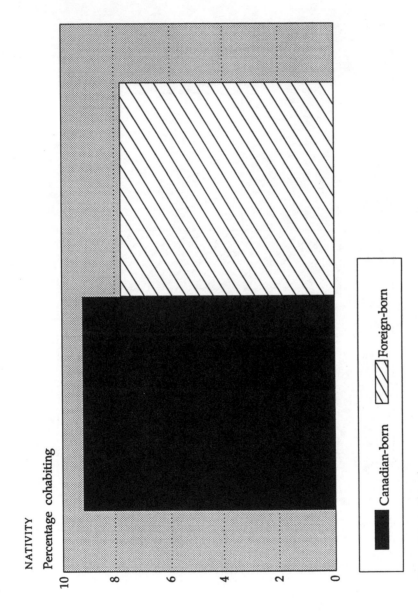

Figure 5.2 continued

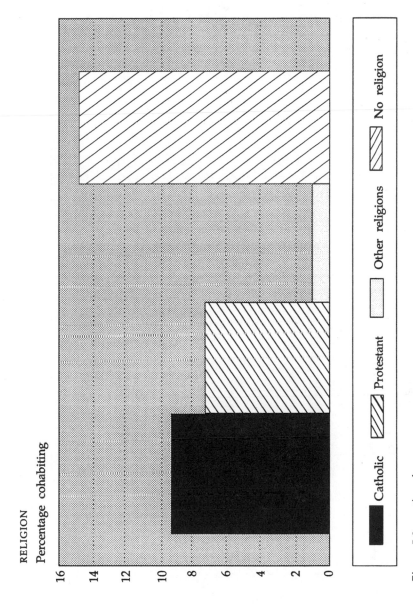

RELIGION
Percentage cohabiting

Catholic   Protestant   Other religions   No religion

Figure 5.2 continued

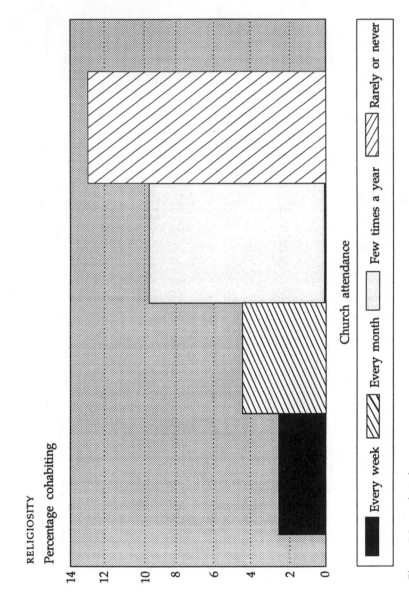

RELIGIOSITY
Percentage cohabiting

Church attendance

Every week Every month Few times a year Rarely or never

Figure 5.2 continued

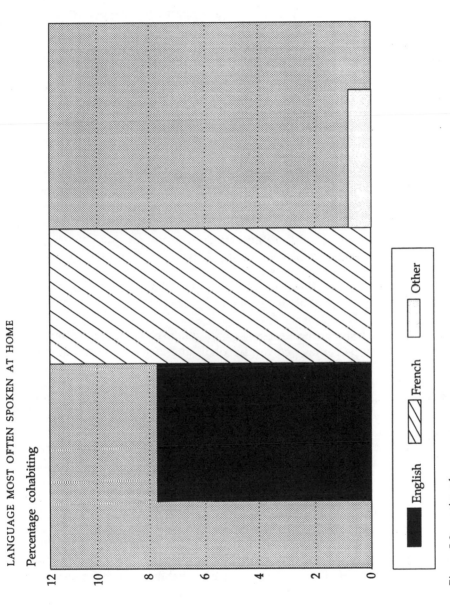

LANGUAGE MOST OFTEN SPOKEN AT HOME

Percentage cohabiting

English   French   Other

Figure 5.2 continued

The incidence of current cohabitation is more than double among native-born Canadians compared with the foreign-born, the percentages being 9.1 and 4.3 respectively. The proportion ever cohabiting was also higher among the native-born.

Both religion and religiosity are related to cohabitation. Though there was no significant difference in the proportion ever cohabiting between Protestants and Catholics, the proportion currently cohabiting is higher among the Catholics: 9.6 per cent of them were currently in a cohabitation, while only 7.3 per cent of the Protestants were in such a union. One should however be careful in attributing this difference to their religious beliefs. Most of the Catholics in Canada are in Quebec, where cohabitation seems to be much more popular than elsewhere in Canada. For example, we see also in table 5.4 that 12.0 per cent of women who speak French most often at home are cohabiting, compared with only 7.7 per cent among those whose home language is English. One needs to compare Catholics and Protestants in Quebec and outside Quebec to examine the influence of religion. Cohabitation was most common among those who stated they belonged to no religion. Though they formed only about 8.6 per cent of the total sample, more than half of them have cohabited sometime in their lives and 14.7 per cent were currently cohabiting.

The factor that shows the strongest correlation to cohabitation is church attendance. The percentage currently cohabiting increases from 2.6 per cent to 13.2 per cent as the frequency of church attendance decreases from every week to rarely or never. Part of this, however, is the age effect. Church attendance is higher among the older women, who are also less likely to be in a cohabitation. It is necessary to analyse the data in a multivariate context in assessing the relationships of the individual variables to cohabitation status.

Stability of common-law unions

Of considerable interest is the stability of common-law unions. They can result in a marriage, get broken, or continue to be a consensual union. Again multiple-decrement life tables have been constructed for CFS data for such unions from the date of formation of the union. Table 5.5 and figure 5.3 present the cumulative probabilities of different outcomes derived from such life tables using single years of duration as time intervals. In the CFS, data on outcomes were gathered only for a duration of eight years.

In the oldest cohort, the incidence of cohabitation was very low, but

TABLE 5.5

Cumulative probabilities of survival, marriage, or separation for common-law unions by duration for age groups

Duration (years)	Survival	Marriage	Separation
	18–29 (*N* = 861)		
1	.74	.10	.16
2	.52	.21	.27
3	.37	.28	.35
4	.26	.34	.40
5	.20	.37	.43
6	.14	.40	.46
7	.08	.44	.48
8	.07	.44	.49
	30–39 (*N* = 515)		
1	.78	.14	.08
2	.57	.27	.16
3	.42	.38	.20
4	.32	.42	.26
5	.27	.44	.29
6	.20	.48	.32
7	.17	.49	.34
8	.13	.51	.36
	40–49 (*N* = 173)		
1	.84	.13	.03
2	.70	.22	.08
3	.64	.26	.10
4	.57	.30	.13
5	.50	.33	.17
6	.47	.34	.19
7	.45	.36	.19
8	.43	.36	.21

N = sample size

the unions themselves were much more stable than in the younger age cohorts. At the end of eight years, 43 per cent of the cohabitations can be expected to be intact, 36 per cent to have resulted in a marriage, and the remaining 21 per cent to have broken up. In the youngest cohort, aged 18–29, only 7 per cent can be expected to survive, 44 per cent to end in a marriage and almost half, 49 per cent, to break up by the end of eight years.

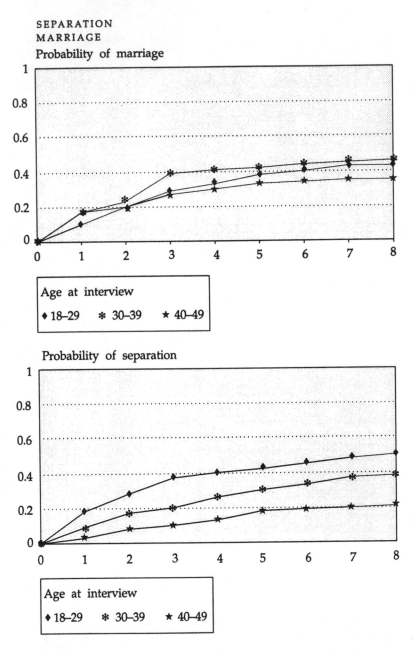

Figure 5.3 Cumulative probabilities of marriage and separation for common-law union by duration

Though age captures some of the period effects of union formation, it may be worthwhile to look at the stability of cohabitations by the time period in which they were entered into. Cohabitations began to become popular and socially more acceptable only in the last decade. Therefore, those who entered such unions before 1970 may be different from those who did so after. The stability of the unions may reflect this fact. Table 5.6 presents the cumulative probabilities of survival, marriage, or separation for common-law unions by duration for the two period cohorts, pre-1970 and 1970–84, for the CFS sample. Those who entered a common-law union before 1970 were more likely to remain in the union compared to those who entered after 1970. At the end of eight years, only 13 per cent of the recent common-law cohort can be expected to be still in the union, as against 25 per cent for the earlier cohort.

First marriage[2]

We have already seen the importance of the proportions entering marriage and of age at entry in the reproductive behaviour of Canadian women. The later the age at marriage, the lower the lifetime fertility and the more delayed childbearing. It is therefore particularly relevant to examine the trends in first marriage. Because detailed marital histories were collected in the Canadian Fertility Survey, we could construct life table estimates of first-marriage patterns as well as examine some of the correlates of first marriage.

Table 5.7 and figure 5.4 present the life table estimates of the cumulative proportion of women married by selected ages for various birth cohorts. It is apparent that the tempo of first marriage has slowed down considerably. Among the older cohorts (aged 35 or more), slightly more than half married before the age of 22. By age 24, the probability of entering first marriage was almost three-fourths among these women. Most of them married in the late 1950s or early 1960s, the period of the baby boom. In contrast, among the youngest cohort, aged 20–24 at the time of the survey, only 17 per cent were married by age 20, compared with 34 per cent among the oldest cohort, 45–49 years old. Only 50 per cent can be expected to be married by age 24. If one were to extrapolate,

---

2 The analysis on first marriage was carried out by K.V.Rao and is more fully described in his doctoral thesis, 'Demographic models of age at first marriage and age at first birth,' University of Western Ontario, 1987.

TABLE 5.6
Cumulative probabilities of survival, marriage, or separation for common-law unions by duration for common-law-union cohorts

Duration (years)	Survival	Marriage	Separation
CLU cohort 1970–84 (N = 1390)			
1	.77	.11	.12
2	.56	.23	.21
3	.42	.31	.27
4	.32	.36	.32
5	.25	.39	.36
6	.19	.42	.39
7	.15	.44	.41
8	.13	.45	.42
CLU cohort pre-1970 (N = 159)			
1	.72	.21	.07
2	.50	.31	.19
3	.42	.36	.22
4	.34	.40	.26
5	.32	.41	.27
6	.28	.43	.29
7	.27	.43	.30
8	.25	.44	.31

N = sample size

it is very unlikely that the young women in 1984 would reach the ever-marrying proportion of .95 seen among the older women by age 40.

Table 5.8 shows the median age at first marriage as obtained from the single state life tables for various covariate categories for all the six age cohorts. The covariates are place of residence, education, religion, religiosity measured in terms of church attendance, and work status.

Urban women in all age cohorts have higher medians than rural women and the differences between the two categories are significant at the 5 per cent level. The median age at first marriage among urban women ranges from 24.4 years for the 20–24 age cohort to 21.8 years for women aged 40 and above. The trend in median age at first marriage among rural women is less pronounced. The median age among rural women ranges from 22.6 for the youngest cohort, 20–24, to 20.8 for the 45–49 cohort. As expected, more-educated women tend to have a higher median age at first marriage, irrespective of the age cohort they belong to. Again, the differences between the three categories were statistically

TABLE 5.7
Life-table estimates of cumulative proportion of women married by selected ages for various birth cohorts

	Birth cohort					
Selected ages	1935–39 (45–49)	1940–44 (40–44)	1945–49 (35–39)	1950–54 (30–34)	1955–59 (25–29)	1960–64 (20–24)
15	0.006	0.007	0.009	0.003	0.002	0.001
17	0.041	0.047	0.035	0.022	0.022	0.018
19	0.196	0.193	0.148	0.150	0.151	0.097
20	0.341	0.319	0.284	0.255	0.259	0.172
22	0.566	0.570	0.534	0.521	0.468	0.357
24	0.744	0.759	0.728	0.684	0.637	0.494
26	0.827	0.846	0.827	0.780	0.729	–
30	0.903	0.908	0.911	0.827	0.818	–
35	0.942	0.944	0.941	0.844	–	–
40	0.954	0.954	0.950	–	–	–
Median	21.4	21.6	21.8	21.8	22.4	23.4
Sample size	516	590	897	1029	1114	949

Note: Figures in parentheses indicate age span for each cohort in 1984.

significant at the 5 per cent level. Women who had a grade 11 or lower education have the lowest median age at first marriage throughout, and the difference between the highest and lowest median in this group is about a year. Also, women with grade 14 or higher education have higher medians, and the difference between the highest and lowest median within this group is about two years. The next interesting covariate considered is religion, which is found to be important for older cohorts of women, that is, older than 35. Below age 35, the differences in marriage patterns of Catholics and non-Catholics were insignificant. There was no clear pattern by religiosity. Though the less religious have a tendency to marry late in the younger cohorts, there seems to be little difference among the older women. The differences between the categories of religiosity were statistically significant only in the 25–29, 30–34, and 40–44 age cohorts.

Among the younger women, those who were working at the time of the survey had higher median ages at first marriage. This relationship does not hold among older women. However, cause-effect relationships are hard to establish. Women who delay marriage are more likely to be in the labour force. Since work status only measures work at the time

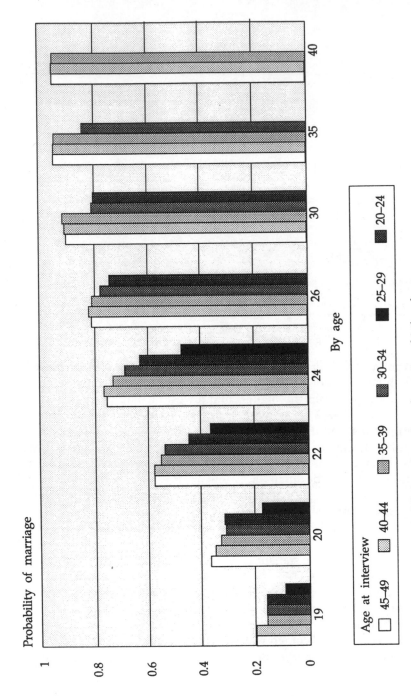

Figure 5.4 Cumulative probabilities of marriage for various birth cohorts

TABLE 5.8
Median age at first marriage (obtained from life-table analyses)

Covariates	Age cohorts					
	20–24	25–29	30–34	35–39	40–44	45–49
Place of residence						
Urban	24.42	23.17	22.33	22.33	21.83	21.83
Rural	22.58	21.00	21.16	21.08	21.42	20.75
Education						
≤ Gr. 11	21.75	20.75	20.33	20.33	20.58	20.67
Gr. 12–13	23.67	21.33	21.50	21.67	21.42	20.75
Gr. 14+	22.67*	24.33	23.41	23.08	22.75	23.33
Religion						
Catholic	24.58†	22.67**	22.08**	22.16	21.92	21.92
Other	23.42	22.17	21.58	21.50	21.50	21.00
Religiosity						
Weekly	22.83**	21.75	21.25	22.00†	22.25	21.83†
Sometimes	23.17	22.08	21.75	22.00	21.50	21.17
Rarely	24.58	23.33	22.58	21.33	21.08	21.08
Work status						
Employed	24.33	23.25	22.17	21.92**	21.50†	21.16†
Unemployed	23.33	21.58	21.50	21.75	21.67	21.75
Sample size	1004	980	922	845	642	590

* Represents first quartile.
** Significant at 10% only
† Differences between the categories are not significant.

All other differences between covariate categories are significant at 5%.

of the survey, it is possible that many older women may have entered the labour force after completing their fertility.

Table 5.9 presents the proportional hazards coefficients for age at first marriage by age cohort. Coefficients greater than or less than 1.00 indicate higher or lower probabilities of first marriage compared with the reference category, controlling for other variables. Rural women are likely to marry earlier than urban women in all the age cohorts. For example, in the 25–29 age cohort, the coefficient of 1.414 indicates that these women have a 41 per cent higher risk of first marriage compared with urban women. The variable with the highest impact on age at first marriage seems to be education. Those with grade 14 or higher education are less likely to marry than those with grade 11 or lower education. This is true in all the age cohorts, but the differences are greatest in the

TABLE 5.9

Proportional-hazards coefficients (e^β) for age at first marriage in Canada (sample: all women in CFS)

Covariates	Age cohorts					
	20–24	25–29	30–34	35–39	40–44	45–49
Place of residence						
Urban	1.000	1.000	1.000	1.000	1.000	1.000
Rural	1.369*	1.414*	1.284*	1.384*	1.268*	1.375*
Education						
≤ Gr. 11	1.000	1.000	1.000	1.000	1.000	1.000
Gr. 12–13	0.680*	0.916	0.773*	0.738*	0.903	0.793*
Gr. 14+	0.345*	0.546*	0.505*	0.494*	0.588*	0.533*
Religiosity						
Weekly	1.000	1.000	1.000	1.000	1.000	1.000
Sometime	0.750*	0.908	0.817*	0.889	1.210	1.031
Rarely	0.599*	0.678*	0.686*	0.989	1.314*	1.041
Religion						
Catholic	0.782*	0.813	0.815*	0.781*	0.776*	0.752
Other	1.000	1.000	1.000	1.000	1.000	1.000
Work status						
Unemployed	1.000	1.000	1.000	1.000	1.000	1.000
Employed	0.785*	0.740*	0.829*	0.938	0.938	1.076
Log L	2341.6	5406.3	5542.1	4961.1	3078.7	2625.5
Global χ^2	94.5	172.1	137.9	99.8	50.0	49.7
df	7	7	7	7	7	7
Sample size	1004	980	922	845	642	590

* Significant at 5 per cent

younger cohorts. These findings confirm the earlier findings from the single life table analyses (table 5.8) in a multivariate setting. Unlike education and place of residence, religiosity shows mixed results across the age cohorts. Except for the 40–44 and 45–49 age cohorts, women who frequently attend church services have higher chances of marrying compared with those who attend sometimes or rarely or never. In general, religiosity is significant for younger women and its effects are in the expected direction. In contrast to religiosity, religion shows a consistent pattern. Catholics have lower risks of marriage across all the age cohorts. The coefficients vary from 0.752 to 0.815, with most of them being statistically significant. Employed women (working continuously for more than six months at the time of the survey) have lower risks of first marriage, the coefficients being significant for younger women, less than 35 years of age. This shows that young women who are actively participating in the labour force are postponing their marriages.

The results in table 5.9 allow us to identify the high- and low-risk groups of women for first marriage for various age cohorts. Women with lower education who are non-Catholic, unemployed, and residing in a rural area or a small city are more prone to early marriage compared with women in urban areas, with grade 14 or more education, who are Catholic, attend church sometimes or rarely, and are working.

Though remarriage is becoming an increasingly important factor in the study of the family in the developed countries, we have not examined it in this study. The main reason is that there were only 231 women in our sample who were married a second time, a number too small for in depth analysis and reliability of the estimates for subgroups. Besides, because our upper age cut-off was 49, there will be the possibility of excessive bias owing to censoring. Many women may not have had enough exposure time since their first marriage and its dissolution to be remarried before age 49. Larger samples with a broader age range will be more appropriate.

First-marriage dissolution

Of the 5315 women in our sample, 3884 have been ever married. Of these first marriages, 96 (2.5 per cent) were dissolved owing to the husband's death and 727 (18.7 per cent) by separations, with most resulting in divorce by the survey date (69 per cent). For our analysis here, we define date of dissolution as the date of death of the spouse or date of separation, whether followed by the divorce by survey date or not. Because many women in our sample are still young and may experience marriage dissolution later in life, we need to use life table techniques to adjust for the effects of censoring.

Table 5.10 and figure 5.5 present simple or 'single-state' life table results calculated separately for each category shown. The values are estimates of marriage dissolution and indicate the proportions of first marriages terminating by various marital durations. For instance, 26 per cent of the women who marry before the age of 20 will have their marriages terminated by 15 years; this proportion increases to 37 per cent by the end of 25 years. For those who marry at ages 22–24, the proportion of marriages terminated by the end of 25 years is 24 per cent. The slightly higher rate of dissolution for those who marry after the age of 24, found in some U.S. studies, is not found in the Canadian sample (Teachman 1982). Premarital births, and to a lesser extent pre-marital conceptions, significantly increase the chances of marriage dis-solution. Women with a premarital birth have a 37 per cent chance of being separated after 15 years, compared with 30 per cent for those with a premarital conception and only 18 per cent for those who had neither.

Of the marriages entered into before 1965, only 3 per cent were dissolved by 5 years and 8 per cent by 10 years of duration. For the 1965–74 marriage cohort, these proportions were estimated as 8 per cent and 16 per cent respectively. The proportion at 5 years' duration for those married after 1975 is even higher, at 13 per cent. One should realize, however, that all of these figures are affected by an age-at-marriage bias arising from censoring and should be interpreted with caution. For example, the cross-sectional nature of the survey means that those who married before 1965 have to be married before age 30, and those who marry in 1975 or after could marry at any age between 18 and 49. In our sample, however, 98 per cent of the ever-married women married before the age of 30. Therefore, this bias is not too serious. Subject to this limitation, we can clearly see that the marriage dissolution probabilities of recent marriage cohorts have substantially increased.

Most of the marriage history of our sample group of women refers to the period 1960–84, a time of rapid increase in divorce rates. Though divorces have been increasing in Canada since the early 1960s, the lib-eralization of the laws in 1968 resulted in a somewhat greater increase in the rates during the years 1970–4 than in the 1960s. The early duration dissolution rates for those in our sample who were married before 1965 may therefore be affected downward by the fact that divorces were relatively harder to get at that time. This period effect should have disappeared by 10 years' duration for early marriage cohorts and should not affect later marriage cohorts. It is, however, unlikely that marriage dissolution rates would have been much higher among the older women in our sample in the early 1960s given the long-term secular trends in divorce and the social mores existing at that time. In any case, small numbers preclude any detailed analysis of this period effect in the early marriage dissolution probabilities among the older women.

The life tables in table 5.10 show that women who cohabited before their first marriage have much higher probabilities of marriage disso-lution. Thirty-five per cent can be expected to have terminated their first marriage before 15 years, compared with only 19 per cent among those who did not cohabit before marriage. We realize that, though not in-

TABLE 5.10

Life-table estimates of probabilities of first-marriage dissolution by specific durations by selected characteristics of women

| Characteristic | Years since first marriage | | | | | |
	N	5	10	15	20	25
Ages at first marriage						
19 or less	1235	0.11	0.21	0.26	0.32	0.37
20–21	1108	0.07	0.15	0.20	0.25	0.29
22–24	987	0.06	0.11	0.15	0.22	0.24
25 or higher	539	0.05	0.07	0.14	0.15	–
Year of marriage						
Before 1965	1046	0.03	0.08	0.13	0.19	0.24
1965–74	1509	0.08	0.16	0.22	–	–
1975–84	1313	0.13	–	–	–	–
First-birth status						
Premarital birth	276	0.23	0.30	0.37	0.47	–
Premarital conception	375	0.15	0.22	0.30	0.35	0.43
Not conceived before marriage	3217	0.06	0.13	0.18	0.23	0.27
Cohabitation status						
Cohabited before marriage	666	0.17	0.31	0.35	0.40	0.48
Did not cohabit	3202	0.08	0.14	0.19	0.25	0.30
Religion						
Catholic	1790	0.08	0.12	0.17	0.24	0.26
Non Catholic	2074	0.11	0.18	0.24	0.30	0.35
Religiosity (church attendance)						
Weekly or more often	1113	0.04	0.07	0.10	0.13	0.18
Sometimes	1467	0.09	0.15	0.19	0.24	0.27
Rarely or never	1284	0.16	0.25	0.33	0.42	0.47
Place of residence						
Large urban	2346	0.11	0.18	0.24	0.31	0.36
Small urban	1213	0.07	0.13	0.18	0.23	0.28
Farm	304	0.06	0.08	0.10	–	–
Educational attainment						
≤ grade 11	1358	0.08	0.15	0.20	0.26	0.29
Grades 12–13	1374	0.08	0.16	0.20	0.24	0.30
14 or more years	1135	0.07	0.14	0.21	0.27	0.35

Note: Differences between dissolution probabilities for the categories are statistically significant at the .01 level for all covariates except eductional attainment.

cluded here, duration of cohabitation could influence probabilities of dissolution. We believe, however, that to cohabit or not to cohabit is a

Figure 5.5 Cumulative probabilities of marriage dissolution by selected characteristics

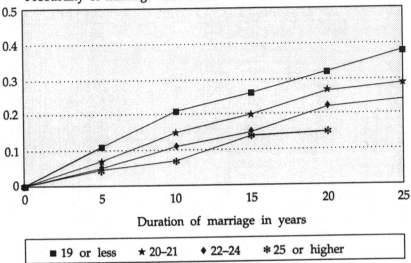

AGE AT FIRST MARRIAGE
Probability of marriage dissolution

Duration of marriage in years

■ 19 or less   ★ 20–21   ♦ 22–24   ✳ 25 or higher

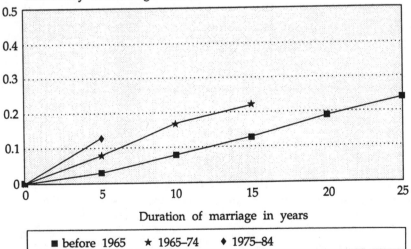

YEAR OF MARRIAGE
Probability of marriage dissolution

Duration of marriage in years

■ before 1965   ★ 1965–74   ♦ 1975–84

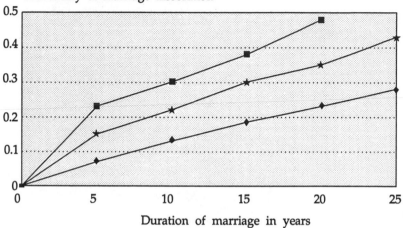

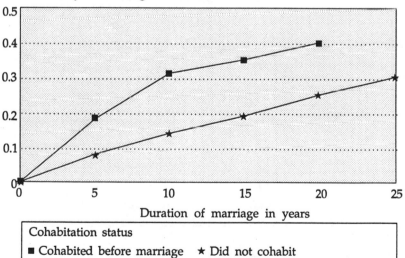

Figure 5.5 continued

RELIGION

Probability of marriage dissolution

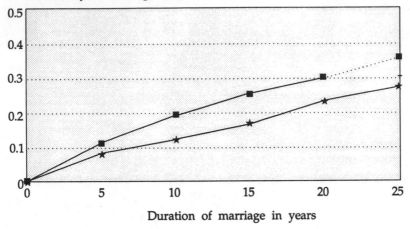

Duration of marriage in years

Religion
★ Catholic   ■ Non-Catholic

RELIGIOSITY

Probability of marriage dissolution

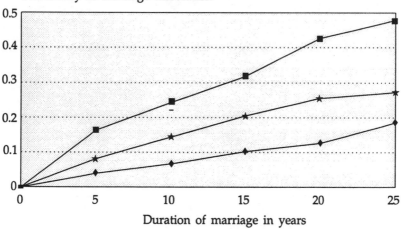

Duration of marriage in years

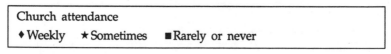

Church attendance
♦ Weekly   ★ Sometimes   ■ Rarely or never

Figure 5.5 continued

PLACE OF RESIDENCE
Probability of marriage dissolution

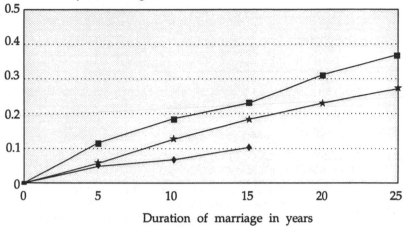

Duration of marriage in years

Place of residence
■ Large urban   ★ Small urban   ♦ farm

EDUCATION
Probability of marriage dissolution

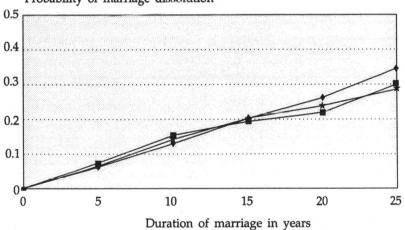

Duration of marriage in years

Years of schooling
★ Less than grade 11   ■ Grades 12–13   ♦ 14 or more grades

Figure 5.5 continued

factor worthy of consideration in itself in the analysis of subsequent marital stability.

Religion seems to have a noticeable effect on dissolution probabilities, the higher probabilities for non-Catholics being statistically significant. Religiosity has a stronger influence on marriage dissolution than religion per se. Among those who went to church at least once a week, 18 per cent can be expected to have terminated their marriage before 25 years, whereas this proportion is 47 per cent among those who rarely or never go to church. One criticism of the religiosity variable is that it measures church attendance at the time of the survey and is only a surrogate for religiosity during the entire marriage period. Our assumption is that religiosity is acquired in early childhood socialization, and those who are religious at the time of the survey are likely to have been religious at the time of the marriage and later. The strong relationship is an indication of the importance of religiosity to marital stability.

As expected, women who reside in large urban areas have experienced much higher rates of marriage dissolution than those in smaller urban areas or in rural farm communities. Here again, place of residence is measured as at the time of the survey and does not necessarily mean that the respondents have lived in such communities for the whole marriage duration, though such an assumption is implicit in the models. Single life tables for education categories do not show much difference, and one would have to see whether they do when other factors are controlled.

Tests of significance of the differences in the dissolution probabilities among categories were performed separately for each covariate. These tests showed that the differences were significant except for the educational attainment categories.

Since many of the covariates considered above in marriage dissolution are interrelated, their independent effects are masked in the single life tables presented in table 5.10. Life tables must therefore be constructed for subgroups of populations with differing characteristics to see whether the chances of marriage dissolution vary among them. When more than two or three variables are of interest, this approach quickly leads to small-sample size problems. Therefore, hazard model analysis is used to consider the effects of covariates on dissolution probabilities at various durations. The details of the application of proportional hazard models have been presented elsewhere in great detail, so they are not outlined here (see especially Menken et al. 1981 and Teachman 1982 for a step-by-step exposition). Basically, the model allows the risk to depend not only on time, as in a simple life table, but on the personal characteristics

TABLE 5.11
Hazard coefficients for marital dissolution

Variable	Category	Model 1	Model 2
Age at marriage	≤ 19	1.394*	1.376*
(20–21)	22–24	0.666*	0.674*
	25 or over	0.422*	0.435*
Year of marriage	Before 1965	0.470*	0.473*
(1965–74)	1975 or after	1.622*	1.592*
Cohabitation before marriage (did not cohabit)	Cohabited	1.482*	1.495*
First-birth status (did not	Premarital birth	2.357*	2.349*
conceive before marriage)	Prem. conception	1.489*	1.495*
Religion (non-Catholic)	Catholic	0.885	
Religiosity	Weekly	0.610*	0.610*
(church attendance sometimes)	Rarely or never	1.768*	1.836*
Place of residence	Small urban	0.662*	0.665*
(large urban)	Farm	0.348*	0.355*
Education	≤ grade 11	1.126	
(grades 12–13)	14 or more years	1.120	
Log likelihood		−5239.9234	−5243.2296
Model χ square		473.67*	468.20*
Degrees of freedom		15	12
Number of women	N = 3852		

* Significant at 5 per cent

Note: Reference categories are given in parentheses.

of the individual. The duration-dependent risk is calculated for a baseline or reference group. The hazard function enables one to estimate the relative risks of other groups in relation to this baseline group.

The hazard coefficients are presented in table 5.11 for two different models. The proportionality assumption was tested by plotting ln[−ln(proportion remaining married)] for the various categories, which were found to be nearly parallel and hence taken to be valid. Values greater than 1 indicate that the relative risk of marriage dissolution is greater for this group, compared with the reference group. Thus, when the survival probabilities for the reference group is known at various durations, the survivorship probabilities for the other groups can be found easily, subject to the assumption that the relative risks remain the same at all durations. The coefficients in the two models in table 5.11 were tested for statistical significance, and those for religion and education were found to be not significant. The first model includes all eight variables. For example, in model 1 the figure of 1.394 for those who married on or before age 19 means that their risk for marriage dissolution is 1.394 times greater than the risk of those who married between 20 and 21, other characteristics being the same. The second model drops the two variables that have the lowest effect and were found to be not statistically significant. We can look on model 2 as more efficient because it explains almost as much as model 1 but with two fewer variables. Likelihood ratio statistics show that both models are improvements on the model that assumes that covariates have no effect; in other words, the probability of dissolution is the same for all the women at various durations. We will refer to model 2 in the subsequent discussions.

The coefficients in model 2 show that age at marriage is significantly related to marriage dissolution. The coefficient is only 0.435 for those who married after the age of 25, but increases steadily to 1.376 for those who married before 20. In other words, other things being equal, the probability of dissolution is more than three times greater for those who marry before 20, compared with those who marry after 25. The same trends can be observed for the marriage cohorts. The coefficient is three times as large for those who married in 1975 or later as for those who married before 1965. Women who cohabited before marriage have about a 50 per cent higher risk of marriage dissolution than those who did not cohabit before marriage. The coefficients show that premarital birth or conception significantly increases the chance of dissolution of marriage, the relative risks being 2.349 and 1.495, respectively. Religiosity has a strong relationship, as predicted. The coefficient for those who rarely or never attend church is about three times that for those who attend church at least once a week. Those residing in large urban areas at the time of the survey were much more likely to have had a divorce, compared with those living on a farm.

Age at first marriage and fertility

In a developed country such as Canada the effect of the increase in age at first marriage on fertility decline is difficult to assess. In the past, age at first marriage had a strong inverse relationship to completed fertility (Balakrishnan et al. 1979). One reason for early marryers to have a higher completed fertility has been their socio-economic profile, which may be related to desire for a larger family and the inefficient use of contraception. A second reason for early marryers to have a higher fertility is the fact that they are exposed to a longer duration of potential child-bearing (Freedman and Casterline 1979). Besides, they are more exposed to the risk of pregnancy in the highly fertile years of their twenties. In contrast, women who marry late experience fertility when their fecundity is on the decline. However, in Canada, where the desired family size is low and contraception is efficient, the effect of the length of exposure time on final fertility is more problematic. Later-marrying couples may speed up their reproductive behaviour to catch up with the younger women (Grindstaff 1984). When the total desired family size is only about two children this is easily possible. A decline in the proportion married in the earlier years may be compensated for by the higher fertility of late marryers.

A serious problem in establishing a relationship between age at first marriage and fertility is that there may be a common set of factors influencing age at marriage and fertility, making the simple correlation spurious. One needs to control for these factors to make conclusions on the independent effect of age at marriage on reproductive behaviour (Balakrishnan et al. 1979). Table 5.12 presents the mean number of births by age at marriage for the various age cohorts after controlling for other factors such as religion, religiosity, ethnicity, education, nativity, pre-marital birth status, and place of residence. Comparison of the unadjusted and adjusted mean number of births by survey date indicate that the negative relationship between age at first marriage and cumulative fertility persists and is only slightly diminished when controlled for other factors. The effect of controls is even smaller in the case of total expected fertility, implying that the negative effect of age at marriage on cumulative fertility is largely independent of other factors.

The cumulative fertility of women aged 45–49 is, on the average, about one birth more than that of women 35–39 years old, who also have largely completed their fertility, expecting only an additional 0.10 children. The differences between early and late marryers are also similarly larger, 1.49 births in the 45–49 cohort versus 0.89 births in the 35–39 age cohort. Controls do not change these differences significantly, the new differences being 1.62 births and 0.81 births, respectively, for the two age cohorts.

The importance of age at marriage on cumulative fertility is indicated by the proportion of variance it explains. About a third of the variance

TABLE 5.12
Unadjusted and adjusted cumulative fertility and total expected fertility by age at first
marriage and age at interview

Age at inter-view/Age at first marriage	Number of women	Cumulative fertility by survey data		Total expected fertility	
		Unadjusted	Adjusted*	Unadjusted	Adjusted*
18–24					
≤ 19	171	1.07	0.94	2.39	2.39
20–21	123	0.70	0.76	2.49	2.48
22–24	67	0.22	0.46	2.15	2.18
≤ 25	–	–	–		
R^2			.46		.13
25–29					
≤ 19	233	1.88	1.75	2.31	2.31
20–21	206	1.41	1.43	2.36	2.33
22–24	215	1.00	1.05	2.26	2.27
≥ 25	79	0.55	0.77	2.23	2.26
R^2			.43		.11
30–34					
≤ 19	223	2.25	2.17	2.35	2.31
20–21	241	1.91	1.94	2.17	2.19
22–24	198	1.68	1.73	2.08	2.11
≥ 25	140	1.18	1.17	1.85	1.82
R^2			.31		.20
35–39					
≤ 19	217	2.50	2.42	2.58	2.51
20–21	227	2.13	2.15	2.20	2.22
22–24	219	2.03	2.09	2.17	2.22
≥ 25	127	1.61	1.61	1.79	1.80
R^2			.24		.22
40–44					
≤ 19	199	3.18	3.09	3.21	3.12
20–21	170	2.52	2.64	2.52	2.63
22–24	146	2.42	2.43	2.42	2.43
≥ 25	100	1.76	1.72	1.83	1.80
R^2			.26		.26
45–49					
≤ 19	187	3.80	3.79	3.83	3.81
20–21	143	3.13	3.21	3.13	3.21
22–24	140	2.94	2.97	2.94	2.98
≥ 25	94	2.31	2.17	2.32	2.18
R^2			.26		.26

* Adjusted by Multiple Classification Analysis for religion, religiosity, ethnicity, education, nativity, premarital birth status, and place of residence

in cumulative fertility is explained by age at first marriage alone. Age at marriage alone explains 14 per cent of variance in the 18–24 age group; 18 per cent in the 25–29 age group, 12 per cent in the 30–34 age group, 6 per cent in the 35–39 age group; 11 per cent in the 40–44 age group, and 8 per cent in the 45–49 age group (not shown in table). In most age cohorts age at marriage explains more variance than any other variable. The other variables of importance to cumulative fertility are education, work status, and premarital birth status of the woman.

Cohabitation and fertility

One of the significant trends in recent years in Canadian society is increasing cohabitation, especially among young single persons. Reliable statistics on the extent of cohabitation are difficult to gather. The Canadian Fertility Survey shows that about 25 per cent of single women in the age group 18–29 were cohabiting. The effect of cohabitation on overall fertility levels is complex (Roussel 1986). Cohabitation of single persons will have a positive effect on fertility compared with single persons not in a cohabiting union if only because there is a continuous exposure to pregnancy. On the other hand, cohabiting women may have a lower fertility than married women because women may avoid pregnancy during cohabitation, if it is seen as a trial period without, as yet, a sense developed of commitment to proceed to legal marriage. The Canadian Fertility Survey found a very high use of contraception among cohabiting single women, which indicates a desire to avoid pregnancy, in this presumably transitional stage.

Table 5.13 presents the mean number of children ever born by cohabiting status. Cohabiting women have only slightly higher fertility than single non-cohabiting women in all the age cohorts. Cohabiting single women have much lower fertility than married women in the same age category. Single cohabiting women in the age group 20–24 had an average of 0.29 births, compared with 0.78 for married women and 0.20 for single non-cohabiting women in this age group. One of the reasons for increased cohabitation among single women is that it is more widely accepted than in the past. The effect of this on fertility is likely to be negative, as couples keep fertility low in the cohabitation period.

Among separated, divorced, and widowed women, cohabitation makes little difference to fertility. Almost 27 per cent of these women were cohabiting at the time of the survey. Their fertility was not too different from that of the married women. Most of their fertility probably came

TABLE 5.13
Mean number of children ever born by marital status and age

Age group	Single		Currently married	Separated, divorced, widowed	
	Non-cohabiting	Cohabiting		Non-cohabiting	Cohabiting
18–19	0.02 (254)	0.05 (36)	0.45 (23)	* (3)	* (0)
20–24	0.20 (542)	0.29 (129)	0.78 (303)	1.12 (30)	* (3)
25–29	0.21 (172)	0.54 (77)	1.38 (646)	1.25 (61)	0.98 (31)
30–34	0.19 (87)	0.49 (32)	1.86 (680)	1.68 (83)	1.41 (41)
35–39	0.53 (43)	0.81 (8)	2.19 (663)	1.79 (99)	1.72 (34)
40–44	0.10 (22)	* (5)	2.55 (513)	2.36 (74)	3.83 (30)
45–49	0.08 (22)	* (1)	3.23 (457)	2.87 (88)	3.02 (23)
Total	0.17 (1142)	0.37 (289)	2.02 (3283)	1.95 (438)	2.07 (162)

* Mean not presented where number of women is fewer than 5.

Note: Numbers in parentheses denote number of women.

from their marriage and is, therefore, irrelevant to their current cohabitation. Because of the small sample size no attempt is made to calculate fertility within and after marriage by any selective socio-economic characteristics of these women. On the whole, it can be safely said that it is cohabitation among single women that is mainly relevant for fertility and increased cohabitation is likely to have a depressing, rather than a positive, effect on fertility.

From the Canadian Fertility Survey it can be estimated that roughly half the cohabitations among single women end up in a legal marriage. It will be instructive to see whether the fact of cohabitation before marriage has an effect on overall cumulative fertility. While couples may avoid childbearing while cohabiting, accidental pregnancy in a cohabiting union may lead to an immediate marriage. Moreover, while cohabitation may delay age at marriage, in low-fertility societies such as Canada, the couple may have enough exposure time in marriage to attain their desired family size. Studies done in Norway and France have shown that while fertility in cohabitation is small the final fertility of those who have or have not cohabited before marriage is basically the same (Festy 1979).

The mean number of children for ever-married women who have or have not cohabited with their husbands before marriage is presented in table 5.14. Since these women may vary significantly by age at marriage, mean ages at first marriage and mean duration from first marriage to survey date are also shown in the table. Among women over 30 years of age, those who cohabited before marriage married later and had fewer children compared with those who did not cohabit. In the 40–49 cohort only about 2 per cent had cohabited. These women married very late and had only 1.62 children on an average, whereas those who did not cohabit married early and had 2.89 children. The differences are smaller in the 30–34 cohort, but still noticeable. Eighteen per cent of these women had cohabited with their husbands before marriage. Those who cohabited married about three years later and had an average of 0.23 fewer children than those who did not cohabit. Among the younger cohorts, 18–24 and 25–29, there does not seem to be an appreciable difference in fertility. However, these women have a substantial portion of their reproductive life in front of them. Therefore, it is too early to say whether there will be a significant difference in their final fertility. The much lower fertility of their older sisters is no guide, because they also had a much shorter duration in the married state, while the cohabiters at younger ages will have durations not much shorter than non-cohabiters, and longer exposure to sex if the duration of cohabitation is added (three years on the average).

Marriage dissolution and fertility

The relationship between marital disruption and fertility is complex, especially in a developed society where contraception is widely used (Bumpass 1989; Martin and Bumpass 1989). The negative relation of marital disruption to fertility in the past has been explained mainly by its effect of reducing the exposure time to childbearing. This may not be too relevant in situations where the family-size norm is low, so that even a short marriage can produce the desired number of children. Childless couples may be more prone to divorce, under the assumption that unhappily married couples may avoid having children. (Balakrishnan et al. 1987). The mean duration of marriage for divorces taking place in 1985 in Canada was 12.5 years (Dumas 1985). If all the fertility had taken place before divorce, then obviously divorce has no effect on final fertility. However, there is a great deal of variance in the marital duration before divorce, and many divorced women do not reach the fertility level they would have reached if they had stayed in their marriages.

While the fertility of women when divorced may be low, those who remarry may experience substantial fertility depending on their age at remarriage and the children they and their spouses may have had in any earlier marriages. In 1985, about 20 per cent of women marrying were previously divorced or widowed (Statistics Canada 1987). The ef-

TABLE 5.14
Mean number of children by cohabitation status with husband before first marriage

	No cohabitation before first marriage			Cohabited with husband before first marriage		
Age at interview	No. of women	Mean age at 1st marr.	Mean marital dration*	Mean no. of children	No. of women	Mean age at 1st marr.	Mean marital duration*	Mean no. of children ever born
18–24	252	19.39	2.97	0.78	109	20.29	2.37	0.84
25–29	549	20.46	6.76	1.37	186	20.51	4.53	1.30
30–34	657	20.98	11.02	1.86	146	23.69	7.91	1.63
35–39	728	21.22	15.67	2.16	66	25.48	11.05	1.71
40–49	1159	21.28	23.22	2.89	24	28.75	13.49	1.62

* Refers to duration from date of first marriage to interview date.

fect of remarriage on total fertility is not known. The decrease in exposure time owing to divorce may be compensated for by a desire to have a child in the second marriage.

The Canadian Fertility Survey collected detailed data on marriage history, and therefore exact duration can be calculated for each marriage. The mean number of children ever born are presented in table 5.15 for age cohorts of women classified by their marital status. Currently married women were divided into those once married and continuously married and those who were married more than once. One may argue that multiple marriages may produce more children if there is a tendency to have children in each marriage. Overall means show that women who were married more than once had an average of 2.12 children, compared with 2.02 children for those married only once and 1.98 for those who were separated, divorced or widowed. But this result is largely a function of age distribution. Women married more than once are likely to be older, and hence one has to control for age before comparing their fertility with once-married women. Among women over 30, in each age category, women married more than once have a smaller number of children. But among the younger women the pattern is reversed, probably because those women married more than once are also likely to have married early the first time. Because of the effects of age at first marriage and marital duration on fertility, these two variables were controlled through Multiple Classification Analysis in reassessing the effect of marital status on fertility. The adjusted mean numbers show a very different pattern than the unadjusted means. The mean number of children for separated, divorced, and widowed women adjusted for age at

TABLE 5.15
Children ever born by age and current marital status

Age at interview	Once married, currently married	Separated, divorced, widowed	More than once married, currently married
18–24	0.76 (322)	1.08 (37)	1.05 (3)
25–29	1.37 (613)	1.13 (92)	1.74 (31)
30–34	1.88 (632)	1.58 (125)	1.65 (46)
35–39	2.21 (594)	1.79 (132)	1.93 (69)
40–44	2.56 (469)	2.78 (104)	2.52 (44)
45–49	3.26 (418)	2.91 (111)	2.94 (38)
Total	2.02 (3048)	1.98 (601)	2.12 (231)
Adjusted total*	2.00	2.14	1.92
Mean age at first marriage	21.53	20.23	19.10
Marital duration (years)†	13.02	9.40	11.49

* Adjusted by Multiple Classification Analysis for age at first marriage and marital duration

† Actual years spent in a legal marital union

first marriage and marital duration was 2.14, compared with 2.00 for once-married, currently married women and 1.92 for those women more than once married and currently married. The differences are small and furnish no evidence that multiple marriages increase the fertility of women, or that marriage dissolution decreases fertility, once duration is controlled.

Conclusion

In Canada not only are nuptiality patterns changing, but their linkages to fertility are weakening. The main changes in nuptiality are an increasing age at first marriage and a decreasing proportion ever married in the various age groups. The final proportion marrying is expected to go below .90 for the young cohorts. On the surface, it seems that these trends will have an effect of lowering the fertility. One might, however, argue that in a society where desired family-size norms are very low, such as two children, even a short marriage duration is enough to produce this level of fertility. There is some evidence that the influence of age at first marriage on total cumulative fertility has declined, but it still exists. Late marryers do not catch up with early marryers.

The weakening of the link between marriage and fertility also arises because of increased cohabitation especially among young women. Cohabitation alone can be expected to have a positive effect on fertility. However, fertility in a cohabitation is much lower than in a legal union. Cohabitation in lieu of legal marriage has a negative effect on overall fertility, because it delays entry into a legal marriage.

Not only are there proportionately more single women in the age group 15–24, but their fertility is higher than in the past owing to increased sexual activity and greater social acceptance of birth outside of marriage. However, the level of fertility is still very low compared with marital fertility. Besides, the individual and social costs of childbearing to young single women are too high for this to be a healthy trend.

The increasing extra-nuptial fertility indicates that in Canada not only are sexual activity and reproduction getting separated, but the links between legal marriage and reproduction are also weakening. An obvious implication is that public policies related to fertility should not be addressed towards married women only.

A powerful factor affecting the linkage between nuptiality and fertility is the increasing labour-force participation of women. In the past, marriage and childbearing came first in priority and women entered or left the labour force according to the timing of these events. Now, not only is this causal link considerably weaker, but it may not exist at all in many cases. It may even operate in the reverse direction: entry into the labour force has priority and childbearing is facilitated, as a subsequent consideration, by the ease or difficulty of interrupting the labour-force participation. The need to understand this connection is crucial in estimating future fertility trends.

It is clear that a large part of the fertility declines in recent decades is due to nuptiality changes. The institutions of marriage and family are in a great state of flux, and fertility trends in coming years will continue to reflect these changes.

6

Attitudes towards family and marriage

The study of opinions and attitudes regarding fertility and marriage provide insight for a better understanding of the reproductive behavior of Canadian women.* The exploration of these attitudes and opinions also provides a way of grasping the much broader reality of the underlying value system. Many demographers have recently underscored the pertinence of studying values in order to explain the reproductive behaviour of women in Western societies (Lesthaeghe and Meekers 1986; Lesthaeghe and Surkyn 1988; Simons 1986; Roussel 1987). These studies not only emphasize the importance of recent transformations in the family value system, but more important, they also put forward the idea that these societies are also undergoing a cultural mutation. Accordingly, a general process of institutional devaluation is in progress, a 'disinstitutionalization' such that 'l'institution est devenue pour une part de la population simple formalité sociale' (Roussel 1987: 443). According to Simons the term 'secularization' symbolizes the motor of cultural change; it embodies the formal changes undergone by religion as well as the reduction of societal influence on individual behaviour. Lesthaeghe and his colleagues supplement this concept of secularization with the reorientation of ideals towards individualism and 'post-materialism.' At the level of family and procreation, these cultural mutations entail a devaluation of marriage, a growing pluralism of demographic behaviour (unmarried cohabitation, voluntary infecundity, divorce, abortion, and so on), a greater tolerance towards these new forms of behaviour and the establishment of a new procreation rule of conduct, the two-children norm.

Economic explanations (microeconomic theory and Easterlin's theory

* This chapter was written in collaboration with René Houle.

of cycles) are not completely rejected, but rather they are qualified: first, transformations at the family level are not independent of the societal object (Roussel 1987: 445–6); second, the rational choice calculations applied to fertility interact with and are mediated by values (Simons 1986). Lesthaeghe and Surkyn take this argument even further: 'the transmission or reordering of meaning-giving (ideational) goals ... through agents of socialization and through the individual's search for meaning-giving beacons in life contributes to the specification of the content of what is understood under the blanket term 'utility.' In short, universes of meaning specify the object of economic optimization (Lesthaeghe and Surkyn 1988: 2).

Thus, the questions from the 1984 Canadian Fertility Survey will be analysed in the perspective of a transformation of family values. Questions related to various themes including marriage, unmarried cohabitation, divorce, children, life as a couple, and abortion, as well as questions pertaining to the sharing of housework associated with children and to the organization of life as a couple, are relevant.

All 5315 women surveyed were asked these questions. Two demographic factors are particularly relevant for the descriptive analysis of attitudes about the family: age and marital experience. In order to take into account the fact that women belong to various generations and have reached various stages in their marital life, selected groups only were retained, as is shown in table 6.1. In total, 7.7 per cent of the sample have been excluded from the detailed analysis, but were still included in the total distribution in each table, so it may reflect adequately the Canadian women aged 18 to 49. The decision of excluding some groups was based on the small number of cases and on the fact that some of them are relatively marginal in the society.

There are, however, some women who did not provide answers for the questions relating to opinions and attitudes. On average, they represent 1.5 per cent of the sample. The questions on abortion in particular received inferior coverage (the total of 'don't know' and 'no answer' responses ranging from 1 to 6 per cent), whereas in other cases less than 1 per cent declined to answer.

Most of this chapter contains descriptive material; it seems relevant to present detailed data on attitudes and opinions on the family since the Canadian literature is relatively poor on the subject. More sophisticated analysis of some of these data has already been published. These articles have dealt with some socio-economic correlates of attitudes towards cohabitation and marriage (Wu and Balakrishnan 1992), with the attitudes of young women in Québec (Lapierre-Adamcyk, Balakrishnan,

TABLE 6.1
Distribution of women surveyed by age and marital experience

| | Total 18–49 | First marriage in progress | | | | | First marriage broken | | Single | | | | |
| | | | | | | | | | Cohabitants | | Alone | | |
		18–19†	20–29	30–39	40–49	Total 18–49	18–29†	30–49	18–29	30–49†	18–29	30–49†	NK*†
Number	5315	23	914	1227	887	3051	164	670	242	46	968	174	1
%	100.0	0.4	17.2	23.1	16.7	57.4	3.1	12.6	4.6	0.9	18.2	3.3	0.0

* Marital experience not known
† Subgroups that will be excluded from tables 6.2 to 6.18

and Krótki 1987), and with the relatively low degree of consistency between groups determined by their attitudes towards various dimensions of family life (Lapierre-Adamcyk 1989). This chapter will deal successively with attitudes on marriage and children, on the relationship of the couple, and on the importance of family life for happiness.

Marriage and children

In the past, when a woman and a man decided to live together, they were obliged to marry and by the same token to set up a household. Unmarried cohabitation was out of the question, even on a trial basis. Moreover, with the exception of particular circumstances, marriage was expected to blossom with the creation of a family and the bearing of children. In this context divorce was very difficult to obtain and figured as an exceptional if not tragic event. As we know, behaviour and the law have changed in these respects, and so have women's opinions and attitudes. We shall see that this evolution has affected to a varying degree all women aged 18 to 49. Regarding marriage, children, and divorce, perceptions have become far more equivocal than past behaviour would have sanctioned.

1. Marriage. Is marriage on the verge of becoming an obsolete institution? De Boer (1981) brought forward this question in the light of results from numerous public-opinion studies executed in Western countries of Europe and North America at different points in time. In the case of West Germany for instance, in 1949 approximately 90 per cent of the population considered marriage as a 'necessary' institution; however, in 1978 this figure had plummeted to 40 per cent, while for those under twenty years old it was below 30 per cent. For De Boer, this trend will in all likelihood persist in the years to come (1981: 263).

A similar tendency also emanates from the important attitude and opinion surveys, which are more complete and thus permit one to differentiate attitudes. In his analysis of a 1969 French survey, Roussel concludes that 'd'un groupe de cohorte à l'autre, quelque chose a "bougé" dans les attitudes et les mobiles relatifs au mariage et à la vie familiale' (1971: 131); he adds that this transformation originates from recent cohorts, therefore from the young (and from women in particular). A few years later Roussel and Bourgignon (1978) established that only 20 per cent of French youth (under 30 years old) believed that marriage 'adds something positive,' while a majority of them reduced marriage to being a simple formality. Not only has something 'moved'; rather, a major transformation has occurred in the 'representations related to marriage': the institutional aspect of marriage has been devalued and marriage has been reduced to the couple.

This modification of attitudes towards marriage has also been confirmed in the American context. As expressed by Thornton and Freedman: 'the majority apparently considered the decision to marry or to remain single as a real and legitimate choice between acceptable alternatives; this perception of the relative merits of marriage and single life is quite different from that held by Americans in the past' (1982: 299).

This does not however imply a massive rejection of marriage: it continues to be valued although it no longer appears as the only possible way of life. The attitudes of Canadian women follow this pattern. When women aged 18 to 49 were asked to judge the importance of marriage for life as a couple, a quarter of them considered it to be very important, while a third estimated that it was not very or not at all important (table 6.2). Hence, the majority of women continue to believe that marriage is valuable for the family setting. However, notable differences appear according to age groups and marital experience. In fact, the only group for which marriage continues to be of great importance for life as a couple is that of currently married women between 40 and 49 years old: 42 per cent of them think that it is very important, whereas 20 per cent feel that it is of little or no importance.

Conversely, over 50 per cent of separated/divorced/widowed women and of women living with a partner (cohabitants) volunteer the opinion that marriage is of little or no importance for life as a couple. Marital experience, and in particular being part of a stable marriage, strongly influences the perception one has of marriage. Even the young first-time married women aged 20–29 lend greater importance to marriage than do unmarried women, including those separated/divorced/widowed 30–49 years old; only 7 per cent of cohabiting women are firmly convinced of the pertinence of marriage for life as a couple. These diverging points of view between married women on the one hand and unmarried women (separated/divorced/widowed or cohabiting) on the other can be easily ascertained: the former are currently living in the state of marriage, while the latter have either breached their contract or have chosen not to commit themselves in the same way.

The women were also asked what were the 'necessary conditions' when two people decide to get married; seven conditions or propositions were submitted to them for this purpose. Table 6.3 presents the portion of women who judged these conditions to be 'absolutely necessary.' The most obvious feature of these results is the high degree of consensus

TABLE 6.2

Percentage distribution of women according to the importance of marriage when a man and a woman live together, by marital experience and age group

| | First marriage in progress | | | | | First marriage broken 30–49 | Single | |
	Total 18–49	20–29	30–39	40–49	Total 18–49		Cohabitants 18–29	Alone 18–29
Very important	25.6	24.3	30.4	41.9	32.0	17.4	7.4	21.8
Important	34.3	39.5	35.5	36.3	37.0	29.9	25.6	34.9
Not very or not at all important	38.9	35.7	33.0	20.4	30.1	50.3	65.4	42.2
Don't know/no answer	1.2	0.5	1.1	1.4	0.9	2.4	1.6	1.1
Total	100.0	100.0	100.0	100.0	100.0	100.0	100.0	100.0

Q201: In your opinion, when a man and a woman decide to live together, is it very important, important, not very important, or not at all important for them to get married?

among the various groups of women for each condition taken separately. The most important prerequisite for marriage is that the woman and the man 'love each other strongly': 70 to 80 per cent of women consider this condition absolutely necessary.

Two-thirds of the sample felt that two other conditions were absolutely necessary for marriage: that the two people 'feel the same way about wanting or not wanting to have children' (67 per cent) and that 'they intend to stay married for the rest of their lives' (65 per cent). Cohabitants here differ from the sample as a whole in that they lend a bit less importance to these two propositions (58 per cent). Furthermore, that 'there is a strong sexual attraction between them' and that 'the couple has the financial means to support itself' received support in the 'absolutely necessary' category of respectively 40 per cent and 50 per cent of the women.

For three out of the seven indicators no change has been reported from older to younger generations. But it is interesting to note that, for the younger women, the importance of love increased by 10 percentage points, while the desire for and importance of children declined respectively by 6 and 4 percentage points; the importance of social background decreased by 10 points; all four changes are significant to the observer of the social scene. As if freed of the substance of previous attitudes and norms, the respondents had to fill in the vacuum with substitutes, however ephemeral.

Finally, around a fifth of the respondents considered it absolutely necessary for marriage that the couple have a similar social background and that they want to have children (16 and 22 per cent). Such a low percentage for the condition regarding having children is quite surprising; in fact, for nearly half the women surveyed the desire to have children is of no importance with respect to a couple's decision to marry. This result is opposed to the conventional view of marriage whereby the creation of a parent/children family is presumed. Nevertheless, the perspective of a romantic marriage where 'love is king' remains well entrenched in women's views, surpassing sexual attraction and financial security. A strong feeling of love almost succeeds in achieving unanimity among the women regarding its importance for marriage: 97 per cent consider it absolutely or fairly necessary.

Hence, according to womens' opinions, to marry it is absolutely necessary to be in love, but not requisite to want to have children. However, if children are desired, must the couple place itself within the legal framework of marriage? The majority replied 'yes' (71 per cent of the women in table 6.4). An affirmative reply was given by 85 per cent of

TABLE 6.3

Percentage of women who consider the condition mentioned 'absolutely' necessary for a man and a woman to decide to marry, by marital experience and age group

| | Total 18–49 | First marriage in progress | | | | First marriage broken 30–49 | Single | |
		20–29	30–39	40–49	Total 18–49		Cohabitants 18–29	Alone 18–29
a) love strongly	74.1	80.0	72.3	70.3	74.0	78.3	76.1	79.1
b) strong sexual attraction	41.3	41.9	38.4	41.0	40.2	44.2	43.2	40.7
c) want to have children	21.9	22.5	21.8	28.5	24.0	18.1	20.4*	20.5
d) feel same way about children	67.0	66.7	67.9	70.9	68.3	66.7	58.4	65.3
e) stay married for life	64.6	69.3	64.3	70.5	67.7	54.9	58.3	68.0
f) sufficient financial means	52.1	51.0	49.1	54.7	51.4	54.1	46.3	54.0
g) similar social background	15.8	13.1	15.2	23.4	16.9	22.9	9.8*	9.8

Q203: When two people decide to get married, is it absolutely necessary, fairly necessary, or not necessary that ...?

* Estimate based on less than 50 cases

married women aged 40–49, but by only 45 per cent of cohabiting women. The position of cohabiting women can clearly be understood in terms of their choice of living arrangement; although they do not desire to engage in a legal marriage, they do not wish to renounce having a family or bringing children into the world. This near opposition between the elder married women and the young cohabiting women clearly exhibits the limitations of the evolution that the perceptions of the role of marriage and the family are undergoing in our society.

The majority of women (over 85 per cent) nevertheless persist in believing that marriage 'adds something positive to the relationship that helps the couple get through difficult times' (table 6.4). The contrast between the results for first-time married women (93 per cent) and cohabiting women (62 per cent) once again deserves mention. Marital experience also influences the perception of marriage as creating obligations for the couple; according to table 6.4, about 36 per cent of married women consider that 'marriage creates certain obligations which have a negative effect on the relationship,' while for the three other groups 50 per cent of the women fall into this category.

The perception of marriage among the Canadian female population in 1984 is evidently highly diversified. For some women, marriage has ceased to be the only way of life. Both attitudes and behaviour have changed markedly. Although marriage remains an important institution, its absolute pertinence is being challenged. Young people, particularly when cohabiting, seem to be at the forefront of this transformation; these women have a somewhat different view of the couple whereby this institution makes way for an 'informal' agreement.

2. *Cohabitation.* In our society, especially among the young, cohabitation has become an increasingly prevalent way of life for couples. To a certain extent, cohabitation therefore opposes itself to the 'white' wedding that governed the formation of new families until just a few years ago. Unlike what can be observed over the abortion issue, for instance, today premarital sexual relations and cohabitation are no longer the subject of important societal debates. In fact, these 'new behaviours' have become largely accepted by the population (De Boer 1981: 263; Roussel and Bourguignon 1978; Singh 1980; Clayton and Bokemeier 1980). This permissiveness is not restricted to specific groups or social classes; the apparent tendency is rather towards a convergence of attitudes. Hence, on premarital sexuality Roussel and Bourguignon write that 'la grande majorité de la population interrogée [18–29 ans] estime "qu'il est bon" que des relations existent avant le mariage' (1978: 111) and that the contrary

TABLE 6.4

Percentage of women by their perception of the importance of marriage for having children and for the quality of their relationship, by marital experience and age group

	First marriage in progress					First marriage broken 30–49	Single		
	Total 18–49	20–29	30–39	40–49	Total 18–49		Cohabitants 18–29	Alone 18–29
To have children it is necessary to marry (Q211)	70.8	70.0	75.4	84.8	76.3	67.5	44.6	69.6
Marriage adds something positive to relationship (Q209)	85.2	94.4	91.2	93.2	92.8	69.9	62.1	84.8
Marriage creates obligations (Q210)	42.1	36.3	33.7	39.6	36.3	50.8	45.0	50.0

Q211: When a couple decide to have children, do you think that it is necessary that they get married?

Q209: Would you say that being married adds something positive to the relationship that helps the couple to get through difficult times?

Q210: Would you say that being married creates certain obligations which have a negative effect on the relationship?

appears almost abnormal. Singh (1980: 392) arrived at a similar conclusion in his study of the American case. Cohabitation, however, did not receive unconditional relative acceptance; although cohabitation is easily tolerated as a prenuptial lifestyle, it is much less so in the context of family life, that is, when children are involved: 'when the question arises of having children in such a situation, a sharp rise is noted in the percentage of the population who consider this morally wrong' (De Boer 1981: 263).

In the 1984 Canadian Fertility Survey, a few questions were asked in order to ascertain the women's opinion on this subject. For women aged 18 to 49 taken as a whole, over 70 per cent find premarital sexual relations acceptable (table 6.5). The degree of acceptance for this practice is however slightly greater for young men (75 per cent) than for young women (71 per cent). This disparity seems significant, although slight; moreover, with the exception of cohabiting women, gender differences are apparent for all age groups of women, though the increase in acceptance in young cohorts is rather marked. Also, the propensity for cohabitants to state their approval of premarital sex is markedly higher (nearly 95 per cent) than for the other women. This distinction can be explained by their youth (18 to 29 years old) and by their cohabitation, since they constantly live their sexuality outside the bonds of marriage. These results, however, do not indicate whether young cohabiting women would consent in similar proportion to a sexual life outside a relationship.

Conversely, it is among married women, and particularly among those aged 30–49, that the least acceptance is expressed for premarital sexual relations; for instance, less than 50 per cent of those between 40 and 49 years of age approve of such behaviour. Let us also note that almost 80 per cent of women whose first marriage broke up and of single women living alone approve of premarital sex, against 74 per cent of young women married for the first time.

Another qualification must be added regarding the acceptability of cohabitation; opinions differ depending on whether the objective of the cohabitation is to ensure the success of the future marriage, or whether it simply results from a reciprocal attraction between the man and the woman without entailing any long-term commitment. In the first case 76 per cent of women state their approval for cohabitation, whereas this figure drops to 60 per cent regarding the second situation (table 6.5). Once again, strong variations appear according to age group and marital experience. Married women, especially those aged 30–49, appear to reject cohabitation the most, in particular if it does not imply a long-term

TABLE 6.5
Acceptance of premarital sex, cohabitation, and cohabiting couples same as married couples, by marital experience and age group

		First marriage in progress				First marriage broken 30–49	Single	
	Total 18–49	20–29	30–39	40–49	Total 18–49		Cohabitants 18–29	Alone 18–29
Premarital sex acceptable for young women (Q206)	71.2	73.7	65.9	47.1	62.8	77.4	93.7	80.3
Premarital sex acceptable for young men (Q206)	74.6	76.6	69.7	51.9	66.6	81.0	94.0	84.2
Cohabitation acceptable as an insurance that marriage will last (Q205)	76.3	79.1	71.6	59.6	70.5	81.8	93.8	87.7
Cohabitation acceptable if there is attraction but do not want to make long-term commitment (Q205)	59.4	64.1	56.7	41.3	54.6	64.0	84.7	72.2
Cohabiting couples accepted same way as married couples (Q212)	73.0	72.1	72.4	65.7	70.4	81.2	92.3	83.3

Q206: In your opinion, is it acceptable for (a) young women and (b) young men to have a sexual life before getting married?
Q205: Do you find that it is acceptable or not acceptable for a man and woman to decide to live together without marriage ...?
Q212: Among the people you known, are couples living together accepted in the same way as married couples?

commitment. This result is quite understandable given their personal choice of a more conventional union.

Cohabitants are at the other extreme. However, all of them do not accept cohabitation, as one might expect: rather 94 per cent do in the case of a trial marriage, and 85 per cent do when there is no long-term commitment. Two plausible hypotheses may explain this seemingly paradoxical situation. First, one of the spouse's marital situation may prevent remarriage, if at least one of them is separated without being divorced. Second, it is possible that one partner must submit to the will of the other partner who for some reason does not wish to commit him- or herself to marriage.

Unfortunately, the survey does not provide information regarding the acceptance of cohabitation in relation to procreation. Results just examined (in table 6.4) nevertheless allow us to presume that with the exception of cohabitants, extramarital fertility continues to be negatively perceived. Moreover, we know that the arrival of a child within a cohabiting union often brings it to legitimize the relationship (Leridon and Villeneuve-Gokalp 1988; Roussel and Bourguignon 1978) and that, more generally, a successful cohabitation often results in marriage (Bower and Christopherson 1977). On the other hand, 92 per cent of cohabitants indicate that their social circle accepts cohabitation in the same way as marriage; 65 per cent of married women aged 40–49 and 73 per cent of women from the sample as a whole fall into this category.

The positions of the women surveyed regarding cohabitation and premarital sexual relations fit quite well with their views on marriage in general. These opinions are in fact not independent. Cohabiting women appear to be living in the most liberal circles, along with, to a lesser extent, single women living alone and women whose first marriage broke up. Married women live especially in more conservative circles, particularly those 40–49 years old.

3. *Children*. According to Philippe Ariès, the motivations that nowadays push individuals and couples to reduce their fertility are very different from those that previously existed. Today, the child's place within the couple has been reduced and its existence 'is related to plans for a future in which he is no longer the essential variable, as he was during the nineteenth century' (Aries 1980: 650).

Hence, American women value education and work before marriage (Thornton and Freedman 1982: 301–2), while in France, 'les attitudes à l'égard de l'enfant sont ... plutôt négatives chez la plupart de ces jeunes couples "mariés" qui ont d'abord envie de vivre pour eux' (Roussel and

Bourguignon 1978: 46). Children would seem to require too much emotional and material investment and present a challenge to the overall lifestyle of the household. However this does not mean that the presence of children has become an unfavourable situation. On the contrary, if children are no longer the finality of marriage, they have nevertheless become a necessity for the parents (Blake 1979; Roussel and Bourguignon 1978): they are of instrumental value and contribute to the happiness of the couple.

Their economic importance remains very limited however (not to say being null or negative), and current family size seems to be converging toward two children. Roussel and Bourguignon in fact speak of 'une certaine idée irrévocable de la taille "idéale" de la famille.'

Regarding opinions on children, the results from the 1984 Canadian Fertility Survey do not show the recurrence of the pattern that emerged from women's opinions on marriage and cohabitation: there is no opposition between the more conservative married women and the more liberal cohabitants.

Table 6.6 illustrates this point. For 72 per cent of the women surveyed, 'having a child provides a goal in life that nothing else can replace,' while for 84 per cent of the sample it supplies 'an irreplaceable source of affection.' However, 94 per cent believe that becoming a parent 'means taking on heavy responsibilities,' whereas a small fraction (18 per cent) feel that 'having children tends to distance the spouses from one another.' These proportions vary little according to age group or marital experience, with perhaps the exception of married women aged 30–49 whose first marriage is broken. These women tend to attribute a bit less gratification to the presence of children and consider in markedly greater proportion that their presence 'tends to distance the spouses from one another'. The opinions of the women in the three other groups – married women, cohabitants, and single women living alone – are relatively homogeneous regarding the four propositions in table 6.6. Women from all groups agree in their almost unanimous support (94 per cent) of the claim that parenthood entails heavy responsibilities, although a majority of them concurrently recognize the happiness it brings. It is thus not surprising that present fertility is rather hesitant! We would like to add that the argument about the hesitancy in fertility is valid only in certain interpretations. Over the years the standard of living has increased by leaps and bounds, while the numerical burden of children declined. The feelings of responsibility increased then only because the value system turned in other competing directions, not because the responsibilities themselves have become greater. In terms of the number of children, they declined.

TABLE 6.6

Percentage of women who say they 'strongly agree' or 'agree' with the statement mentioned about children, by marital experience and age group

| | Total 18–49 | First marriage in progress | | | | | First marriage broken 30–49 | Single | |
		20–29	30–39	40–49	Total 18–49			Cohabitants 18–29	Alone 18–29
A child:									
a) provides irreplaceable goal in life	71.7	78.8	72.6	69.4	73.6		65.4	71.1	73.6
b) distances spouses	17.7	16.0	17.8	15.8	16.6		27.2	17.2	13.9
c) means taking on heavy responsibilities	93.7	92.9	94.1	93.3	93.5		94.6	90.9	94.3
d) provides irreplaceable source of affection	83.9	88.8	85.2	80.6	85.1		78.2	84.8	85.8

Q217: On the whole, would you say that you strongly agree, agree, disagree or strongly disagree with the following statements ...?

Women were also asked their opinion on the presence of an only child and, in this context, on the relevance of a second child (table 6.7). According to half the respondents, there is a risk that an only child will have more problems than a child in a family with other children. Little variation occurs with women's age group or marital experience.

The women who disagreed with the preceding statement were further asked if they believed on the contrary that an only child will in fact have *fewer* problems than a child in a family with many children. Only slightly more than 20 per cent of the women replied 'yes.' In total, 10 per cent (that is 20 per cent of 50 per cent) of the women surveyed believe that an only child will have relatively fewer difficulties than other children, whereas, as we saw above, 50 per cent feel that he or she will have more problems.

The women were subsequently questioned on the necessity of a second child, either to ensure a better family environment or for the parents' satisfaction. A majority consider that a second child must 'create a better environment for the children,' which coincides with the opinion volunteered regarding the well-being of an only child. However, over 40 percent of respondents feel that a second child will be conceived for the couple's personal satisfaction.

The most remarkable element pertaining to women's opinions on children is their homogeneity across age and marital experience categories, in contrast with what has been observed regarding marriage and cohabitation. In any event, these results seem to confirm that fertility motivations have undergone a profound evolution, distinct from that experienced by attitudes towards marriage. This matter will be reviewed in our concluding discussion.

4. *Divorce.* Divorce is a legal procedure that terminates a marriage, although in principle marriage is supposed to be a permanent union. Since the beginning of the 1960s an impressive change in attitudes regarding marriage dissolution has occurred in the United States (Thornton 1985). This evolution is assumed to have followed the growing incidence of divorce. In Canada, where the tradition of divorce is more recent, it seems to be attitudes (motivations and necessity) that led to the legal reform of 1968 (Péron et al. 1987: 62). The integrity of marriage nevertheless remains a value largely shared by Canadian women: for 90 per cent of the women surveyed, marriage is conceived of as a permanent union that should only be broken for very serious reasons (table 6.8). This is particularly true for married women (93 per cent), while understandably less so for women whose first marriage is broken (80 per cent).

TABLE 6.7

Percentage of women by their perceptions of problems with an 'only' child and a second child, by marital experience and age group

| | First marriage in progress | | | | | First marriage broken 30–49 | Single | | |
	Total 18–49	20–29	30–39	40–49	Total 18–49		Cohabitants 18–29	Alone 18–29
a) Only child has more problems.	49.1	52.2	46.6	50.1	49.5	46.0	53.1	50.8
b) Only child has fewer problems.	21.3	21.8	19.2	19.3	19.9	25.6	23.4*	22.0
c) Second child:								
– for child	49.2	50.4	48.7	51.1	50.0	50.1	47.0	47.5
– for parents	38.6	34.9	38.4	47.9	36.7	38.7	42.5	43.1
– for child and parents	9.4	13.2	9.9	8.7	10.5	7.7	7.7	7.9

a) Q225: In your opinion, is there a risk that an only child will have more problems than a child in a family with other children?

b) Q226: Do you believe on the contrary that an only child will in fact have fewer problems because his parents will be able to devote more time to him?

c) Q227: In your opinion, do parents have a second child in order to create a better environment for the children or rather for their own personal satisfaction?

* Estimate based on less than 50 cases

TABLE 6.8
Attitudes towards divorce, by marital experience and age group

	Total 18–49	First marriage in progress			Total 18–49	First marriage broken 30–49	Single	
		20–29	30–39	40–49			Cohabitants 18–29	Alone 18–29
More or less agree that marriage should be broken only for very serious reasons (Q202)	89.9	92.7	92.3	93.1	92.6	79.9	85.0	86.4
Likely to get divorced if no love but only friendship (Q213)	24.6	25.1	19.8	15.3	20.2	28.0	32.3	31.6
Likely to get divorced if husband unfaithful (Q213)	60.2	64.8	52.7	51.4	56.2	62.0	67.0	69.1
Likely to get divorced if no common interests except financial security (Q213)	64.6	63.2	62.4	52.2	59.7	69.2	78.8	66.3

Q202: In general, would you say you more or less agree or disagree with the following statement: 'Marriage is a permanent union which should only be broken for very serious reasons'?

Q213: If you were in the following circumstances, would you be likely to get divorced? Try to put yourself in the situation described.

There are numerous circumstances that may lead a married couple to divorce. Three of these were suggested in the survey, and the women were asked if, in each of the situations described, they would consider divorce (table 6.8). First, nearly 25 per cent of respondents state that they would divorce if the initial strong love no longer exists and there is only friendship and respect left. This percentage is higher for the non-married women (about 30 per cent) and weaker for married women (20 per cent). Second, for 60 per cent of the women, an adulterous husband would be a circumstance justifying divorce. Finally, if there were no longer any common interests in the union other than financial security, 65 per cent of the women would consider terminating their marriage. In all these situations, cohabitants and single women living alone would divorce in a greater proportion than would the other groups of women. Undoubtedly, being married makes the perspective of a breakup more difficult to imagine; likewise, having already been married influences one's perception of divorce. Age may also have an effect on women's opinions on this subject. Where married women are concerned, we notice that the younger they are, the higher the percentage of them willing to consider divorce in either of the three circumstances mentioned. But even in this case, the determining factor could be marital experience, specifically marriage duration. In fact, in Thornton's study, (1985: 868) this variable appears as the most discriminating to explain attitudes towards divorce. The issue remains complex and a satisfactory under-standing of the facts would require more in-depth analysis of the results.

Another interesting feature appears in table 6.8. Regarding women's opinions on marriage, we observed earlier in table 6.3 that the funda-mental condition for a couple in deciding to get married was that the man and the women 'love each other strongly' (74 per cent). Interest-ingly, if within the marriage over time love ceases to exist and is replaced by friendship, this situation is not judged as sufficiently dramatic for the majority of women to consider divorce. Only 25 per cent said that they are likely to get divorced.

Reality is evidently always more complex: in fact, if there is no longer any love within a union, there are certainly other underlying problems. Moreover, getting divorced is a complex decision to make. Among other things, the children become an issue of considerable importance; the degree of women's approval of divorce thus varies depending on whether or not children could be present within the union (table 6.9). Among the respondents, 17 per cent approve of divorce without reservation in the presence of young children, but this figure reaches 28 per cent when the children are adolescents and climbs to almost 65 per cent in the

TABLE 6.9

Percentage of women who would approve of divorce 'without reservation,' by the presence of children, marital experience, and age group

| | Total 18–49 | First marriage in progress | | | | | Single | |
		20–29	30–39	40–49	Total 18–49	First marriage broken 30–49	Cohabitants 18–29	Alone 18–29
– With very young children	17.1	13.0	15.9	12.3	13.9	32.7	20.3	13.6
– With teenaged children	27.7	26.8	24.9	17.9	23.4	41.6	36.1	26.5
– Without children	64.4	59.6	63.7	62.5	62.0	74.3	71.1	60.2

Q215: Do you approve without reservation, approve with reservations or completely disapprove of divorce in the following circumstances ...?

TABLE 6.10
Percentage of women who think that couples
should be allowed to get divorced simply
according to their will, by marital experience
and age group

	%
Total, 18–49	50.2
First marriage in progress	
20–29	47.0
30–39	47.8
40–49	41.6
20–49	45.9
First marriage broken, 30–49	58.7
Single cohabitants, 18–29	65.2
Single alone, 18–29	50.2

absence of children. Hence, women's opinion on divorce is considerably tempered when the presence of children is considered, and this holds for all groups of women.

Lastly, let us mention that half the female population surveyed believes that couples should be able to divorce simply according to their wishes, and not for reasons specified by law (table 6.10). Among cohabitants and divorced/separated/widowed women, this proportion reaches 65 and 60 per cent respectively, which reflects their greater acceptance of divorce as such. These attitudes must of course be related to those on marriage and cohabitation: they are various aspects of the perceptions and values pertaining to family life as a whole.

The couple

Although marriage is becoming less and less valued and decreasingly popular, cohabitation nowadays presents a viable alternative to marriage, and life as a twosome continues to be the principal way of life for today's adults. However, the contemporary couple – particularly if the partners are young – differs markedly from former couples. In their study of young French generations, Roussel and Bourguignon (1978) identified six attributes that characterize couples aged 18 to 30 (married or cohabiting):

- privatization of the feelings of love
- growing importance of sexuality and the recognition of the woman as a partner in the pleasure
- realistic and reasonable romanticism
- undramatic acceptance of breakups
- equality of the sexes (no hierarchy between spouses)
- spontaneity of the feelings of love and importance of faithfulness.

The presentation of the pertinent Canadian data is divided into two themes:

- Life as part of a couple
- Role sharing

1. *Life as a couple.* The women were asked to express their opinion regarding the importance of four conditions for ensuring that a couple's relationship lasts a long time (table 6.11). These four conditions are love, affection, sexuality, and faithfulness. Despite a few variations according to the subgroups of women, over 45 per cent of the sample consider that the persistence of the strong love that existed at the beginning of the relationship as well as a satisfactory sexual life are important or very important for a couple's survival.

A third condition, which states that the strong love that existed at the beginning should turn at least into deep affection, is held by 55 per cent of the women, who believe that an enduring relationship depends on more than love and sexual satisfaction. Women attribute the greatest importance to faithfulness: nearly 75 per cent of them consider it important or very important for the couple's relationship to survive. Differences are once again apparent according to marital experience and age group, but the emphasis placed on faithfulness is most noticeable, as it surpasses all other conditions by up to 15 percentage points.

The emphasis on faithfulness in the abstract for 74 per cent of respondents in table 6.11 compares with the 60 per cent in table 6.8 who see unfaithfulness as a cause for divorce. One wonders whether to interpret the difference as a sign of the remaining strength of the marital ties or as another indicator of the declining importance of earlier values.

Cohabitants stand out in that they seem to attribute less weight than do the other respondents to emotional and sexual conditions for a couple's longevity. Cohabiting women are the only ones who ascribe less importance to each of the four conditions than do all women as a whole. Is it the liberality of the cohabiting single women that puts them below

TABLE 6.11

Percentage of women who consider that four conditions are 'important' or 'very important' 'for a couple to live together for a long time,' by marital experience and age group

	First marriage in progress					First marriage	Single	
	Total 18–49	20–29	30–39	40–49	Total 18–49	broken 30–49	Cohabitants 18–29	Alone 18–29
a) love endures	46.1	50.9	45.2	45.8	47.1	42.8	42.1	49.4
b) love vs affection	54.8	53.9	54.0	59.8	55.7	57.8	42.7	52.7
c) satisfactory sexual life	48.6	49.9	48.1	49.4	49.0	52.1	42.2	45.2
d) faithfulness	73.8	79.9	71.3	75.8	75.3	70.5	68.7	76.6

Q204: In order for a couple to live together for a long time, would you say that it is very important, important, not very important or not at all important that ...?

the average expectations of other women or is it the feeling that in their status they must not expect too much from life?

Furthermore, as can be observed in table 6.12, cohabitants are those most in favour of each partner having their own close friends (whom they can see without the other's presence). Single women in general express the least opposition to friendship outside the couple (with over 80 per cent being in favour). Of all the women living as part of a couple, while over 60 per cent of cohabitants replied that they participated in recreational activities outside the home without their husband/partner more than once a month, among the other groups of women this proportion was never above 50 per cent (table 6.12).

Hence cohabitants seem to assign a bit less importance to their relationship than do other women, particularly married women aged 40–49. Moreover, table 6.13 indicates that cohabiting women are the most likely to experience difficulties within their relationship, whether it be regarding spending money, organizing leisure time, sharing housework, or even their sex life. Without further study, it may be premature to conclude that cohabitants experience less satisfying relationships. The problems encountered by these women could in fact result from more combative attempts at achieving equality within the couple. However, this hypothesis remains unverified.

Couples most often face difficulties regarding the way they spend money and share housework. Approximately 9 per cent and 8 per cent of women experience these problems respectively, while for cohabitants these figures reach 13 per cent and 15 per cent. For all groups of women, sexual life appears to be the least troublesome area; we may however be underestimating this particular type of problem, since women might not have been sufficiently at ease in discussing the issue during a telephone interview.

2. *Role sharing.* In the case of a conventional couple, role sharing between the partners is relatively well defined: the man works outside the home while the woman takes care of the children and of household chores (cooking, housework, and so on). In recent years, because more and more women work outside the home and are having fewer children, the situation has rapidly changed. Consequently, the division of household labour has had to be 'renegotiated' in conjunction with this new behaviour, which has brought men (husbands or partners) to participate more in child-related and household chores.

The examination of sex-roles has been the subject of numerous studies, particularly in North America (Thornton, Alwin, and Comburn 1983).

TABLE 6.12
Friendship and participation in recreational activities outside the home without partner, by marital experience and age group

| | Total 18–49 | First marriage in progress | | | | First marriage broken 30–49 | Single | |
		20–29	30–39	40–49	Total 18–49		Cohabitants 18–29	Alone 18–29
Good thing to have close friends without partner (Q220)	75.4	72.0	73.4	68.1	71.4	76.5	85.0	82.3
Recreational activities outside home without partner (Q700)	45.8	46.1	47.5	40.0	44.7	43.9*	62.5	N.A.

Q220: Do you find that it is a good thing for each partner in a couple to have their own close friends who they each see without the other?

Q700: Would you say that you take part in recreational activities outside the home without your husband/partner ...

* Percentages based on the subgroup of women living as a couple

N.A.: Not applicable

TABLE 6.13
Percentage of women who 'often' have a problem in their life as part of a couple, by marital experience and age group

| | Total 18–49 | First marriage in progress | | | | Total 18–49 | First marriage broken 30–49 | Single Cohabitants 18–29 |
		20–29	30–39	40–49				
a) spending money	8.9	9.8	6.4	9.0		8.2	10.4†	12.9†
b) organizing leisure time	3.6	3.2†	2.8†	4.4†		3.4	4.9†	4.7†
c) sharing housework	8.2	9.4	7.4	7.1		8.0	6.4†	15.3†
d) sex life	3.0	1.8†	2.4†	3.8†		3.0	2.8†	3.8†

Q701: In your life as a couple, do you often, sometimes or never have problems in the following areas ...?

* Percentages based on the subgroup of women living as a couple
† Estimate based on less than 50 cases

Since the 1960s, all segments of society seem to have undergone a marked evolution towards greater sex-role egalitarianism (Thornton and Freedman 1979), which has led Thornton and his colleagues to conclude that: 'young women of the 1980s appear to be entering adulthood with considerably more egalitarian sex-role attitudes than was true of their mothers' (Thornton et al. 1983: 213–15).

Although education and female labour-force participation have played an undeniable role in sex-role emancipation, the importance of a generation effect must not be neglected: generations born and socialized during the baby-boom have greatly participated in the social and political debates of the period (sexual liberation, civil rights movement, women's struggle) and have thus contributed to the shaping of new values. Canadian women are no exception. Role-sharing within the couple is an integral part of these new values acquired over the last twenty-five years.

For the majority of women surveyed, there is no doubt that the couple must tend towards a greater equality when it comes to sharing tasks that are necessary to establish a household and to ensure that it functions smoothly (whether or not children are present) (Kempeneers 1992). Thus, over 90 per cent of the sample consider that child-related chores must necessarily be shared equally by both partners, while for household chores 78 per cent of the women express this opinion (table 6.14). These percentages are a bit higher for the groups of single women, either cohabitants or women living alone: they reach 96 per cent regarding children and are a bit below 86 per cent in the case of housework. Married women aged 40–49 show the lowest percentages, although these remain above 85 and 70 per cent respectively.

In reality, however, equality of role- and task-sharing falls short of women's desires. Among those who have children, approximately 70 per cent or 77 per cent of women admit that they are in large part responsible for feeding the baby and changing diapers, and buying clothes for the children, respectively, while 50 per cent state that they oversee the children's school work (table 6.15). The situation is identical regarding housework: about 78 per cent of those surveyed do the cooking and 70 per cent handle the rest of the housework (table 6.15). None of these situations suggests that equality is close to being attained. A minority of women have a living arrangement whereby the partner contributes equally or more than they do to household chores (table 6.16). Young women under thirty, and especially cohabitants, seem to be furthest along the road to parity with men in this respect. However, considerable progress must be made even by these women in order to achieve the sharing they desire. Under such conditions, it is not sur-

TABLE 6.14

Percentage of women who think that child-related and household chores should be shared equally by both partners, by marital experience and age group

| | Total 18–49 | First marriage in progress | | | Total 18–49 | First marriage broken 30–49 | Single | |
		20–29	30–39	40–49			Cohabitants 18–29	Alone 18–29
a) Children: shared equally	92.8	91.8	92.7	87.9	91.1	92.3	96.1	96.4
b) Household: shared equally	78.0	75.9	74.8	70.1	73.7	76.5	85.6	86.4

a) Q218: Do you think that looking after the children should be done only by the woman, mostly by the woman, equally shared by both partners or done mainly by the man?

b) Q219: Do you think that household chores such as the cooking or the housework should be done only by the woman, mostly by the woman, equally shared by both partners or done mainly by the man?

TABLE 6.15

Percentage of women who say that they are 'always' or 'mostly' the one who takes care of the children,* cooking, and housework, by marital experience and age group

| | First marriage in progress | | | | | First marriage broken 30–49 | Single cohabitants 18–29 |
	Total 18–49	20–29	30–39	40–49	Total 18–49		
Care of children (Q703):							
a) feeding and changing diapers	70.7	61.2	68.9	78.9	70.2	79.1	54.5†
b) shopping for children's clothes	77.1	70.7	77.3	81.6	77.1	81.6	64.2†
c) overseeing children's school work	50.1	42.3	46.0	53.9	49.0	59.8	40.0†
Cooking (Q702)	78.8	77.6	82.2	85.3	81.8	73.4	55.0
Housework (Q702)	70.4	66.3	73.3	78.1	72.5	66.8	47.1

Q703: Would you say that it was always you, mostly you, equally you and your husband/partner or mainly your husband/partner who ...?

Q702: Would you say that it is always you, mostly you, equally you and your husband/partner or mainly your husband/partner who ...?

* Concerns only women who have children

** Percentages based on the subgroup of women living as a couple

† Estimate based on less than 50 cases

TABLE 6.16
Percentage of women who state that in their
relationship household chores are shared equally
between the partners or are mainly done by
the man, for five categories of tasks

Cooking	21.7
Housework	29.6
Change diapers	29.4
Shop for children's clothes	22.8
Supervise children's schoolwork	49.9

prising to note that the problems these women most often face in their
life as a couple are attributed to household organization (managing expenses and sharing housework) rather than to their sexual or social lives.

Importance of family life and overall happiness

The following presentation has two distinct objectives: first, we will
attempt to examine the comparative importance women attribute to family life and to personal independence respectively, and second we will
try to measure women's level of overall happiness.

Table 6.17 refers to the first theme. The results represent the proportion of women who stated that five conditions were 'very important'
for a happy life: 'having a lasting relationship as a couple,' 'being married,' 'having at least one child,' 'being able to take a job outside the
home,' and 'being free to do as you wish.' Having a lasting relationship
is the only condition considered very important by an average respondent (65.7 per cent). Proportions for the four other conditions are below
45 per cent. In order to have generally happy lives, women clearly
attribute a lot of weight to their life as part of a couple. Combining the
proportions of women who answered 'very important' and 'important'
to the five statements of table 6.17, we arrive at the following results
for women as a whole:

Statement	*Percentage*
Have a lasting relationship	95.5
Be married	70.4
Have at least one child	71.8
Be able to take a job outside the home	71.9
Be free to do as you wish	87.4

TABLE 6.17

Percentage of women who consider that five conditions are 'very important' for being generally happy in life, by marital experience and age group

	Total 18–49	First marriage in progress				First marriage broken 30–49	Single	
		20–29	30–39	40–49	Total 18–49		Cohabitants 18–29	Alone 18–29
a) have a lasting relationship	65.7	72.6	70.8	73.3	72.2	60.6	56.2	58.0
b) be married	41.2	46.4	47.9	55.0	49.5	28.8	24.3	37.3
c) have a child	40.4	43.7	44.7	52.8	46.6	37.6	28.7	31.6
d) be able to take job outside home	31.6	27.2	28.1	25.3	27.0	32.0	36.8	42.4
e) be free to do as you wish	43.0	41.0	41.0	39.1	40.5	41.6	43.6	49.3

Q207: In order for you to be generally happy in life, is it very important, important, not very important or not at all important ...?

Thus, having a 'lasting relationship as a couple' receives almost unanimous support from respondents. The second most important condition is 'to be free to do as you wish.' Family values – being married and having at least one child – and having a job outside the home ranked third, slightly above 70 per cent. A few differences appear in table 6.17 according to subgroups. Women whose first marriage is in progress place strong emphasis on family values and on life as part of a couple. However, fewer than 30 per cent of these women consider that it is very important to be able to work outside the home. On the contrary, among single women family values are markedly less influential whereas labor-force participation is more highly valued; life as part of a couple nevertheless remains very important for the majority.

Women clearly dissociate family values from life as part of a couple; these dimensions seem to be envisaged as two distinct realities, in the same way as being able to work outside the home and doing as one wishes. With the exception of married women, another feature of these results is the weak contribution that having at least one child makes for 'a happy life,' which must be related to women's attitudes regarding marriage, life as part of a couple, and children. However, the decisive role of the respondents' present situation in their evaluation of the necessary conditions for a happy life must not be neglected: women's answers could simply reflect a posteriori justifications of their lifestyles. The less-than-a-quarter importance attached to 'being married' by cohabiting women could be another case of rationalization of a situation without alternative.

Table 6.18 informs us of the respondents' appreciation of their lives as a whole. The results are interesting although difficult to interpret. In total, 45 per cent of the women declare themselves very happy, while less than 5 per cent feel very unhappy. Married women and single women living alone appear as the most happy (53 per cent and 47 per cent respectively). Cohabitants are the next most happy group (39 per cent), followed by the separated/divorced women (21 per cent). Approximately 14 per cent of this last group stated that they were very unhappy. Many studies highlight this differential happiness according to marital status; their results concur with the finding that married people declare themselves relatively happier (Glenn and Weaver 1979; Mugford and Lally 1981; Gove et al. 1983), although the relationship seems to have undergone recent changes (Glenn and Weaver 1988). These studies inform us that marital status is the best predictor of overall happiness, which is always at a higher level for married women. One explanation

TABLE 6.18
Percentage distribution of women by level of happiness in life, by marital experience and age group

| | First marriage in progress | | | | Total 18–49 | First marriage broken 30–49 | Single | |
	Total 18–49	20–29	30–39	40–49			Cohabitants 18–29	Alone 18–29
Very happy	45.4	53.8	52.5	54.6	53.4	21.5	39.2	47.2
Fairly happy	50.7	44.7	46.1	42.8	44.9	64.9	57.5	49.8
Unhappy	4.9	1.5	1.4	2.6	1.7	13.6	3.3	3.0

Q208: On the whole, would you say that you have had a very happy life, a fairly happy, a fairly unhappy or a very unhappy life up to now?

Note: 'Unhappy' includes 'fairly unhappy' and 'very unhappy' categories.

for these findings is based on the concept of 'dissonance': '[some] married women deny feelings of unhappiness because of cognitive dissonance between their actual situation and that which they have been told to expect' (Mugford and Lally 1981: 969–70). Gove et al. (1983) favour a selection effect: emotionally unstable persons are less likely to marry and, when they do, they stay married in smaller proportions. Consequently, individual well-being does not depend on marriage as such but rather on marriage quality. According to Glenn and Weaver (1977, 1979), marriage – and remarriage alike – provide psychological benefits that make marriage the best alternative to remaining single (or to divorce, as the case may be). However, it would seem that this relationship has changed over the last few years: a dramatic decline in the level of overall happiness of married persons aged 25 to 39 has been observed in American society, while the opposite tendency has appeared in the case of single people (Glenn and Weaver 1988). This reversal, if applicable to Canadian society, is a function of the multiplication of alternatives to marriage (such as cohabitation), the growth of individualism, and the decreasing influence that social groups exert on individual behaviour.

Although in the 1984 Canadian Fertility Survey the differences in overall happiness between married persons and single women living alone are slight, fewer than 40 per cent of cohabitants consider themselves very happy. Following Mugford and Lally's argument (1981: 973), the combativeness of these women regarding sex roles and their generally unconventional behaviour could possibly increase the daily level of social tensions that they must confront. This viewpoint relates to a previous finding, which revealed that cohabitants face problems in their relationship somewhat more frequently than do other women (see table 6.13, for example).

None the less, it is necessary to emphasize that 96 per cent of respondents feel fairly or very happy. Though among those whose first marriage is broken we find the lowest proportion reporting themselves as very happy (21.5 per cent), among the other groups the differences are small. The percentages reporting as 'very happy' among the married, cohabitants, and singles living alone are 53.4, 39.2, and 47.2 respectively. Consequently, excluding women whose first marriage is broken, it is difficult to claim that marital experience can continue to have (assuming it ever did) a significant differential effect on individual happiness. The present multiplication of unconventional family arrangements that is undermining sexual and family roles (Macklin 1980: 915–16) indicates that we are heading towards a lack of noticeable variation in individual satisfaction. This perspective provides insight for understanding why the institution of marriage is decreasingly valued and the cohabitation 'trend' persists. Each person eventually finds the lifestyle that best fits his or her values and aspirations.

Discussion

The detailed presentation of the Canadian Fertility Survey data on attitudes about various dimensions of the family shows that women in general have adopted very nuanced views on marriage and cohabitation, on the importance of having children, on the stability of the family and on the relationship that these realities have with their personal satisfaction and happiness. Although on each dimension examined there are always a good number of women who are attached to the more traditional aspects of the family institution, the features of the changing relationship between men and women and between parents and children are more and more well accepted and seen as valid alternatives to traditional values and behaviour. Not only have cohabitation and divorce become socially acceptable, but having children is not considered any more as the focal point of a woman's life or as the basis of a couple's relationship. In that respect, it is interesting to add that data show a wide acceptance of artificial insemination (65 per cent of the sample agree with the procedure) and a limited acceptance, but not negligible, of surrogate motherhood (24 per cent agree with the practice). Even if the actual recourse to these practices is in fact relatively rare, it could be argued that the social acceptance they enjoy is by itself a major change and a strong indicator of a profound transformation of the Canadian value system.

Moreover, an analysis of the socio-economic correlates of attitudes about marriage and cohabitation shows that, not only age and marital experience are influencing them, but that other factors such as religiosity and educational level, as well as region of residence and total number of desired children, have an effect on how women envisage cohabitation and marriage (Wu and Balakrishnan 1992). The mechanisms through which these factors operate could not be studied, but they cannot be put aside or neglected in any attempt to understand the evolution of attitudes about the family or the evolution of the family itself.

The results consequently highlight the emergence of new family values in our society. However, certain points deserve further discussion:

- the meaning of differing attitudes between married women and cohabitants

- the meaning of the differences observed in values regarding marriage, cohabitation, divorce, etc. on the one hand, and those concerning children on the other hand
- the meaning of these new family values in the context of social-demographic evolution as a whole

The few studies that focus on the attitudes of cohabitants demonstrate that they have a higher tendency than do married people to commit themselves to less formal relationships and to favour less conventional attitudes. Roussel and Bourguignon's (1978) in depth study illustrates these points well, and is confirmed to varying degrees by other works. Thus, Stafford et al. (1977) and Bower and Christopherson (1977) underline the slightly less 'traditional' character of young American cohabitants, although they conclude that such behaviour poses no threat to the institution of marriage; however, these studies are slightly dated. Recent studies of Quebec, France, and the Netherlands reveal more fundamental transformations in attitudes, with the most unconventional aspects of these attitudes originating from young cohabitants (Lapierre-Adamcyk et al. 1987; Leridon and Villeneuve-Gokalp 1988; Latten 1984). In his study of Dutch youth, Latten identifies a conformist-nonconformist continuum regarding attitudes about the family, which he describes as: 'a gradual transition from conformistic attitudes to non-conformistic ones, with at one end young people who want to marry and at the other end cohabiting young people who do not want to marry' (20).

This continuum can be successfully transposed to our results, which continually show that Canadian cohabitants have the least conventional attitudes, followed by separated/divorced/widowed women, single women living alone, and married women. With the exception of this last group, age plays a marginal role. Young married women aged 20–29 undoubtedly have more progressive opinions than their elders, but in comparison with non-married women, they remain relatively conventional.

Roussel and Bourguignon and Latten agree that this continuum more generally and more fundamentally reflects differing positions towards society: ideological variables rather than socio-demographic variables best explain the differential attitudes about the family. We can thus assume that if marriage appears as the symbol of 'traditional' norms, then cohabitation embodies a way of expressing new cultural values (Roussel and Bourguignon 1978: 81–2).

However, this systemization has one exception: the value of children. All groups of women value children, while they also admit that they represent heavy responsibilities. In fact, the motivations of marriage and procreation appear as different 'mechanisms.' There seems to be a sequence of three stages that should be treated separately: union formation, the birth of the first child, and subsequent births (Lesthaeghe and Surkyn 1988: 40–1). According to this reasoning, it would seem that the value of the first child currently remains high, despite the fact that marriage is being called into question. This conclusion is partly reinforced by the still low degree of childlessness, about which much has been written in recent years, and which is still lower than at some other periods in Canadian history. Furthermore, it seems that few couples want to embark upon procreation beyond two children. This dimension is complex and certainly requires further study.

As a final point, what meaning should be attributed to the new values that are taking shape regarding the family? We have already mentioned that Lesthaeghe, Roussel, and Simons consider this phenomenon as part of a major transformation of value systems as a whole. These conclusions do not, however, receive unanimous support. Economic growth, the contraceptive revolution, and the entrance of women on the job market are often cited as the major sources of change in nuptiality and fertility (Cherlin 1981; Westoff 1984; Preston 1986). In this perspective, values have undergone a transformation as a result of the 'modernization' process (urbanization, education of the masses, sex-role egalitarianism, and so on) and cannot be considered as the cause of change in themselves.

It would seem then that the thrust of the debate opposes sociologists and economists, Europeans and Americans. This study does not permit one to conclude one way or the other. We can only accept the facts. Although it is difficult to identify the source of present nuptiality and fertility behaviour, it seems that the opinions and attitudes of young Canadian women in the 1980s have reached a point where a reversal seems unlikely in the near future; present attitudes seem self-contained and they may influence those of following generations.

7

Attitudes towards abortion

Following the changes made in the abortion law in 1969, the incidence of therapeutic abortions in Canada rose from about 8.6 per 100 live births in 1969 to 17.8 in 1979.* The rate, as well as the absolute number, of abortions has since then decreased: the latest figure for 1985 being 16.2 per 100 live births (Statistics Canada 1986). The restrictive law continued until 1989, when the Supreme Court of Canada declared it unconstitutional. The federal government introduced a compromise bill, criticized equally by the pro-life and the pro-choice proponents. Passed by the House of Commons in 1990, it was rejected by the Senate in 1991 (with 43 votes for and 43 against). It is not expected that another attempt at a legislative provision on abortion will be made for some years.

While the mildly restrictive legislation was in existence, in each hospital area a duly constituted therapeutic abortion committee had to approve an abortion. Although the same federal legislation was applicable to the whole country, wide variations were observed in the regional distribution of abortions depending on the interpretation of the law and the attitudes of the abortion committee. One may also surmise that given the lower rates in Canada compared with United States and other developed countries – especially in Western Europe – the reported therapeutic abortion statistics were an understatement of the true numbers. The application of the randomized response technique to a fertility survey in Alberta in 1974 (Krishnan and Krótki 1976) suggested that the true number of all abortions is several times the number of legal and

---

* This chapter is adapted largely from Balakrishnan, Lapierre-Adamcyk, and Krótki 1988.

registered abortions in the same period in the same area (Krótki and McDaniel 1975; Krótki and McDaniel 1977; McDaniel and Krótki 1979). The purpose of this chapter is not to measure abortion per se in Canada, but to analyse the attitudes of women towards abortion. Though attitudes in general cannot be equated with actual behaviour, one can expect them to have some impact on behaviour and on possible legislation, depending on their strength. Politically active groups for and against abortion could also create significant swings in the attitudes of the general public. To the extent that one's attitude towards abortion is a morally and ethically sensitive issue, it is important to know its place in the broader set of social norms regarding family, marriage, and childbearing. In addition, there is clearly a continuing need to measure attitudes in the wider Canadian population for policy reasons in preparation for the time when this issue, dormant in the early 1990s, will come to life again.

A number of local and province-wide studies have been done in Canada since 1967 to measure attitudes towards abortion (Balakrishnan et al. 1972; Barrett 1980; Barrett and Fitz-Earle 1973; Boyce and Osborn 1970; Committee on the Operation of the Abortion Law 1977; Hartnagel et al. 1985; Henripin and Lapierre-Adamcyk 1974; Osborn and Silkey 1980). In addition, Gallup polls have interviewed national samples of women, albeit small (less than 500 women), since 1965. However, owing to a lack of standardization in the questions and the samples covered, no good time series of attitudes on abortion in Canada can be constructed (Boyd and Gillieson 1975). In the United States, a much larger number of studies have been conducted, including annual surveys by Gallup and the National Opinion Research Center (NORC) to assess changes in the attitudes towards abortion (Blake 1977; Blake and Del Pinal 1981; Fuchs, Rose, and Haney 1980; Granberg and Granberg 1980; Henshaw and Martire 1982; Jones and Westoff 1978).

An interesting trend has been observed in the American studies. The level of approval of abortion increased rapidly until 1973, but has since then levelled off. In the NORC surveys, the average approval for six specified reasons (mother's health, rape, defect in baby, low income, unmarried, and does not want another baby) increased from 41 per cent in 1965 to 68 per cent by 1973, but has remained at that level until 1980 (Granberg and Granberg 1980). Analysing NORC as well as Gallup polls, Blake and Del Pinal made a similar observation on the erosion of the liberal abortion platform since the historic Supreme Court decision of 1973 (Blake and Del Pinal 1981). Though the strength of the pro-life movement may have something to do with this, a more enduring cause may be that there is still considerable conflict in matters of personal morality among the American public, and opposition to abortion reflects a conservative approach in these matters. For example, in the NORC surveys from 1972 to 1978, it was found that disapproval of premarital sex, extramarital sex, homosexual relations, interracial marriage, use of marijuana, and pornography were inversely related to approval of abortion (Granberg and Granberg 1980). The conflict between the legality and morality of abortion was more directly measured in a 1981 survey. Though 67 per cent in this national survey of women said that abortion should be legal, 56 per cent also said it is morally wrong (Henshaw and Martire 1982). These studies show that attitudes towards abortion can be understood better in the context of attitudes to other matters of personal morality. Though the Canadian Fertility Survey did not gather information on whether women regard abortion as morally wrong, data on approval or disapproval of behaviour, such as having children out of wedlock and raising a child without a husband or partner were collected that could be examined in relation to attitudes towards abortion.

The objective of this chapter is to analyse the factors associated with attitudes towards abortion in the national sample of Canadian women. First, the relationship of demographic and social-status variables – such as age, marital status, religion, education, religiosity, place of residence, and work experience – to abortion attitudes will be examined. Other studies have found that having a higher education, being non-Catholic, and having an urban residence are positively associated with liberal attitudes towards abortion. Conversely, religiosity and Catholicism have been consistently negatively associated (Granberg and Granberg 1980). One theoretical explanation for this relation offered by Hartnagel et al. (1985) is that the dominant status groups in a society are likely to approve situations where there is a moral conflict, such as there is with abortion. Second, it is hypothesized that while socio-economic background variables are important in the formation of attitudes, proximate determinants – such as an unwanted or an untimed pregnancy, number of children expected, or the type of contraceptive used – may also independently influence one's attitudes towards abortion. In other words, experience of a personal situation where abortion may seem an option may influence one's attitudes in general. Third, it is hypothesized that attitude towards abortion is related to attitude towards marriage, family, and childbearing in general. For example, those who feel strongly that marriage and childbearing are important for happiness in life are likely to be less liberal in their attitudes towards abortion. In other words, those who are family-oriented and more traditional will be less approving of abortion. Conversely, those who value work outside the home and greater personal freedom and who put less emphasis on marriage and children as sources of happiness may be more approving of abortion.

Measurement of attitudes towards abortion

A series of questions on attitudes towards abortion under various conditions were asked of all women interviewed in the Canadian Fertility Survey. The percentage distribution of the responses to the six questions on attitudes towards abortion, which are arranged in descending order of seriousness of the situation, is presented in table 7.1. Non-responses were very low: together with unsure ones, they amounted to only 1 to 5 per cent in the range of questions. The situations were preceded by the phrase 'Assuming abortion were legal, would you be for or against a woman having an abortion if ...' Therefore, the responses are general attitudes and do not measure whether the respondents themselves would get an abortion under the specific situation. To include a larger set of questions to tap such nuances, though important, was beyond the scope of the parent study. As we expected, our deliberately limited attempt to measure the number of abortions actually performed on the respondents was not so successful. The pregnancy histories, which contained information on the outcome of each pregnancy, indicated only 357 abortions, which gives a rate of 4.4 abortions per 100 live births – a substantial underestimate whether counted against legal and recorded abortions or even less against estimates of true and all abortions. It is evident that Canadian women are still reluctant to admit to having had an abortion. Similar results of substantial underreporting were also found in a much earlier study (Krótki and McDaniel 1975). On the other hand, the fact that even that many will volunteer the information on a telephone survey may be indicative of more liberal attitudes than in the past. It is possible that some of the abortions were reported as a miscarriage, which amounted to 16.4 per 100 live births – a slightly higher figure than one would expect in the Canadian population. The responses in table 7.1 reveal a dichotomy. The women overwhelmingly approved of abortion if the mother's life or health was in danger and in the case of rape. Ninety-two per cent approved of an abortion if the mother's life was in danger and 85 per cent if her health was in danger. Eighty-three per cent approved in the case of rape. There is no doubt that when the woman's physical well-being was gravely threatened, there was considerable support for an abortion. If the child was likely to be born physically or mentally handicapped, a lower proportion – 72 per cent

– approved of an abortion. But only about one-third approved of abortion if the mother was not married or for financial reasons. Support for abortion declined considerably in situations where there was no threat to the mother's or child's health.

The consistency of responses to the six questions, assuming an ordinal sequence, was tested using Guttman scalogram analysis. The coefficient of reproducibility was 0.93. An index measuring the attitudes towards abortion was developed using the six questions in table 7.1. The index is the sum of the positive responses and can vary from 0 to 6 for any respondent. The mean of the index for all women was 3.99, with a standard deviation of 1.63. Construction of the index by simple addition implies equal weight for all the questions. The larger the index, the more liberal is the respondent's attitude towards abortion.

Demographic and socio-economic correlates of attitudes

Attitudes towards abortion are influenced to a great degree by the values and norms acquired through early socialization, from reference groups, and through media and social movements. While it is hard to investigate the exact manner in which attitudes are formed, there is no doubt that a wide range of characteristics are found to be correlated. We first examined the relationship between five selected socio-economic factors and three personal situation variables on attitudes towards abortion, taking into account the age and marital status of the respondent at the time of the interview. The five socio-economic factors were religion, religiosity, education, place of residence, and work status. The personal-situation variables were last-pregnancy status (whether planned or unplanned), total expected number of children, and current method of contraception.

Catholics have traditionally been less liberal than Protestants, as documented in many studies (Balakrishnan et al. 1972; Hartnagel et al. 1985; Osborn and Silkey 1980; Ryder and Westoff 1971). In our study, the religious differences, while they existed, were much less influential. The mean abortion index for Catholics was 3.80 and for Protestants, 4.16 (table 7.2). Controlling for all the other predictor variables using Multiple Classification Analysis reduced the difference, the adjusted means being 3.93 and 4.04 respectively. One cannot but speculate that the convergence in the attitudes towards abortion runs parallel to a convergence in fertility and family-planning behaviour between Catholics and non-Catholics found in recent years in Canada. Religiosity turned out to be the most discriminating variable. Those who attended religious services

TABLE 7.1

Percentage distribution of responses to attitudes towards abortions in different situations

Situation	For	Against	Don't know Unsure Non-response
1 ... if the pregnancy is endangering the mother's life	92	7	1
2 ... if the pregnancy puts the mother's health in danger	85	12	3
3 ... if the woman has been raped	83	13	4
4 ... if there were good reasons to believe that the child would be physically or mentally retarded	72	23	5
5 ... if the woman was not married	36	58	5
6 ... if the household does not have the financial means to support a child	32	65	4

Q: Assuming abortion were legal would you be for or against a woman having an abortion ...?

regularly every week were least liberal, with an index of 2.94, compared with 4.56 for those who rarely or never went to church. Only 16 per cent of regular church-goers approved of abortion if the mother is not married, while 52 per cent of those who rarely went to church approved of abortion for the same reason. Controlling for the other variables hardly changed these figures, indicating that the effect of religiosity on attitudes towards abortion is largely independent of other factors. This parallels a recent U.S. study where religious attendance was the most highly correlated variable with attitudes towards abortion (Henshaw and Martire 1982).

As reported in other studies, education and place of residence of the respondent were found to be related to the attitudes towards abortion (Balakrishnan et al. 1972; Ryder and Westoff 1971). Better-educated women were more liberal than those with less education. Those who had at least some college education had a mean abortion index of 4.27, compared with 3.56 for those with less than eight years of schooling. Women in larger cities were more liberal (4.12) than women living in small towns (3.79) or on farms (3.56). Though those with a greater commitment to work seemed to be more liberal, when controlled for other factors, work differences were found to be minimal.

Age did not show any clear pattern. Younger women in the age group 18–24 were more conservative in their attitudes towards abortion than

TABLE 7.2
Mean abortion index (unadjusted and adjusted) by selected demographic and socio-economic characteristics

Characteristics	Number approving						Mean abortion index		
	Mother's life	Mother's health	Rape	Child handi-capped	Not married	No financial means	Unadjusted	Adjusted for the predictors	Number of women
Age at interview									
18–24	90	84	86	64	34	31	3.73	3.73	1301
25–29	95	87	86	76	41	33	4.12	4.01	969
30–34	95	90	88	79	41	37	4.24	4.14	908
35–39	95	86	81	74	37	34	4.00	4.06	835
40–44	93	84	80	74	31	26	3.82	3.98	635
45–49	92	86	77	74	37	28	3.89	4.22	587
Marital status									
Single	92	88	90	70	41	38	4.10	4.07	1394
Married	94	85	81	72	34	28	3.89	3.94	3248
Widowed, separated, divorced	94	87	87	81	45	41	4.29	4.07	594
Religion									
Catholic	91	83	81	71	30	27	3.80	3.93	2522
Non-Catholic	95	89	86	74	43	36	4.16	4.04	2713
Religiosity									
Attend services weekly	84	71	63	50	16	12	2.94	3.07	1345
Attend services every month or a few times a year	95	90	89	78	37	33	4.17	4.16	2023
Attend services rarely, never	97	93	93	84	52	45	4.56	4.47	1867
Education									
≤ 8 years	88	83	69	71	25	22	3.56	3.82	404
9–11 years	92	85	80	71	29	26	3.79	3.79	1193
12–13 years	93	85	85	71	37	32	3.96	3.95	1950
14 or more years	96	89	89	76	46	39	4.27	4.22	1689

Place of residence									
Large city or town	94	87	86	75	41	35	4.12	4.04	3378
Small town	93	86	80	69	30	26	3.79	3.92	1512
Farm	90	80	73	67	31	23	3.56	3.81	345
Work status									
Never worked for more than 6 months	91	85	81	63	31	28	3.72	3.96	763
Previously worked for 6 months or more but not now	92	85	79	70	34	29	3.82	3.95	1584
Currently working	94	88	87	77	40	35	4.16	4.02	2889
Total expected number of children									
0	95	93	89	81	53	48	4.52	4.31	501
1	95	88	91	81	49	41	4.39	4.21	539
2	94	87	86	74	37	33	4.07	4.03	2193
3	93	85	81	71	31	26	3.84	3.93	1296
4	91	77	75	60	26	22	3.45	3.65	477
5+	87	66	60	56	19	16	3.05	3.41	299
Last pregnancy status									
Number failure (unwanted)	95	87	82	79	47	43	4.31	4.30	422
Timing failure	93	85	85	75	40	33	4.05	4.01	603
All others	93	86	84	72	35	31	3.95	3.96	4210
Current method of contraception									
Pill and IUD	95	89	91	77	44	41	4.33	4.14	1305
Barrier (condom, diaphragm)	94	87	87	77	45	38	4.21	4.04	416
Sterilization (tubal ligation, vasectomy, hysterectomy)	94	86	80	75	36	29	3.99	4.05	2105
Rhythm, withdrawal, others	86	87	72	55	21	18	3.18	3.54	146
None, at risk	87	83	82	62	31	28	4.39	3.67	789
Not at risk	93	86	82	70	28	26	3.79	3.96	474
Total							3.99		5235

older women, contrary to the conventional wisdom that people grow conservative as they become older. This age pattern on attitudes towards abortion has also been evident in earlier studies (Balakrishnan et al. 1972; Ryder and Westoff 1971). One may hypothesize that younger women have not experienced the pressures of birth control or unwanted pregnancies and therefore can afford to take a more casual attitude towards abortion than older women. Married women were more conservative than single or previously married women in their attitudes towards abortion, but the differences by marital status were small.

One of the main premises of this investigation is that attitudes towards abortion are likely to be strongly correlated with personal desires and experience with childbearing. There is a clear inverse relationship between mean abortion index and total expected number of children. Those who expected to be childless were most liberal with a mean index of 4.52, which decreased uniformly to 3.05 for those who expected five or more children. It was even more striking in certain situations. For women who were not married, 53 per cent of those who expected to be childless approved of abortion, while only 19 per cent of those who expected five or more children did so. This is probably just one more example of the pristine clarity of the answers being muddied by what we variously called wishful thinking – 'do as I say, not as I do' – and rationalization after the event. Social surveyors are wary of such influences in reported opinions. Similarly, when financial means were lacking, the corresponding figures were 48 per cent and 16 per cent respectively. Controlling for other factors does not alter the trend or the figures significantly, confirming that personal reproductive experience and expectations are important determinants of attitudes towards abortion.

The planning status of the most recent pregnancy was also clearly related to attitudes towards abortion. For each pregnancy, women were asked whether they planned that pregnancy, would have preferred to have a child some other time, or preferred not to have another child. Number failure denotes an unwanted pregnancy, and timing failure a pregnancy not wanted at that time. Women were classified according to whether their recent pregnancy was unwanted, unwanted at that time, and all others. Those who had an unwanted pregnancy or did not want a pregnancy at that time were more pro-abortion than others. Number failure was more significant (4.31) than spacing failure (4.05) in the determination of the attitudes towards abortion. Women who were using more effective contraceptive methods were also more liberal than those using less effective methods. Women who were using the pill or an IUD were most liberal, with a mean abortion index of 4.33, compared with 3.18 for those who depended on rhythm or withdrawal for birth control.

Those who are serious about family planning seem to be more likely to approve of abortion than those who are not.

Attitudes towards abortion and towards marriage, family, and childbearing

As seen in chapter 6, in the Canadian Fertility Survey a large section was devoted to assessing the attitudes towards marriage, family, and childbearing. Questions were asked about the importance of marriage, children, work outside the home, and autonomy of spouses for happiness in life. Attitudes towards premarital sex, having a child outside of marriage and the importance of having a child for life satisfaction were also ascertained. It should be interesting to see whether the attitudes towards abortion are related to these broader attitudes towards life in general. Table 7.3 presents the mean abortion index for women by their responses to questions on other attitudes.

Very clear relationships are to be found among the attitudes, in the direction one would expect. Those who felt that to be happy in life one had to be married and should have at least one child were less liberal towards abortion (3.66) than those who felt that these were not very important or not at all important (4.65). Women who felt it is very important to be able to take a job outside the home had a mean abortion index of 4.30, compared with women who thought work outside the home is not important at all (3.24). Such wide differences were also found according to whether the respondents felt that women should be free to do as they wish in order to be generally happy.

How strongly or not one feels that it is necessary for a couple to get married when they decide to have children is a measure of the extent of permissive attitudes. Those who considered it necessary to get married to have children had a mean abortion index of 3.83, compared with those who did not feel that way (4.38). One could also hypothesize that those who found it acceptable to have a child without a husband/partner were likely to be more liberal and approve of abortion under more circumstances. This was supported by the data, the mean abortion index being 4.45 for those who found it acceptable to raise a child without a husband/partner, compared with 3.65 for those who said that it is not acceptable.

Those who felt strongly that having a child provides a goal in life that nothing else can replace and an irreplaceable source of affection were less in favour of abortion than those who did not feel so strongly. It is again not surprising that a more positive attitude towards childbearing is related inversely with approval of abortion.

TABLE 7.3

Mean abortion index by attitudes towards marriage, family, and childbearing

Attitude	Mean abortion index			
	Very important	Important	Not very important	Not at all important
1 In order for you to be generally happy in life, is it very important, important, not very important, not at all important				
a) to be married?	3.66	3.98	4.40	4.65
b) to have at least one child?	3.67	3.99	4.34	4.75
c) to be able to take a job outside the home?	4.30	4.04	3.67	3.24
d) to be free to do as you wish?	4.25	3.89	3.51	3.22
		Yes	No	
2 When a couple decide to have children, do you think that it is necessary that they get married?		3.83	4.38	
3 Do you find it acceptable for a woman to decide to have a child without husband/partner in the house?		4.45	3.65	
4 Could you make such a decision to have a child without the presence of a husband/partner in the house?		4.32	3.88	
	Strongly agree	Agree	Disagree	Strongly disagree
5 On the whole, would you say that you strongly agree, disagree or strongly disagree with the following statements:				
a) Having a child provides a goal in life that nothing can replace.	3.81	3.91	4.24	4.61
b) Having a child provides an irreplaceable source of affection.	3.94	3.94	4.22	4.75

Multivariate analysis

In the earlier sections, we have seen that three sets of factors – namely socio-economic, personal situation, and attitudes towards marriage and childbearing – affect attitudes towards abortion. We will now examine the relative importance of these factors using Multiple Classification ,I0xAnalysis (MCA). Our interest will be to look at the beta coefficients and the variance explained in the attitudes towards abortion. Table 7.4 presents the coefficients and the variance explained. Computer-software capabilities restricted the maximum number of predictors in the MCA to ten variables. The five socio-economic and three personal-situation variables, along with age and marital status, explain 21.6 per cent of the variance. This figure is very close to the 21.0 per cent variance explained by a large set of predictors in a U.S. study (Westoff et al. 1969), but lower than the variance explained of 31 per cent in an earlier Toronto study (Balakrishnan et al. 1972) and 27 per cent in a recent Edmonton study (Hartnagel et al. 1985). Religiosity alone explained 15.9 per cent of the variance. The three personal-situation variables of last pregnancy status, expected number of children, and current method of contraception explained 7.8 per cent when considered by themselves. The five selected attitudinal variables explained 10.7 per cent of variance in abortion attitudes as a set. A combination of three socio-economic variables, two personal situation variables, and five attitudinal variables together explained the maximum variance in abortion attitudes amounting to 22.7 per cent. All the variables in this set were statistically significant at the 5 per cent level, as were most at the 1 per cent level as well. They clearly show that attitude towards abortion is a complex variable determined jointly by situational factors, religious behaviour, socio-economic characteristics and attitudes towards marriage and childbearing.

Conclusion

A generally liberal attitude associated with secularism, education, and urbanization means greater approval of abortion. This is consistent with other studies. One also finds in this study that women who have experienced personal situations such as an unwanted pregnancy have more liberal attitudes towards abortion. It is not surprising that those who use more effective contraception, such as the pill or IUD, are more pro-choice. These women are particular about avoiding another pregnancy, and if found pregnant with an unwanted child are likely to resort to abortion.

TABLE 7.4
Beta coefficients of predictors and variance explained on abortion index

Predictors	Beta coefficients				
	One	Three	Ten	Five	Ten
Religiosity	0.40**		0.34**		0.32**
Religion			0.03*		
Education			0.11**		0.08**
Place of residence			0.05**		0.04*
Work status			0.0		
Age at interview			0.10**		
Marital status			0.04		
Last pregnancy status		0.09**	0.07**		0.09**
Total expected births		0.21**	0.12**		0.10**
Current contraception		0.15**	0.10**		
Child important for happiness				0.14**	0.08**
Job outside home important for happiness				0.14**	0.08**
Marriage necessary to have children				0.07**	0.03*
Child provides goal in life				0.05**	0.03*
Acceptable to have child without husband/partner				0.18**	0.11**
Multiple correlation coefficient	.399	.279	.465	.327	.476
Variance explained	15.9%	7.8%	21.6%	10.7%	22.7%

* Statistically significant at 5 per cent level
** Statistically significant at 1 per cent level

Note: The beta coefficients presented here are derived from Multiple Classification Analysis. They indicate the relative importance of the various predictors in their joint explanation of the dependent variable. For a technical discussion of the MCA, see Andrews, Morgan, and Sonquist 1969.

Attitudes towards abortion are clearly a subset of a wider range of attitudes towards life in general: towards marriage, family, and childbearing. Women who place less value on marriage and childbearing and more value on work and personal freedom are more liberal towards abortion. Thus, in spite of the rhetoric of pro- and anti-abortion groups, attitudes towards abortion are probably rooted more in general social change in the area of family and marriage. In the absence of comparable national statistics, it is impossible to talk about trends. One may, however, speculate that the trend towards greater permissiveness in cohabitation, premarital sex, childbearing out of wedlock, and so on may also imply a more liberal attitude towards abortion.

8

Contraceptive practice

One of the main purposes of the Canadian Fertility Survey was to ascertain the extent of contraceptive practice in Canada.* The rapid decline in the fertility rates in Canada since the early 1960s, which is only now stabilizing at replacement levels, is obviously due in large part to the extensive use of contraception among Canadian women. However, we know little about the trends and extent of use at the national level. The last two decades were also a period that saw rapid advances in contraceptive technology. We know a lot more about oral pills, both about their merits and dangers. More sophisticated methods of sterilization have been developed and public awareness and acceptance have drastically improved. Nevertheless, there are many subgroups where unwanted pregnancies persist. As in other developed societies, substantial shifts in the distribution of methods must have been taking place in Canada as well. We need to know the extent and impact of some of these trends in Canada. This chapter will first examine the extent of contraceptive use, both ever use and current use among women by method, and later investigate in greater detail oral contraception and sterilization, as these are the predominant methods used by Canadian women.

Knowledge of contraception

As knowledge of contraception is likely to be very high in Canada, not too much effort was spent on its assessment in the Canadian Fertility Survey. A simple question – 'As you know, there are various methods

* Parts of this chapter have been published in Balakrishnan, Krótki, and Lapierre-Adamcyk 1985.

to either postpone or prevent pregnancy. I am going to mention several contraceptive methods and I would like you to tell me whether you've heard of them ...' – produced the distribution shown in table 8.1.

Though abortion cannot be considered strictly as a contraceptive method it was presented as a last method, in the interest of knowing the extent of knowledge among Canadian women of abortion as a way of preventing a birth. Clearly, hearing about a method does not indicate the extent of knowledge. However, the figures in the table show that almost all Canadian women are probably aware of most methods.

Contraceptive use

Ever-use. Ever use by method and marital status is shown in table 8.2. Oral contraception is the most often used method, both among married and single women. However, we will soon see that many women do not stay on the pill. Of the ever-married women, 82.7 per cent have at one time or other used the pill, which is much higher than for any other method. It is surprising that the condom, which has been in use for a long time and is relatively easy to use, is mentioned by only 55.8 per cent of the women. It is equally surprising to note that almost one-third, 32.3 per cent of the women, report having been sterilized. Only a fourth, 26.3 per cent, report having ever used the rhythm method. Even among Catholics, ever-use of rhythm was only 34.9 per cent, compared with 19.0 per cent among the non-Catholics (table not shown). Though no national data are available for earlier periods, limited information for localized studies in Canada and national surveys from other developed countries such as the United States lead to the inference that rhythm as a viable birth-control method has lost much of its appeal. Among single women also the pill is the most popular method, with 71.3 per cent having used it sometime or other. As a percentage of single women who have used any method at all, this amounts to 89.5 per cent. It is not surprising that there are very few single women who have undergone sterilization, only 2.4 per cent, especially as most of them are young, below 25 years of age.

Current use. Current contraceptive status (including male and female sterilization) was measured as of the time of the interview. Information on ever-use, on use of a birth control method in the open interval, and on sterilization procedures was used to double-check the accuracy of the findings on current contraceptive status. If a woman used more than one method of birth control, the most effective method was considered

TABLE 8.1
Percentage distribution of women who have heard of the
contraceptive method

Contraceptive method	Heard of method
The pill	99.6
IUD (intra-uterine device)	94.1
Foam, jelly, or cream	93.5
Condom	97.1
Diaphragm	92.1
Female sterilization	96.6
Male sterilization (vasectomy)	97.1
Rhythm methods (e.g., temperature or calendar)	93.7
Withdrawal	85.3
Douching after intercourse	90.6
Abortion	98.8
Number of women	5315

as her current method. The hierarchy of effectiveness used was female
sterilization, male sterilization, pill, IUD, diaphragm, condom, foam,
rhythm, abstinence of more than a month, withdrawal, and other. If
both the woman and her husband or partner had been surgically sterilized, only the woman's procedure was counted in the use estimates.

Extent of contraceptive use becomes more meaningful when it is restricted to fecund women exposed to the risk of pregnancy. In the CFS,
information on current sexual activity was not gathered. Therefore, it is
not possible to describe the contraceptive practice of women exposed to
the risk of pregnancy. In particular, many previously married women
who obtained a tubal ligation while they were married and who count
therefore as current users of a method, may not have been sexually
active at the time of the survey. In the absence of data on sexual activity,
an attempt was made to identify the fecund women on the basis of other
criteria. Thus, all women other than current users are classified into
three groups: those who are currently pregnant, have recently given
birth or are seeking pregnancy; women who are sterile for non-contraceptive reasons (including those experiencing difficulty in conceiving,
those who have had a hysterectomy or other operation that has made
them sterile, and those whose husbands are sterile as a result of an
operation other than a vasectomy); and women who are presumably
fecund, not seeking a pregnancy, but using no method of contraception.

Women who had a hysterectomy following a tubal ligation were con-

TABLE 8.2
Percentage distribution of women by marital status and
ever-use of contraception by method

Contraceptive method	Ever married	Single
Number of women	3884	1430
Any method	96.7	79.6
Pill	82.7	71.3
IUD	25.7	12.0
Condom	55.8	40.8
Diaphragm	10.3	4.5
Foam, jelly, cream	21.6	9.4
Rhythm	26.3	12.1
Withdrawal	30.8	26.9
Female sterilization	32.3	2.4
Male sterilization (vasectomy)	14.6	2.0
Douche	13.2	10.8
Other	20.5	21.0

sidered to be users of a contraceptive method. However, those who only had a hysterectomy were classified as non-users of a method, among the non-contraceptively sterile. Almost half of the women who have had a hysterectomy said that if they had not had that operation they would have had a tubal ligation. Women who said that they were not practising contraception because they were post-partum made up a very small proportion of the sample.

Patterns of current use

As table 8.3 shows, among all Canadian women aged 18–49 in 1984, 68 per cent said that they were using a method of birth control at the time of the interview. A further 9 per cent were pregnant, post-partum, or seeking pregnancy, and 7 per cent were non-contraceptively sterile. Fifteen per cent were non-users. The table reveals large differences in contraceptive prevalence by the woman's marital status. Currently married women show the highest overall level of use (73 per cent), followed by the previously married (69 per cent) and the never-married (57 per cent). Moreover, only 5 per cent of currently married women are not using a method of birth control. The high level of current contraceptive practice among the previously married can be explained largely by the fact that these women are somewhat older than average and, therefore,

TABLE 8.3
Percentage distribution of women in reproductive years by current contraceptive status according to marital status, Canada

Canada, 1984, aged 18–49

| | Total | Never married | | | Currently married | Separated, divorced, widowed | | |
		Total	In cohabitation	Not in cohabitation		Total	In cohabitation	Not in cohabitation
Number of women (sample)	5315	1430	289	1141	3283	601	162	439
Contraceptive users (%)	68.4	57.4	83.1	50.8	73.1	68.8	78.9	65.2
Pregnant, post-partum or seeking pregnancy (%)	9.2	3.0	11.0	1.0	13.0	3.2	8.7	1.1*
Non-contraceptively	7.0	1.5	1.4*	1.7	8.7	10.6	11.2	10.2
Other non-users (%)	15.4	38.1	4.5	46.6	5.2	17.4	1.2*	23.4
Total	100.0	100.0	100.0	100.0	100.0	100.0	100.0	100.0

* Denotes percentages with relative standard errors of 0.03 or more.

are more likely to have been contraceptively sterilized while they were still married. Thirty-six per cent of previously married women and 29 per cent of the currently married women were 40 or older. Similarly, the higher average age of the previously married also helps to account for the fact that these women report a higher incidence of non-contraceptive sterility (mostly hysterectomy) than do the other groups.

Levels of contraceptive use among single cohabiting women are high in Canada (83 per cent), and even somewhat higher than the level reported among the previously married now living with a partner (79 per cent). An interesting observation is that women in cohabiting unions have much higher use levels than do those who are legally married. The levels of contraceptive use among single women not cohabiting (51 per cent) suggests that at least half of the women in this group are sexually active. This finding indicates that there is no longer any justification for excluding single women from contraceptive-prevalence surveys.

Table 8.4 summarizes patterns of contraceptive use by method. The leading method in Canada – accounting for almost half of all use – is sterilization, both male and female. The pill is the second most widely used method, accounting for 28 percent of all use, followed by the condom and the IUD (9 per cent and 8 per cent, respectively). Use of other methods is so low as to be of no importance.

As table 8.4 illustrates, there are considerable differences in the choice of a method between never-married and married women. Never-married women predominantly rely on the pill (71 per cent of users), while married women overwhelmingly rely on sterilization (59 per cent); the pill, condom, and IUD assume considerably less importance among married women as ways of avoiding pregnancy (15, 11, and 8 per cent respectively). Much of this pattern among currently married women, when compared with that of single women, is, of course, a function of the differing age structure of the two groups. The finding that a large proportion of married women resort to sterilization is consistent with conclusions of an earlier study carried out in Quebec (Marcil-Gratton and Lapierre-Adamcyk 1983), and reflects the fact that many of these women have already had as many children as they want. The high level of female sterilization among the previously married reflects this same relationship. Reliance on male methods (vasectomy and the condom) is, as one might expect, lower among the separated, divorced, and widowed women than among those still living with a husband.

TABLE 8.4
Percentage distribution of women in reproductive years practising contraception by current method, according to marital status, Canada

	Canada, 1984, aged 18–49	Never married			Currently married	Separated, divorced, widowed		
	Total	Total	In cohabi-tation	Not in cohabitation		Total	In cohabi-tation	Not in cohabitation
Number of users (sample)	3635	821	241	580	2400	414	127	287
Distribution (%)								
Female sterilization	35.3	4.3	4.1	4.3	41.8	59.7	53.5	62.4
Male sterilization	12.7	1.7	3.3*	1.0*	17.6	6.3	11.8	4.2
Pill	28.0	71.2	66.0	73.4	15.0	17.4	16.5	17.8
IUD	8.3	7.9	9.5	7.2	8.0	10.6	11.0	10.5
Diaphragm	1.7	2.8	2.1*	3.1	1.4	1.2*	3.9*	0.0
Condom	9.1	7.9	9.1	7.4	10.8	2.2**	2.2	2.1*
Foam	0.8	0.4*	0.4*	0.3*	0.7	2.2*	0.8*	2.8*
Rhythm	2.3	1.7	2.1*	1.4*	3.0	0.2*	0.0	0.3*
Withdrawal	1.2	1.3*	2.9*	0.7*	1.3	0.2*	0.8*	0.0
Other	0.6	0.9*	0.4*	1.0*	0.6	–	0.0	0.0
Total	100.0	100.0	100.0	100.0	100.0	100.0	100.0	100.0

* Denotes percentages with relative standard errors of 0.03 or more.

Differentials in current use

Levels of contraceptive use according to selected background characteristics and method are presented for all women and for currently married women in tables 8.5 and 8.6. These tables add further evidence to
the finding that a woman's age is by far the most important determinant
of her method choice. For example, among all women, the proportion
of users who become contraceptively sterilized increases sharply after
the age of 30; by ages 30–34, 36 per cent of users have obtained a tubal
ligation, and by ages 45–49 this proportion has climbed to 68 per cent.
If the incidence of vasectomy is also included, 83 per cent of women
40–49 rely on sterilization to prevent pregnancy. Even among those aged
35–39, combined male and female sterilization constitutes more than
two-thirds of all use. Correspondingly, reliance on the pill among older
women almost disappears, with only 3 per cent of contraceptive users
in the 40–44 range depending on this method. Even among women aged
30–34, pill use amounts to only 17 per cent of all contraceptive practice.
It is clear, then, that the pill in Canada is now predominantly used only
during the early years of a woman's reproductive life.

Sixty-four per cent of all women in the survey do not expect to have
any more children (excluding the current pregnancy), as table 8.5 shows.
Among these women, overall contraceptive use is very high (75 per
cent). Moreover, among users who expect no more children, 68 per cent
are protected against pregnancy by female or male sterilization.

The traditional differences observed between Catholics and Protestants have all but disappeared in Canada, as table 8.5 reveals. Sixty-
seven per cent of Catholics and 71 per cent of Protestants were using
some form of contraception at the time of the survey, and method choices
are remarkably similar. For example, 35 per cent of the Catholic users,
compared with 39 per cent of Protestant women using a contraceptive
method, had been sterilized. No appreciable religious differences can be
seen in the use of vasectomy, the pill, the IUD, or the condom. Moreover,
the rhythm method, which used to be widely relied on by Catholics,
accounts for only 3 per cent of current use among Catholics, compared
with 1 per cent among Protestants (not shown). In fact, the differences
found in the use of the various methods between Catholics and Protestants are less than if either of these two groups were compared with
other religious groups.

However, religiosity, as measured by church attendance, does appear
to be associated with some differentials in contraceptive use. Women
who go to church at least once a week have lower overall levels of use

TABLE 8.5
Contraceptive use by method and selected characteristics (all women)

Characteristic	Total number of women	Using contraception (%)	Distribution of users (%)						
			Total	Female steril.	Male steril.	Pill	IUD	Condom	All others
All women	5315	68.4	100.0	35.3	12.7	28.0	8.3	9.1	6.6
Age groups									
18–24	1323	56.9	100.0	2.1	1.6	76.6	6.5	8.1	5.0
25–29	986	67.7	100.0	16.5	7.9	39.2	11.7	14.5	10.2
30–34	925	74.8	100.0	35.7	16.8	17.3	13.4	10.0	6.8
35–39	846	78.5	100.0	54.1	17.8	6.5	8.6	7.4	5.7
40–44	644	76.2	100.0	61.3	21.6	2.9	3.9	4.7	5.7
45–49	591	63.6	100.0	67.6	15.4	0.3	1.6	8.8	6.4
Expect more children									
Expect more	1898	57.0	100.0	0.0	0.0	66.0	10.2	14.3	9.5
Expect no more	3375	75.4	100.0	50.2	18.2	11.9	7.5	6.9	5.3
Religious affiliation									
Catholic	2548	67.3	100.0	34.5	12.2	30.0	8.0	7.9	7.4
Protestant	1871	70.7	100.0	38.7	14.8	25.7	7.7	8.7	4.4
Other and no religion	886	66.3	100.0	30.7	10.1	27.6	10.4	14.0	7.3
Church attendance									
Weekly	1367	60.9	100.0	43.8	14.8	15.2	5.9	9.7	10.6
Sometimes	2047	70.2	100.0	33.1	12.3	31.8	8.1	9.2	5.4
Rarely or never	1893	72.1	100.0	32.4	11.9	31.6	9.9	8.7	5.4
Education									
8 years or less	408	62.0	100.00	68.8	9.1	10.7	3.2	3.6	4.7
9–11 years	1207	70.4	100.0	47.4	16.5	21.1	6.1	5.2	3.8
12–13 years	1977	69.0	100.0	30.0	13.7	33.3	8.2	8.4	6.4
14 years or more	1721	67.9	100.0	25.5	9.5	30.5	11.0	13.9	9.6
Nativity									
Native-born	4576	68.8	100.0	34.8	12.8	30.2	8.4	8.0	5.9
Foreign-born	738	66.5	100.0	38.7	11.8	13.8	7.9	16.3	11.4

* Denotes percentages with relative standard errors of 0.03 or more.

TABLE 8.6
Contraceptive use among currently married women by method and selected characteristics

Characteristic	Total number of women	Using contraception (%)	Distribution of users (%)						
			Total	Female steril.	Male steril.	Pill	IUD	Condom	All others
All women	3283	73.1	100.0	41.7	17.6	15.0	8.0	10.8	7.0
Age groups									
18–24	326	61.3	100.0	6.0	4.0	58.5	10.5	14.5	6.5
25–29	645	68.2	100.0	18.4	10.2	33.0	10.9	16.1	11.4
30–34	679	75.4	100.0	36.5	20.1	13.1	12.9	11.3	6.2
35–39	663	81.4	100.0	53.1	20.7	4.1	7.8	8.5	5.7
40–44	513	78.0	100.0	58.5	26.0	2.0	2.8	5.5	5.3
45–49	457	68.1	100.0	65.0	16.4	0.3	1.6	10.6	6.1
Expect more children									
Expect more	761	53.2	100.0	0.0	0.0	49.0	12.5	23.0	15.5
Expect no more	2509	79.4	100.0	50.2	21.2	8.1	7.1	8.1	5.3
Religious affiliation									
Catholic	1544	72.2	100.0	42.2	17.4	16.2	7.8	8.8	7.6
Protestant	1224	74.4	100.0	44.1	19.4	13.6	7.4	10.2	5.4
Other and no religion	511	73.6	100.0	34.4	13.8	14.8	10.1	18.0	9.0
Church attendance									
Weekly	1017	69.4	100.0	46.1	17.2	9.9	6.0	10.9	9.9
Sometimes	1277	75.2	100.0	40.9	16.7	17.6	8.4	10.8	5.6
Rarely or never	985	74.3	100.0	38.6	19.2	16.6	9.4	10.5	5.6
Education									
8 years or less	296	64.9	100.0	71.0	11.9	7.3	2.6	4.7	2.5
9–11 years	810	73.1	100.0	50.3	22.1	11.5	5.2	5.9	5.0
12–13 years	1174	73.8	100.0	37.0	19.0	19.0	8.1	10.1	6.8
14 years or more	1003	74.8	100.0	32.6	13.8	15.2	11.5	16.8	10.1
Nativity									
Native-born	2751	73.3	100.0	42.0	18.3	16.3	8.2	9.2	6.0
Foreign-born	532	72.4	100.0	40.5	14.0	8.6	7.0	18.7	11.2

(61 per cent) than do all others (70–72 per cent). In addition, regular church attenders report higher rates of sterilization and lower levels of pill use than do other groups.

Wide differentials in the use of various methods are to be found by educational level. Women with eight or fewer years of schooling report the lowest overall level of contraceptive practice (62 per cent) and appear to depend very heavily on tubal ligation (69 per cent of all users in this educational group). The proportion sterilized among all users then decreases with rising levels of education, to 47 per cent of those with 9–11 years of schooling, 30 per cent among women who attended school for 12–13 years, and 26 percent among those with at least some university education. In contrast, use of the IUD and the condom rises with increased education and use of the pill reaches its peak level among high-school graduates. However, a strong relationship between education and type of method cannot be inferred in the absence of controls for age. A long-term secular trend in developing countries is for young women to be more educated than their older counterparts. Therefore, the higher level of sterilization seen among less-educated women is due partly to the fact that older women are heavily represented in this group. A multivariate analysis later in this chapter clarifies these relationships.

A substantial portion of the Canadian population is made up of foreign-born residents. In the CFS sample, 14 per cent of all women were born outside Canada, somewhat smaller proportion than in the total population. During the last two decades, the countries of origin of immigrants to Canada have changed dramatically. A larger proportion are now coming from Asia and Third World countries in other continents than from Western Europe, and this factor probably accounts for the somewhat different pattern of method use seen among women born outside of Canada when compared with that of native-born women. Although the levels of overall use and the proportions relying on sterilization do not differ greatly, pill use is much lower among the foreign-born (14 per cent of all use vs 30 per cent), while condom use is much higher (16 per cent vs. 8 per cent).

Since 62 per cent of all women in the CFS sample (and 77 per cent of those over the age of 30) were married, the findings in table 8.6 with reference to married women do not differ greatly from those for all women. Among the currently married, as with all women, pill use declines rapidly after age 30. Only 13 per cent of married users aged 30–34 rely on this method, and yet further declines occur with increasing age. Overall contraceptive use among currently married women who do not expect to have any more children is very high (79 per cent); moreover,

71 per cent of these women are protected against pregnancy by male and female sterilization.

Table 8.7 presents the findings on contraceptive use among all unmarried women (never-married and previously married), in terms of their age and religion. Since never-married women tend to be concentrated among the younger age groups, and previously married women among the older age groups, in this table the age groups have been collapsed into three categories: 18–24, 25–34, and 35–49. Two thirds of single women are in the age group 18–24. Of these, 17 per cent said that they were living with a partner (cohabiting). Even if these cohabitants were removed from the denominator and the numerator, contraceptive prevalence among single women is as high as 49 per cent (not shown). Eighty-four per cent of single women aged 18–24 practising contraception use the pill, while only 6 per cent rely on the condom. Pill use decreases with age, even among single women. However, since most single women are relatively young, pill use dominates their overall contraceptive practice – 71 per cent of all use. The analysis reveals virtually no differences by religion in the contraceptive practices of single women.

Except for patterns of use of male methods and somewhat higher recourse to female sterilization, the use of birth control methods among previously married women is very similar to that of currently married women. As might be expected, very small proportions of the previously married rely on vasectomy or the condom. However, in the absence of any information on sexual activity, it is not possible to infer whether this pattern is the result of method preference or whether it stems from the fact that these women are not involved in a sexual relationship.

The rapid decline in fertility in Quebec, where the total fertility rate dropped from 4.0 children per woman, on average, in 1967 to 1.5 in 1983, has received a great deal of attention but no satisfactory explanation. A once traditionally conservative society, under strong Catholic influence with regard to reproductive behaviour, has transformed itself into a society in which fertility levels have reached unprecedented lows. A study of trends in Quebec between 1971 and 1979 revealed a very rapid increase in the incidence of female sterilization, vasectomy, and hysterectomy during that period (Marcil Gratton and Lapierre-Adamcyk 1983). The CFS data have made it possible for the first time to compare patterns of contraceptive practice in Quebec with those in the rest of Canada. As table 8.8 indicates, the differences are minimal. In Quebec, 4 per cent of married women aged 18–49 are using no contraceptive; for the rest of Canada, the proportion is almost 6 per cent. Among

TABLE 8.7
Contraceptive use among unmarried women by method and selected characteristics

Characteristic	Total number of women	Using contraception (%)	Distribution of users (%)						
			Total	Female steril.	Male steril.	Pill	IUD	Condom	All others
NEVER MARRIED									
All women	1430	57.4	100.0	4.3	1.7	71.2	7.9	7.9	7.0
Age groups									
18–24	960	55.1	100.0	0.4*	0.8*	84.1	4.2	5.9	4.6
25–34	369	66.9	100.0	7.4	3.7	51.4	14.0	12.8	10.7
35–49	101	49.5	100.0	32.0	2.0*	24.0	18.0	6.0*	18.0
Religious affiliation									
Catholic	752	57.2	100.0	5.3	1.6	68.9	7.9	7.9	8.4
Protestant	428	60.5	100.0	2.7	2.3	74.5	8.1	8.1	4.3
Other and no religion	246	51.6	100.0	3.9	0.8*	74.0	7.8	7.1	6.4
SEPARATED, WIDOWED, DIVORCED									
All women	601	68.8	100.0	59.7	6.3	17.4	10.6	2.2	3.8
Age groups									
18–24	37	59.5	100.0	9.0	0.0*	59.1	27.3	4.5	0.0
25–34	217	75.1	100.0	43.6	7.4	27.0	14.1	3.7	4.2
35–49	347	66.3	100.0	76.1	6.1	6.5	6.5	0.4	4.4
Religious affiliation									
Catholic	252	67.1	100.0	58.0	4.7	21.9	10.1	1.8	3.6
Protestant	219	73.5	100.0	64.0	7.5	14.3	8.7	0.6	5.0
Other and no religion	129	65.1	100.0	53.6	7.1	14.3	15.5	6.0	3.6

* Fewer than 5 women in category

TABLE 8.8

Percentage distributions of married women 18–49, by current reproductive and contraceptive status, and of currently married users, by method, Quebec and the rest of Canada

Status and method	Total	Quebec	Rest of Canada
Number of women	3283	858	2425
All married women			
Pregnant, post-partum, or seeking pregnancy	13.0	12.7	13.1
Non-contraceptively sterile	8.7	8.9	8.7
Not using a method	5.2	3.5	5.7
Using a method	73.1	74.9	72.5
Users			
Female sterilization	41.7	42.1	41.6
Male sterilization	17.6	17.7	17.5
Pill	15.0	17.0	14.3
IUD	8.0	7.0	8.4
Diaphragm	1.4	0.5*	1.7
Condom	10.8	9.8	11.1
Foam	0.7	0.2*	0.9
Rhythm	3.0	3.7	2.7
Withdrawal	1.3	1.0*	1.4
Other	0.6	1.1*	0.4*
Total	100.0	100.0	100.0

* Relative standard error of 0.30 or more

contraceptive users, 42 per cent of Quebec women and of women in the other provinces had been sterilized, and the incidence of vasectomy is also almost identical. Even rhythm, in the past the traditional method in Quebec, has lost all importance as a method of birth control (4 per cent vs 3 per cent in the rest of Canada).

Because Quebec women are mainly Catholic, it is of some interest to compare the contraceptive practice of Catholics and Protestants in Quebec with the two religious groups living outside of the province (table 8.9). Since there are so few Protestant women in Quebec, detailed comparisons by contraceptive method were not possible for this group. Nevertheless, the table shows that there are slightly greater differences between Catholics in Quebec and those in the rest of Canada than between Catholics in Quebec and Protestants in the other provinces, especially with respect to non-use (8 per cent among Catholic women outside Quebec, compared with 3 per cent among those within and 4 per cent among Protestants elsewhere in Canada). The use of permanent

TABLE 8.9
Percentage distributions of married women 18–49, by current reproductive and contraceptive status, and of currently married users, by method, according to religion, Quebec and rest of Canada

Status and method	Total	Catholics		Protestants	
		Quebec	Rest of Canada	Quebec	Rest of Canada
Number of women	3283	780	764	37	1187
All married women					
Pregnant, post-partum, or seeking pregnancy	13.0	12.9	13.2	†	12.4
Noncontraceptively sterile	8.7	9.1	9.4	†	9.2
Not using a method	5.2	2.9	8.4	†	3.9
Using a method	73.1	75.1	69.0	73.0	74.5
Users					
Female sterilization	41.7	43.8	40.5	†	44.2
Male sterilization	17.6	18.9	15.5	†	19.8
Pill	15.0	16.9	15.5	†	13.4
IUD	8.0	6.3	9.5	†	7.1
Diaphragm	1.4	0.0	0.9*	†	2.1
Condom	10.8	8.2	9.5	†	9.9
Foam	0.7	0.0	0.4*	†	1.2
Rhythm	3.0	3.7	4.9	†	1.2
Withdrawal	1.3	1.0*	2.5	†	0.6*
Other	0.6	1.2*	0.8*	†	0.3*
Total	100.0	100.0	100.0	†	100.0

* Relative standard error of 0.30 or more
† Too few cases for analysis

methods of contraception is slightly lower among Catholics in the rest of Canada, whereas the use of barrier methods is somewhat higher.

Trends in contraceptive use in Canada

Because the 1984 CFS is the first genuinely national fertility survey undertaken in Canada, temporal comparisons are hazardous to make. Table 8.10 presents data on contraceptive use provided by a number of different surveys carried out in Canada since 1968. However, it should be emphasized that the target populations were not the same for all the

TABLE 8.10
Percentage distribution of married women[1] using contraception by method, in selected studies done in Canada

Method	Age	Toronto (1968) 18–45	Quebec (1971) <45	Edmonton[2] (1973) 18–54	Quebec[3] (1976) 20–40	Canada (1976) 15+	Canada (1984) 18–49
Pill		43.2	38.1	45.7	28.8	39.2	15.0
IUD		3.1	3.9	5.7	8.5	6.0	8.0
Diaphragm		9.5	4.2	4.4		2.2	1.4
Condom		16.7	6.6	8.4	8.2	6.0	10.8
Rhythm		9.0	32.0	4.3	15.6	6.1	3.0
Withdrawal		8.8	7.9	2.8	4.3	3.4	1.3
Douche		3.5	1.5	–	–	–	–
Foam, jelly		3.4	2.2	–	1.1	2.5	0.7
Other		–	1.1	28.7	1.8	4.1	0.6
Sterilization							
Female		8.7	1.5	–	21.3	30.5	41.8
Male		1.1	1.0	–	10.0	–	17.6
Both		–	–	–	0.4	–	–
Total		107.0[4]	100.0	100.0	100.0	100.0	100.0
No. of women		1132	386	442	325	approx. 1000	2400

SOURCES: *Toronto* – Balakrishnan et al. 1975, table 34; *Quebec* – Henripin et al. 1981, tables 8.1 and 8.2; *Canada* – Justice Canada, Report of the Committee on the Operation of the Abortion Law, Catalogue J2-30/1977, Supply and Services Canada, table 14.6 (p. 350); *Edmonton* – Krishnan and Krótki, 1976.

Note: Table adapted from Romaniuk 1984, table 3.1 (p. 42). Current Demographic Analysis, Statistics Canada, Cat. 91-524E.

1 Toronto sample included women married only once.
2 Refers to women of all marital statuses. Figures derived from table 4.4 of Krishnan and Krotki report.
3 Sample for Quebec included women aged 20–40 in March 1976 who been married at least 5 years.
4 Total exceeds 100 per cent owing to multiple use in some cases.

surveys and the geographic coverage differed considerably. The national rates for 1976 came from a survey carried out among adults to find our their attitudes towards abortion, but the survey contained only a small section on contraceptive use, and the number of women in the survey who were of reproductive age was quite small. Bearing these shortcomings in mind, certain trends emerge, particularly with regard to the dramatic increase in dependence upon sterilization that has taken place in

TABLE 8.11
Contraceptive use in live-birth intervals among ever-married women

Interval	Number	Using contraception in the interval (%)
Marriage to first	3266	58
First to second	2566	68
Second to third	1206	62
Third to fourth	460	53
Fourth to fifth	164	46

Canada over the past seventeen years or so. In Quebec, for example, male and female sterilization rates increased thirteen-fold between 1971 and 1976 alone. Since that time, the incidence of sterilization appears to have increased substantially at the national level. Even allowing for the fact that the 1984 CFS includes tubal ligations performed both for non-contraceptive and contraceptive reasons, the increase is nothing less than spectacular. The second major conclusion to be drawn from the examination of trends in contraceptive practice is that use of the pill has declined over time, and increased recourse to sterilization took place among women over the age of 30. The IUD and the condom are still important methods, but all other techniques of birth control appear to have lost their relevance for today's Canadian women.

Contraceptive practice in birth intervals

Contraceptive use can vary substantially in the different birth intervals. If use is meant largely to limit the number of births rather than to space them, women are less likely to use contraception before they have had the number of children they would desire to have. This would mean that the use will be low, especially in the first two birth intervals. On the other hand, a higher level of use early in the reproductive life would indicate that women are also concerned about the timing of their births. Table 8.11 presents data on contraceptive use in live-birth intervals among the ever married women in the sample. Among those who went on to have another birth, use level increased from 58 per cent in the first closed interval to 68 per cent in the second closed interval and then showed a decrease. However, those who went to higher parities decreased use substantially after the second birth. Slightly less than a third of the women went on to have three or more births. Lower use levels in the higher closed intervals may have occurred because many of these women, coming from the older cohort of women who were in their prime reproductive years during the baby-boom period, may have desired more children.

An analysis controlling for age will show better whether use in the intervals has increased. Table 8.12 presents contraceptive use in the first and second birth intervals by age at interview. Distinct patterns of increase can be noticed in the younger cohorts of women. Among the oldest cohort of women, 45–49 years of age, only 34 per cent used contraception before their first birth. In comparison, 77 per cent of women aged 25–29 report using contraception before they had their first birth, a proportion that shows a steady decline with age. There is a slight decrease in the youngest cohort, 18–24 years of age, to 68 per cent – possibly because they are recently married and have not yet gotten around to using contraception.

Contraceptive use in the second interval, namely between the first and second births, is found to be higher than in the first interval for all the age cohorts of women. This indicates that once the first baby is born women are more concerned about timing the second birth. Overall, two-thirds of the women have used contraception in the second interval, a proportion that steadily increases from 51 per cent in the oldest cohort, 45–49 years of age, to 83 per cent in the youngest cohort, 18–24 years of age.

Planning status of pregnancies

A number of questions were included in the CFS to measure the planning status of each pregnancy. The relevant question asked of all women who had a first pregnancy was, 'When you became pregnant the *first* time ... did you want to become pregnant at that particular time; ... would you have preferred to become pregnant at some other time; ... would you have preferred not to have a child; ... Don't know?' Similar questions were asked for each of the following pregnancies. Responses from these questions were used to assess the extent of unplanned and unwanted pregnancies. Those who said they would have preferred to become pregnant at some other time indicate a timing failure and those who preferred not to have a child were considered as having unwanted births. Table 8.13 presents the distribution of pregnancies by planning status for the first six orders of pregnancies. It shows that only about two-thirds of the pregnancies are planned. Rationalization after the event, powerful as it is in the experience of the CFS, must not have been very strong in this case, if all those children running around the household during the

TABLE 8.12
Contraceptive use in first and second-birth intervals among ever-married women by
age at interview

Age at interview	Marriage to first birth			First to second birth		
	Number	Used (%)	Did not use (%)	Number	Used (%)	Did not use (%)
18–24	196	68	32	77	83	17
25–29	548	77	23	343	78	22
30–34	702	72	28	543	79	21
35–39	704	59	41	601	73	27
40–44	571	42	58	500	56	44
45–49	545	34	66	495	51	49

telephone interview were declared unplanned. There are some noticeable variations by pregnancy order. Planned pregnancies increase from
65.9 per cent for the first order to 76.7 per cent for the second order,
after which they show a steady decline.

The separation of the unplanned pregnancies, according to the timing-
failure or unwanted status, shows expected patterns. Only 8 per cent of
the first pregnancies were unwanted, while 25.2 per cent were wanted
but at some other time. Unwanted pregnancies were even lower at the
second order, 4.2 per cent, while timing failures amounted to 18.2 per
cent. The composition changes for later pregnancies. The percentage of
unwanted pregnancies increases from 10.3 for the third order to 16.6
for the fourth and 22.8 for the fifth. Timing failures show a moderate
decline.

Contraceptive-use failure

A rough measure of contraceptive use failure is the proportion of women
who become pregnant while using a method. In the CFS, after a sequence
of questions about method use before each pregnancy, the question was
asked, 'When you became pregnant the nth time, were you still using
the contraceptive method, or had you forgotten to use it, or had you
chosen to stop using it?' Those who reported getting pregnant while still
using a method indicate a failure. This should not be confused with
contraceptive effectiveness in the strict sense of the term, as we are
ignoring duration of use. It is at best a crude measure of the extent of
unplanned pregnancies arising from contraceptive failure. Table 8.13
shows the distribution of unplanned pregnancies by contraceptive-use
status at the time of pregnancy.

TABLE 8.13
Planning status of pregnancies by order

Planning status	Order of pregnancy					
	1	2	3	4	5	6
Number of pregnancies	3595	2844	1650	800	378	175
Planned at that time (%)	65.9	76.7	69.8	63.9	56.8	54.3
Unplanned (preferred not to have the pregnancy at that time or not at all) (%)	33.2	22.4	28.1	33.8	39.2	38.9
– timing failure	25.2	18.2	17.8	17.1	16.4	13.1
– unwanted	8.0	4.2	10.3	16.6	22.8	25.8
– using a method at time of pregnancy	9.4	9.3	12.8	14.5	20.1	6.9
– not using a method at time of pregnancy	23.8	13.1	15.3	19.3	19.1	32.0

In the case of the first pregnancy, about three fourths of the unplanned pregnancies were due to women not using a method at all. Twenty-four per cent of the first pregnancies occurred where the woman was not using any method, compared with 9 per cent where a method was still being used. It is possible that since the women have not had the desired number of children, they are rather careless in the use of contraception and less concerned about timing. The accidental pregnancy rate while using contraception steadily increases with order from nine at the second order to twenty at the fifth order. Though the sample size for the sixth order is small, the low figure of 7 per cent warrants a comment. These women are likely to be old and probably thought themselves to be less at risk of getting pregnant. The high figure of 32.0 per cent having an unplanned pregnancy while not using a method suggests this explanation.

Age at first use of contraception among young women

Age at first use of contraception has important implications for subsequent events such as entry into a sexual union and start of childbearing. For women who had never been pregnant, there was a direct question in the survey asking the age when they started the use of contraception. For those who have been pregnant, the calculation was more complex. Women were asked whether they used contraception before their first pregnancy and how long they used it. Where they have used more than one method there was information on duration for the longest and the last method used. Some approximations had to be made in the case of women who had been ever pregnant to estimate the starting age of use.

TABLE 8.14
Percentage distribution of young women (20–29) by age at start of contraceptive use

Age at start of contraceptive use	Present age (survey date)	
	20–24	25–29
15 years or less	9.9	7.1
16	10.2	7.9
17	13.9	11.2
18	18.1	13.5
19	11.2	15.2
20	10.5	11.8
21	6.7	11.5
22 years or more	4.8	19.1
Non-users	14.8	2.6
Number of women	1001	976

The analysis was restricted to young women aged 20–29 at the time of the survey, as early use, especially among unmarried women, and greater cohabitation are more of a recent phenomenon. About half the women in this group had never been pregnant.

Table 8.14 presents the percentage distribution of young women (20–29) by age at the start of contraceptive use. It is clear that use is starting earlier among the 20–24 cohort compared with the older cohort of 25–29 years. About 10 per cent reported the start of use at age 15 or younger among the 20–24 cohort, as against 7 per cent in the next older cohort. By age 18, more than half, 52.1 per cent, have used contraception among the very young, compared with 39.7 per cent among the 25–29 cohort. Figures after age 20 for the 20–24 cohort and after 25 for the 25–29 cohort are biased owing to censoring. For example, some of the non-users in the 20–24 group are younger than age 25 and still have time to start use before reaching that age.

It is of considerable interest to examine whether women use contraception before they enter a sexual union, either a legal marriage or a common-law relationship. About a sixth of the births in Canada occur outside a legal marriage. Where the woman is sexually active, many premarital births will be prevented if contraception is used before marriage. Taking all the 20–29-year-olds as a group who have ever used contraception, 20.5 per cent were never in a union (table 8.15). For about a third of the women, the start of contraceptive use coincided with the start of the sexual union. Slightly more, 45.6 per cent, have started contraceptive use before entering a union. Considerable variation can

TABLE 8.15
Percentage distribution of young women (20–29) by the relationship between the start of contraceptive use and the start of a sexual union

Age at start of contraceptive use	Relationship between start of contraceptive use and start of sexual union†			
	Coincide	Contraceptive use before union	Never in union	Total
16 or less	9.4	79.9	10.5	100 (347)
17–19	27.2	46.6	26.0	100 (822)
20–21	47.1	30.5	22.4	100 (399)
22 or more	69.8	17.2	13.0	100 (235)
Total*	33.7	45.6	20.5	100 (1803)

* Excludes 173 women in ages 20–29 who have never used contraception.
† Union includes legal marriage as well as cohabitation.

be noticed by age at the start of contraceptive use. To some extent, this is a statistical artefact, as the variance in age at the start of contraceptive use is much greater than in the age at the start of a sexual union. Still some of the observations are worth a comment. Those who start contraceptive use early, at age 16 or younger, are mostly in a union – 89.5 per cent. Partly because of their early use, in only 9.4 per cent of the cases did they also enter a union at the same time. In comparison, in the modal group who start contraceptive use at ages 17–19, only about 74 per cent are in a union, and in 27.2 per cent of the cases contraceptive use started at the time of entry into the union. As is to be expected, among those who started contraceptive use very late, after the age of 22, the majority, about 70 per cent, did not start use before the start of the union.

The relationship between the start of contraceptive use and the start of reproductive life is examined in table 8.16. Among the women 20–29 years old, about half have had at least one pregnancy. Of these women, slightly fewer than a third, 30.1 per cent, did not use any contraception before their first pregnancy. As is to be expected, those who started the use of contraception early are more likely to have used it before their first pregnancy. Thus, the percentage who did not use contraception before their first pregnancy increases from 23.3 per cent among those who started contraceptive use at 16 or younger to 43.5 among those who waited to use contraception until they were 22 or older. An interesting finding in table 8.16 is that early use of contraception need not

TABLE 8.16

Percentage distribution of young women (20–29) by the relationship between the start of contraceptive use and the start of reproductive life

Age at start of contraceptive use	Number of women	Ever pregnant	Did not use contraception before first pregnancy	Failures among contraceptive users*
≤ 16	348	66.1	23.3	38.6
17–19	822	47.6	28.6	22.9
20–21	399	54.6	29.7	18.2
≥ 22	235	71.5	43.5	13.7
Total†	1977	50.7	30.1	24.9

* Failures include those who got pregnant while using the method as well as those who got pregnant forgetting to use the method. The percentage thus reflects more use failure than method failure.

† Total includes 173 women who never used contraception.

mean effective use. The extent of failures as measured by accidental pregnancies was high, at 38.6 per cent, among those who started use at 16 or younger, a proportion that decreases to 13.7 per cent among the late starters. One should however be cautious in interpreting this trend. In the absence of data on sexual activity, the higher percentage may just indicate a higher level of sexual activity for a longer duration, increasing the risk of accidental pregnancy among the early starters, and not necessarily a careless or incompetent use of contraceptives.

The two variables strongly associated with the starting age of contraceptive use are education and entry into the labour force. Among those who started use at 16 or younger, only 7.6 per cent had some university education, a proportion that steadily increases to 35.5 per cent among the late starters (table 8.17). Of course the important intervening variable is age at first marriage. Those who start contraceptive use early are more likely to enter into a sexual union at a younger age (an important reason as to why they may have started use in the first place), a factor which may hamper their higher education. This logic can be extended to entry into the labour force as well. It is higher education that largely delays entry into the work force. Among those who started contraceptive use at 16 or younger, 37.8 per cent started work before the age of 18, a proportion that declines to 13.2 per cent among the late starters of use.

TABLE 8.17
Percentage distribution of young women (20–29) by age at start of contraceptive use, education, and starting work before age 18

Age at start of contraceptive use	Level of education			Starting work before age 18
	Secondary or less	College and other	Some university or higher	
≤ 16	77.6	14.8	7.6	37.8
17–19	62.9	24.0	12.6	32.8
20–21	48.4	29.1	22.5	21.5
≥ 22	52.4	12.0	35.5	13.2
Total*	58.6	22.7	18.7	26.7

* Includes a small number who have never used contraception.

Further analysis of oral-contraceptive practice

Since the introduction of oral contraceptives in the early 1960s, the level of their use increased steadily in the developed countries until about 1975, when their use peaked. Since then there has been a decline in the use, until what seems to be a levelling off by the early 1980s (Population Information Program 1982). One of the obvious reasons for the decline in popularity has been health and medical problems associated with the use of orals and, more important, the fear of possible serious problems in the future. The recent dramatic increase in sterilizations, both tubal ligations and vasectomies, must have been a consequence of disillusionment with the use of orals. Simplistically, the sterilized have no need for orals, or for any other kind of contraceptive for that matter. To the extent that oral contraception continues to be an important birth-control method, and its use varies widely even among the developed countries, there is a need to know more about the characteristics of oral-contraceptive users, the reasons for the stopping of oral use, and the subsequent contraceptive behaviour of those who discontinued oral contraception.

We saw earlier, in tables 8.5 through 8.7, that oral contraception is adopted largely by young single women. Married women depend on the pill when they are in their twenties but not in the later years of their reproductive life. After the age of thirty-five they hardly use the pill, and use decreases with age among all categories of women. Lower ever use among older women (40–49) could be due to a number of factors. Some of their fertility took place in the late 1950s and early 1960s before orals came into the market. Besides having depended on other methods and been satisfied with them, they may have been reluctant to shift to

TABLE 8.18
Percentage use of oral contraception among ever-married women
by year of first marriage

Year of marriage	Number of women	Ever used	Currently using
Before 1956	145	53.8	0.0
1956–60	460	63.7	0.7
1961–5	553	75.0	1.3
1966–70	746	85.1	4.4
1971–5	808	91.8	10.0
1976–80	758	90.5	21.2
1981–4	406	88.2	36.0
Total	3875	82.8	11.1

the pill. Being already older in their late twenties or early thirties, when the pill became available, they may also have been apprehensive of its use because of possible health complications.

That the oral pill is primarily a method used by the young is also evident from table 8.18, which presents data by marriage cohorts. Those who married recently (1981–4) depend more heavily on oral contraception. Thirty-six per cent were using the pill at the time of the survey, compared with 21.2 per cent among those who married in 1976–80. Among those who married before 1970, who are also much older, current use is extremely low.

Reasons for stopping. As many women who start using the pill soon after marriage, when they are young, stop use after a few years, there is considerable interest in understanding the discontinuation rates by duration of use and the specific causes associated with the stoppage. Earlier studies in the United States and Canada have shown that use usually levels off at about 30 per cent (Balakrishnan et al. 1975; Westoff and Ryder 1977). The main reasons for stopping had been health problems, followed by the desire to become pregnant and other causes, both being equally important. In this study, as information collected is limited to what could be ascertained over the telephone, duration-specific discontinuation could not be measured. The question on stopping was, 'Have you ever stopped using the pill for a reason other than wanting to get pregnant?' This question, while it is adequate where the pill use has been stopped only once, is clearly deficient where there had been more than one segment of use, as one would not know to which segment of use the answer refers. The response to the question therefore gives only a general idea of the magnitude of the causes involved. Given the short duration of pill use in most cases, it is however unlikely that there will be too many cases of multiple segments of use.

In the total sample of 5315 women, 4237 or 80 per cent have ever used the pill. Of these, 1018 women or 24 per cent of ever users were using the pill at the time of the survey. This was made up of 609 women (14 per cent) who were continuously using the pill without stopping and 409 women who had stopped and started again and are currently on the pill. Assuming that second- and higher-order closed or completed intervals of pill use are not significant in number, one may roughly estimate from the data that of those 3219 women who stopped using the pill and were currently not using it, 29 per cent stopped to get pregnant, another 49 per cent stopped for health reasons, and 22 per cent for all other reasons.

Present contraceptive status of past users. Because oral contraception is adopted by a large number of young women who later stop using it, it is necessary to assess the impact of discontinuation. Orals are extremely effective as a birth-control method, and therefore the decline in their use can have a significant impact on fertility rates in general and on accidental pregnancies for individual women. In the absence of complete contraceptive histories, one can only look at the current status of past users. Table 8.19 presents the current contraceptive status of women who used orals in the past and stopped for reasons other than to get pregnant. Of past users, 15.1 percent were back on the pill and using it at the time of the survey. The largest group, amounting to 26.1 per cent, was women who got a tubal ligation subsequently. In the case of another 10.7 per cent, their husbands/partners had a vasectomy, making a total of 36.8 percent of couples not exposed to the risk of pregnancy owing to sterilization operations. Of those who had stopped using the pill, 21.4 per cent switched to other methods of contraception, primarily the condom and IUD. Once we exclude those who became non-contraceptively sterile, mainly through hysterectomies, and those who were pregnant, post-partum, or seeking pregnancy at the time of the survey, only 10.8 per cent of those who stopped using orals were non users of contraception.

Regression analysis of current oral contraceptive use. It was seen earlier in tables 8.5 through 8.7 that oral-contraceptive use is associated with such variables as religion, religiosity, education, and nativity, in addition to age and marital status. Since many of these factors are correlated, it is

TABLE 8.19
Present contraceptive status of women who have used pill in
the past and stopped for reasons other than to get pregnant

Present contraceptive status	Percentage
Using oral contraception	15.1
Had tubal ligation	26.1
Husband/partner had vasectomy	10.7
Using contraception other than pill	21.4
Condom 8.4	
IUD 7.7	
Diaphragm 2.0	
All others 3.3	
Non-contraceptively sterile	6.1
Pregnant, post-partum, or seeking pregnancy	9.9
Non users	10.8
Total	100.0
Number of women	2705

hard to assess the individual effects of these on oral use. To facilitate
the interpretation, a dummy variable multiple regression analysis was
performed on oral use among women who were not sterilized, whose
husbands/partners had not had a vasectomy, and who were not pregnant, seeking pregnancy, or in post-partum at the time of the survey.
In other words, these women were exposed to risk and did not want
another child at the time of the survey. There were 1391 ever-married
women, and 1317 single non-cohabiting women who were in this category in our sample. Among this select group, 80.3 per cent of the ever
married were using some form of contraception, and of these, 31.1 per
cent were using the pill (table 8.20). Among the single women, 58.6 per
cent used contraception, with 44.4 per cent using the pill. The lower use
in this group is probably due to the fact that many of these women,
having no partners at the time of the survey may not need to use a
method owing to lack of exposure.

The regression analysis with six variables shows a multiple correlation
coefficient of .41 for the ever-married women, explaining 16.9 per cent
of the variance in oral contraceptive use. For the single women, the
correlation coefficient was lower, at .29, explaining only 8.3 per cent.
The significant variables were age at interview, nativity, religion, and

TABLE 8.20
Regression of pill use among women not sterilized (self or husband/partner) and not
pregnant, seeking pregnancy, or in post-partum on selected socio-economic variables

	Ever-married women	Single women
Number (excluding sterilized couples and those pregnant, seeking pregnancy, or post-partum)	1391	1317
Not using contraception (%)	19.7	41.4
Using contraception (%)	80.3	58.6
Using oral pills (%)	31.1	44.4
Regression coefficients for oral use		
Age at interview	−.022*	−.011*
Native-born	.110*	.228*
Catholic	.049*	.007
Weekly church attendance	−.054	−.286*
Sometimes church attendance	.030*	−.027
Less than grade 9 education	.058	−.093
Grade 9–11 education	.063	.042
Grade 12 education	.059	.023
Small city	.038	.136
Urban	.049	.100
Constant	.824*	.435*
Multiple Correlation Coefficient	.41	.29

Note: Reference categories are foreign-born, non-Catholic, rarely or never attend
church, some university education, and farm.
* Statistically significant at 5% level.

education for ever married women, and age at interview, nativity, and
religiosity for single women. As seen earlier in the tabular analysis, the
regression coefficient for age at interview was negative, indicating that
older women use the pill less often. Native-born status has a significant
positive relationship to pill use. Regular church attendance has a negative relationship to oral use, which is more pronounced among single
women than among ever-married women.

Further analysis of sterilization

As seen earlier (table 8.10), the most significant of all the trends in
contraceptive use in Canada is the rapid increase in the proportion of
women protected by sterilization. Both tubal ligation and vasectomy
have become much more popular. A method that was very rare even

TABLE 8.21
Proportion of ever-married women, sterilized by age and age at interview

	Age at interview					
By end of age	18–24	25–29	30–34	35–39	40–44	45–49
24	3.3	4.9	3.4	1.0	0.6	0.5
29	–	12.8	17.9	12.8	6.2	2.1
34	–	–	28.2	34.1	28.2	11.8
39	–	–	–	42.3	42.0	31.6
44	–	–	–	–	45.5	39.9
49	–	–	–	–	–	40.4
Number of women	362	736	805	795	617	569

as late as 1970 has become in a short span of about fifteen years the most used method. This is all the more remarkable because it is almost always an irreversible method and persons have to be confident in their decision not to have more children. One of the factors we found associated with sterilization is the age of the woman (table 8.5); the proportion sterilized rapidly increases after the age of thirty. In the CFS information was collected on the date the sterilization operation was performed on the woman, which enables us to see for each age cohort the cumulative proportion sterilized by various ages. Table 8.21 presents the data on the proportion of ever-married women having a tubal ligation by the selected ages. In the table the figures in the lowest diagonal are underestimates, as some of the women have not reached the end age and can have a tubal ligation before reaching it. However, the other figures are comparable across the age cohorts. They clearly show that not only are more women opting for tubal ligation, but they are doing so at a younger age. For example, in the oldest cohort, 45–49 years of age, only 11.8 per cent got sterilized before the age of 35. This increased to 28.2 per cent among the 40–44 cohort and 34.1 among the 35–39 cohort. It is surprising to see that among the 30–34 age cohort 17.9 per cent are already sterilized before age 30, whereas in the oldest cohort this proportion was insignificant, at 2.1 per cent. If the trends were to continue this would indicate that among the younger cohorts as many as half the women may resort to tubal ligation before the end of their reproductive period.

The above cohort analysis can only be done for tubal ligation. The extent of sterilization is greater when we include vasectomies, which add up to approximately a third of the tubal ligations, not counting the few cases where both partners have been sterilized. Among the 3884

TABLE 8.22

Percentage of ever-married women sterilized (tubal ligations plus vasectomies without double counting) by age at interview and number of children

Number of children	Age at interview						
	18–24	25–29	30–34	35–39	40–44	45–49	Total
0–1	0.9	3.8	16.8	36.5	40.9	32.4	15.3
2	20.1	32.3	49.7	64.7	73.2	50.4	52.2
3+	50.0	61.4	69.0	68.1	69.7	60.4	65.6
Total	6.1	20.5	43.3	58.7	65.2	54.5	43.8
	Base number of women						
0–1	285	393	262	192	115	74	1321
2	63	254	372	334	194	135	1352
3+	14	88	171	270	307	361	1211
Total	362	736	804	796	617	569	3884

ever-married women, 32.2 per cent have had a tubal ligation and an additional 11.6 per cent have been protected by a vasectomy done on the partner, for a total of 43.8 per cent protected by sterilization. Apart from age, the factor most related to sterilization is number of children. We have already seen earlier that among those women who do not expect to have any more children more than half are sterilized. The relationship between parity and sterilization is examined in table 8.22 and figure 8.1. More than half the women are protected by sterilization, either through a tubal ligation or a vasectomy on their partner, once they have had three children. This is true even in the youngest cohort of women, 18–24 years old; though the sample size is small it fits into the pattern created by the others. Even among women with only two children, more than half are sterilized after the age of thirty. The proportion reaches a figure as high as 73.2 per cent for the 40–44 age cohort. What is more dramatic is the fact that even among those who had only one child or none, the proportion who are sterilized is more than a third once the woman is past the age of thirty-five. There seems to be a strong reluctance to have a pregnancy later in life, even if the prevalent norm of two children is not attained.

Regression analysis of sterilization

Sterilization, as we have seen up to now, is influenced by such factors as marital status, age, and number of children and by socio-economic

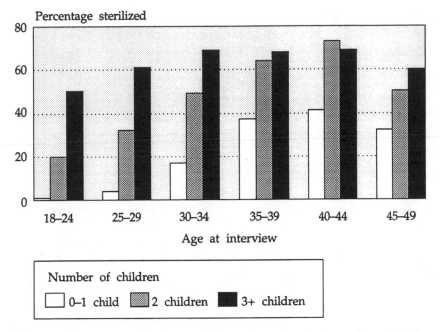

Figure 8.1 Percentage of ever-married women sterilized by number of children

factors such as education, nativity, religion, church attendance, place of residence, and regional location. To assess the relative importance of these variables on the adoption of sterilization, logistic regressions were performed separately for the different age cohorts using these factors as independent variables and sterilization as the dependent variable. Two sets of regressions were done, one considering tubal ligations only and the other both tubal ligations and vasectomies. The seven independent variables were (1) place of residence (urban, small town, or farm), (2) education (number of years of schooling), (3) nativity (native born and foreign-born), (4) religion (Catholic and non-Catholic), (5) religiosity (church attendance: weekly or more often, less than weekly, rarely, or never), (6) region (Quebec, outside Quebec), and (7) number of children (number of live births).

Table 8.23 presents the results of the logistic regression in summary form, indicating the coefficients and their statistical significance. It can be seen that the factor that is highly significant in all the age cohorts is number of children (parity), which is positively related to sterilization. Next to parity, the factor that seems to be of importance is education.

Education is negatively related to sterilization in all but the two oldest cohorts and is statistically significant in the three middle age cohorts of 25–29, 30–34, and 35–39. The more educated are less inclined to get a sterilization. It may well be that the more educated have better success with the other methods and are less reluctant to commit themselves to an irreversible method such as sterilization. The third factor that is consistent across cohorts and of reasonable significance is church attendance. Those who go to church regularly, once a week, or more often have a lower rate of sterilization. These women are likely to desire a larger family size and are more prone to follow the church doctrine against the use of certain birth-control methods.

Summary and conclusions

Canadian women practise contraception extensively, both with in and outside of marriage, and they mainly use the most effective methods, sterilization and the pill. Though the use of oral contraceptives has decreased rapidly among the married, especially after the age of thirty, it continues to be the main birth control method for single women. Not only are more and more married women opting for sterilization, they are doing so at younger ages than before. More than half the women who had two or more children are sterilized themselves or their partner has had a vasectomy. This has virtually eliminated late childbearing for these women, despite there remaining many years of reproductive life. Canada has the highest sterilization rates of any country in the world, a third higher than in the United States and much higher than in Europe. A possible first explanation is that Canadian women are reluctant to use the pill and do not want to depend on less-efficient methods, but that cannot be the complete explanation because women in other countries also know of the problems with the pill and do not rush into sterilization to the extent Canadian women do. Divorce and remarriage are increasing in Canada, and many women who have had a tubal ligation during their first marriage may regret the decision later (Marcil-Gratton 1988). About 10 per cent of the women in the CFS sample reported that if they were to make the decision now, they would not elect to become sterilized.

Differentials in contraceptive use by such factors as religion, church attendance, education, and nativity have narrowed in comparison with the past. For example, there is practically no difference between Catholics and non-Catholics, not only in the extent of use, but even in the methods used. The only noticeable trend is in the case of education, with the more educated being reluctant to adopt sterilization compared

TABLE 8.23

Logistic regression of sterilization among ever-married women on selected socio-economic variables for the different age cohorts

Independent variables	Age at interview					
	18–24	25–29	30–34	35–39	40–44	45–49
	Dependent variable: Female sterilization					
Urban	−.116	.040	−.127	−.170	−.114	−.002
Education	−.192	−.238**	−.123**	−.089**	.069*	−.001
Native-born	6.928	.030	.599*	.255	.118	.033
Catholic	.966	.044	−.178	.022	−.273	−.293
Weekly church	−1.858	−.248	−.291	−.409*	−.313	−.463*
Quebec	−1.755	−.256	−.284	.131	.388	.534*
Number of children	1.627**	1.095**	.656**	.381**	.272**	.216**
Constant term	−9.936	−.858**	−.839**	.038**	−1.453**	−.806**
p (proportion sterilized)	.039	.137	.296	.438	.481	.443
	Dependent variable: Female and male sterilization					
Urban	−1.030	.025	.060	−.126	−.077	.278
Education	−.121	−.297**	−.108**	−.076**	.080**	.012
Native-born	2.976*	.689	.770**	.576**	.443	−.195
Catholic	.758	−.126	−.137	.030	−.390	−.475*
Weekly church	−2.937*	−.292	−.186	−.538**	−.467*	−.543**
Quebec	−1.570	.099	−.068	−.057	.605*	.456
Number of children	2.238**	1.302**	.814**	.438**	.350**	.238**
Constant term	−6.778	−.597**	−.993**	.207**	−1.282**	−.434**
p (proportion sterilized)	.061	.205	.433	.587	.652	.545
Number of women	362	736	804	796	617	569

* Statistically significant at .05 level
** Statistically significant at .01 level

with the less educated. Age of the woman and number of children are the pre-eminent factors in determining the extent and method of use.

Contraceptive use starts very early, with two-thirds of women using even before the first pregnancy, and higher proportions using between the first and second pregnancy. Thus, Canadian women want to control not only the number but the timing of the births and largely succeed in doing so.

What are the demographic implications of the use patterns observed? Extensive use of effective methods across all segments of the population at younger and earlier parities means that unwanted pregnancies are likely to be low. The small family-size norm of two children is pervasive in Canadian society. These factors, along with delayed age at marriage and increased rates of marital dissolution, have all contributed to the below-replacement level of fertility that has existed in Canada since 1972. Barring a fundamental change in the desired family size and nuptiality patterns, the likely scenario is one of continued low fertility under the current pattern contraceptive use.

9

Intergenerational relations and fertility

In developed countries such as Canada, the decline in fertility and longer life expectancy affect intergenerational relations in important ways. As people get older they have fewer children to relate to. Because they live much longer than in the past, they are more likely to need help from their children for longer years of life owing to various health-related or other problems. Because women live much longer than men, almost nine years in Canada, these changes create a particularly difficult situation for older widows. The emergence of these issues arising from the aging of the Canadian population has recently been studied in depth (Gee and Kimball 1987; Connidis 1989; McDaniel 1986; Marcil-Gratton and Légaré 1988).

It was Caldwell who first brought our attention to the importance of intergenerational dynamics to fertility. He, however, was concerned more with the factors necessary for the start of fertility decline in a society (Caldwell 1982). Concentrating on economic issues, his theory stated that as long as wealth flowed from the young to the old, there will not be a motivation for having a smaller number of children. But somewhere along the development stages of a society, children become more expensive, and the cost of children far outweighs their benefit. High fertility no longer makes sense and the rates continue to fall. His logic clearly holds true for Canada. What is ignored in the theory is the non-economic aspects of children, especially in an aging society such as Canada. There is much evidence that there is close contact between older parents and their children and the predominant care of the aged is in the hands of their children and not in nursing homes (Connidis 1989).

Though it was not one of the main focuses in the Canadian Fertility Survey, a few questions were asked to assess intergenerational expectations because of their relationship to number of children. The questions were limited to the need for financial assistance, living arrangements after retirement, and the willingness to have parents living with oneself for extended periods of time.

Financial assistance

In the Canadian Fertility Survey, the question 'When you retire, do you think you will need financial assistance from your children?' was asked of all respondents. Table 9.1 presents the responses by age. Whether they are very young or middle-aged, Canadian women do not expect, by far, that they will need financial assistance from their children. Only about 5 per cent on average think that they will need such assistance on retirement. Apart from the various old-age security nets in place in Canadian society, the social norm that one should provide for oneself in old age and not depend on children may be reflected in these responses. We do not know how many women will need financial assistance when they are actually retired, but at least they do not expect it.

Older women (35–49 years of age) with four or more children are likely to respond that they might need financial assistance on retirement. But even among them, the proportion who so respond is only 7.1 per cent, compared with 4.3 per cent among those with three or fewer children (table 9.1). Those with lower education or lower income in both the younger and older cohorts are twice as likely to report that they might need financial assistance when they retire. For example, 7.1 per cent of women aged 35–49 with 11 or fewer years of schooling say that they will need financial assistance, while among the college-educated women the percentage is only 3.4. Similarly, of women aged 35–49 with annual household income of less than $25,000 8.3 per cent say that they will need financial assistance from their children on retirement, while among those with incomes greater than $25,000 the figure is only around 3 per cent. The main point, however, is that even among the lower socio-economic class, very few expect to depend on their children for financial help.

Not only do few respondents expect that they will need financial assistance from their children when they retire, but few of their own parents count on them for financial assistance. The question 'Do your parents have to count on financial assistance from their children?' was put to all respondents who had one or both parents alive at the time of the survey. The parents of younger women (18–34 years old) are likely to be still in the labour force, while many of the parents of those aged

TABLE 9.1
Percentage of women who will need financial assistance from their children on retirement by selected characteristics

Age at interview/ characteristics	No. of women	Will need financial assistance				
		Yes	No	Don't know	No answer	Total
18–34	3232	5.3	83.9	10.2	0.6	100.0
No. of children:						
0	1636	5.3	82.7	10.9	1.1	100.0
1–3	1536	5.2	85.4	9.3	0.1	100.0
4+	60	7.9	79.1	13.0	–	100.0
Education:						
≤ 11 yrs	741	8.7	75.8	15.6	–	100.0
12–13	1355	4.1	85.7	9.5	0.8	100.0
14+ yrs	1137	4.6	87.2	7.5	0.7	100.0
Household income:						
< $25,000	1195	7.4	80.0	12.3	0.3	100.0
25,000–34,900	603	3.2	87.9	8.5	0.4	100.0
35,000–49,900	557	2.4	90.3	6.7	0.7	100.0
50,000+	437	4.2	87.6	7.3	0.9	100.0
35–49	2083	4.8	84.4	8.9	1.9	100.0
No. of children:						
0	235	3.4	71.9	8.5	16.1	100.0
1–3	1441	4.3	88.1	7.5	0.1	100.0
4+	408	7.1	78.9	14.1	–	100.0
Education:						
≤ 11 yrs	874	7.1	80.1	11.8	1.0	100.0
12–13 yrs	623	2.7	89.1	6.6	1.6	100.0
14+ yrs	585	3.4	85.9	7.2	3.5	100.0
Household income:						
< 25,000	622	8.3	77.4	11.9	2.3	100.0
25,000–34,900	346	3.3	86.4	8.1	2.2	100.0
35,000–49,900	411	2.3	90.5	5.7	1.6	100.0
50,000+	421	3.0	91.1	4.4	1.5	100.0

35–49 may be retired. But there was little difference between the two age cohorts. Only about 5.9 per cent and 7.4 per cent of the respondents in the two age cohorts reported that their parents have to count on their children for financial assistance (table not shown).

Living arrangements on retirement

Often, the retirement years are a life cycle stage during which a change in living arrangement occurs. This may arise for a number of reasons, such as a desire for a change in lifestyle, lower income, reduced health, or the loss of a spouse. In the Canadian Fertility Survey, the following question was asked:

'When you retire, do you expect to ... (*Only one answer*)
... go and live with one of your children
... live in a senior citizens' home
... live in your own place
... live out your retirement in some other way (specify)?'

Table 9.2 presents the responses to this question. An overwhelming majority, about 87 per cent of respondents in the survey, said that they expect to live in their own place. About 6 per cent expect to live in a senior citizens' home, and another 4 per cent expect other living arrangements. It is remarkable that only 1.5 per cent of the younger women (18–34 years of age) and 0.8 per cent of the older women (35–49 years of age) said that they expected to live with their children. These figures were practically the same when controlled for factors such as education and income (table not shown). It is a sign of our times. Of course, these are only expectations. The actual distributions will be dictated by the existing circumstances.

Though only a very small percentage say they expect to go and live with one of their children on retirement, it may worthwhile to see whether this is a function of their expected financial need. There is a significant difference in expected living arrangement between women who respond that they will or will not need financial assistance from their children. Among those who will need financial assistance, 8.9 per cent said that they expect to live with one of their children on retirement, while among those who do not expect financial assistance this percentage was only 0.6 per cent (table not shown). Thus, moving in with a child may be seen as one way of reducing the financial burden on the retired person. Correspondingly, among those who expect financial assistance only 78 per cent expect to live in their own home, compared with 89.6 per cent among those who do not expect financial assistance from their children (table not shown).

TABLE 9.2

Percentages of women by expected living arrangements on retirement

	Age at interview	
Expected living arrangement on retirement	18–34	35–49
Go and live with one of the children	1.5	0.8
Live in a senior citizens' home	5.6	7.2
Live in own place	87.1	86.1
Live out the retirement in some other way	4.4	3.6
Don't know	1.2	2.0
No answer	0.2	0.2
Total	100.0	100.0
Number of women	3232	2083

Willingness to have parents live with one

Studies have shown that in Canada adult children continue to give considerable support to their aging parents, in spite of various extenuating circumstances such as a higher female labour-force participation rate and, sometimes, their own marital dissolution (Connidis 1989). Some of this support arises out of closeness, but filial responsibility plays a large part. Apart from giving various types of help, are adult children also willing to take in their parents for extended periods of time if need be? The responses to this question asked in the Canadian Fertility Survey are presented in table 9.3. Among the younger women, aged 18–34, 83.1 per cent said that they were willing to have their parents live with them for extended periods of time, with 16.4 per cent saying no. The corresponding proportions among the older women aged 35–49 were 74.8 and 24.0 per cent respectively. The lower percentage among the older women who are prepared to have their parents live with them may be due to the fact that they are closer to a situation that may actually arise, since their parents are likely to be older and in need of greater help. For the young the possibility is farther away, eliciting more casual normative responses rather than those based on pragmatic considerations. The effect of women's education and household income on the willingness to have parents live with them is examined in table 9.4. Among the younger women (aged 18–34) there is, however, practically

TABLE 9.3
Percentage of women willing to have parents live with them for an extended period of time

	Age at interview		
Willingness to have parents live with them	18–34	35–49	Total
Yes	83.1	74.8	80.2
No	16.4	24.0	19.1
Don't know	0.5	1.2	0.7
Total	100.0	100.0	100.0
Number of women	3160	1727	4887

Q: If need be, would you be willing to have parents live with you for an extended period of time?

This question was asked only of those respondents who had at least one parent living at the time of the survey (92 per cent)

no difference between the various categories of education and income. There is a noticeable pattern among the older women aged 35–49. Those who were willing to have parents live with them decreased from 77.6 per cent among the least educated to 72.3 per cent for those with some college education. Similarly, among those whose household income was less than $25,000, 78.6 per cent said that they were willing to have parents live with them, compared with 69.9 per cent among those with incomes of over $50,000 annually. This deserves repeating: the poorer, the more charitable.

Conclusion

This brief analysis of the few questions asked in the Canadian Fertility Survey shows that while the bonds between children and parents may be close and children provide considerable help to their older parents in terms of care and emotional support (Connidis 1989), there are few financial expectations and little desire to live together. Different generations want to keep their independence and think they have the economic resources to do so. Whether this is a sign of a weakening in family ties or its cause is an important research question.

TABLE 9.4
Percentage of women willing to have parents live with them for extended periods of time by selected characteristics

Age at interview/ characteristics	No. of women	Willing to have parents live with them			
		Yes	No	Don't know	Total
18–34	3160	83.1	16.4	0.5	100.0
Education:					
≤ 11 yrs	720	83.6	16.1	0.3	100.0
12–13	1325	83.1	16.2	0.7	100.0
14+ yrs	1116	82.7	16.8	0.5	100.0
Household income:					
< $25,000	1160	83.0	16.5	0.4	100.0
25,000–34,900	590	82.2	16.9	0.8	100.0
35,000–49,900	548	82.7	17.0	0.4	100.0
50,000+	431	82.6	16.9	0.5	100.0
35–49	1727	74.8	24.0	1.2	100.0
Education:					
≤ 11 yrs	697	77.6	21.7	0.9	100.0
12–13 yrs	515	73.6	25.2	1.2	100.0
14+ yrs	513	72.3	26.3	1.6	100.0
Household income:					
< $25,000	491	78.6	20.2	1.4	100.0
25,000–34,900	299	76.2	22.7	1.0	100.0
35,000–49,900	338	72.5	26.9	0.6	100.0
50,000+	365	69.9	28.3	1.7	100.0

This question was asked only of those respondents who had at least one parent living at the time of the survey (92 per cent).

10

Summary and conclusions

The main objective of the Canadian Fertility Survey was rather broad, going beyond the aims of most national fertility surveys. These are usually restricted to an understanding of the dynamics of reproductive behaviour of, primarily, married women. We were more ambitious in wanting to investigate the whole area of the changes taking place in the institution of family and childbearing in Canada from a demographic perspective. This desire was based on the belief that such a broad net is necessary to understand better the changing reproductive behaviour of Canadian women. Thus, we tried to probe attitudes towards – as well as measure behaviour regarding – marriage, cohabitation, childbearing, intergenerational expectations, abortions, and other relevant areas. It was hoped that this approach would provide a greater insight into the profound transformations taking place in Canadian society.

Attitudes towards family and childbearing

We start with attitudes because one would expect that they form the basis, by and large, of one's behaviour. Many recent studies on fertility decline in European countries have led researchers such as Roussel and Festy to question the motives behind marriage and childbearing in modern industrialized societies (Roussel 1987; Festy 1979). Traditionally, marriage and childbearing were almost universal, and the family was an institution founded on the mutual commitment of the spouses and oriented towards reproduction. The commitment of the spouses was sanctioned by legal marriage, a public and almost irrevocable contract. Once married, the spouses had rights and duties that were rather well defined and their union did not depend on the continuation of affection and love. Sexual relations usually began with marriage.

In recent years, a shift in the equilibrium seems to have taken place: the stability of a union is no more ensured by the strength of the institution, but by the continued intensity of love and affection. When love does not exist any more, the union is questioned and divorce often takes place. The importance given to love has meant that sexual relations are justified, even when marriage is not considered. And slowly the need for legal marriage becomes less and less evident, at least up to the point where the couple wants a child. Cohabitation has become popular, and acceptable, though still far from general. From the importance given to love follows the new type of relationship between man and woman, based on more independence and autonomy for each person. For a young person today, getting married and having children are tied less to traditionally expected behaviour than to their perception of the needs for their own happiness. The basic question is, 'Will marriage and children make me happier?'

The extensive section on attitudes towards marriage and family in the Canadian Fertility Survey was intended to assess some of these trends in Canada. In the absence of longitudinal studies, we of course cannot talk with authority on the changes. But we can at least comment on the present state of affairs and, where possible, surmise on trends. Though marriage is still considered important, about a third of our respondents said that it is not very or not at all important when a couple decides to live together. About half of the women surveyed did not think that wanting to have children is of importance in the decision to get married. More than two-thirds of the women said that premarital sexual relations are acceptable for both women and men. Almost the same proportion thought that cohabitation is acceptable.

Although almost 90 per cent said that marriage is a permanent union that should only be broken for very serious reasons, about 65 per cent said that they are likely to get divorced if there were no longer any common interests except financial security. Slightly more than half the women thought that couples should be allowed to divorce simply because they want to. Only about 40 per cent said that being married or having a child is important for being generally happy in life.

It seems that while Canadian women place considerable importance on personal relationships and love as being necessary for happiness, the perceived need for a legal marriage and children has decreased. Values have undergone a transformation as a result of the modernization process – urbanization, higher education, increased labour-force participation, sex-role egalitarianism, and so on. Older institutions are not accepted on face value, but in the light of what they can offer to the individual.

Fertility and nuptiality behaviour

The findings of this study clearly show that such attitudes in the area of family and childbearing are reflected in the behaviour of Canadian women. The commitment to early and universal marriage as the most desired life course is no longer true. Women delay marriage to a later age, and it appears that the proportion who may never get married is on the increase. This does not mean that unions themselves have lost their appeal. The decrease in legal marriages, especially among younger people, is more than made up for by cohabiting unions. It is just that young people are reluctant to enter early into legal long-term commitments. The reasons for this behaviour must be many, but surely some of them arise from the complex changes taking place in the interpersonal dynamics between the sexes. Women's movement for greater equality in the home and workplace, in education, in labour-force participation, and so forth has changed the expectations in marriage. Because behaviour such as premarital sex and childbearing is more and more accepted outside of marriage, some of the functions of marriage itself have lost their importance.

Is cohabitation just a prelude to marriage, or a new way of life in itself? Our study shows that the probability of a cohabitation breaking up is almost as high as that of the couple getting married, in any duration. Moreover, cohabitation is no substitute for marriage as far as childbearing is concerned: very few children are born in cohabiting unions. Levels of cohabitation are twice as high in Quebec compared with the Atlantic or Prairie provinces. Though we still don't know all the reasons for the dramatic increase in cohabitation, our study shows that it is more prevalent among the less religious, urban, and native-born populations. Our findings also show that those who have cohabited are more likely to get divorced when they do get married. The impact of cohabitation on the institutions of marriage and childbearing is far from insignificant.

While we know that marriage dissolutions have been increasing in Canada in the last two decades, the CFS enabled us to investigate this trend in greater depth by looking at the correlates of marital dissolution. Those who marry young, before the age of twenty, are twice as likely to get divorced as those who marry after the age of twenty-five. Those who are very religious are much less likely to get divorced and this is independent of their religion per se. Premarital births and conceptions substantially increase the probability of marital dissolution. This is not to say that such births and conceptions 'cause' dissolutions in any direct manner, though to some extent they might do so through increased stress within the union. More generally, there could be deep, underlying socio-psychological and psychological characteristics of the participants and the milieu surrounding them that mutually reinforce each other on the way to dissolution. The increase in marital dissolutions is symptomatic of the changing attitudes towards marriage that we saw earlier. Just as premarital cohabitation and childbearing outside of marriage is becoming socially acceptable, so also is the norm that, if a marriage is not satisfying from a personal point of view, providing love and happiness, one should feel right and even obligated to oneself to leave an intolerable marriage.

As with marriage, fertility behaviour in Canada also seems to be going through a fundamental change. One of the significant findings of our study is that the norm of a small family of one to three children is very pervasive in Canadian society. Many fertility differences usually linked to such traditional ascribed characteristics as religion, ethnicity, and mother tongue are much less significant than in the past. In contrast, achieved characteristics such as education, place of residence, religiosity, and female labour-force participation continue to influence the level of fertility. But differences even according to these variables have narrowed. What is surprising in this study is that income, when other factors were controlled for, had minimal impact on fertility levels. One is tempted to conclude that though socio-economic differentials cannot be ignored, their overall effect on family size has decreased. This does not mean, however, that their effect on timing is any less important. Education, urban residence, and work delay the age at first birth substantially. Those who delay their first birth never quite catch up with those who started childbearing early. But here again, our analysis shows that the impact of age at first birth on final fertility has weakened in comparison with the past. The main reason is that once the women have reached the desired family size of two or three, they get sterilized even though they are still relatively young.

An unexpected finding of the study is the overwhelming importance of religiosity in the union formation and childbearing behaviour of Canadian women. Though Catholic-Protestant differences have practically disappeared, religiosity as measured by church attendance still seems very significant. Those who are more religious are less likely to cohabit and less likely to get divorced. They also have larger families.

Contraceptive practice

One of the main purposes of the Canadian Fertility Survey was to provide for the first time national estimates of contraceptive use in Canada.
Thus, a great deal of the study was concerned with all aspects of family
planning. It was found that knowledge of various methods is almost
universal in Canada. Canadian women also use contraception widely
and use effective methods. About three-fourths of women currently married or in a cohabiting union were contraceptive users at the time of the
survey. Once we exclude those who are not using contraception because
they are pregnant, post-partum, or seeking pregnancy, or are non-
contraceptively sterile, we are left with only 5 per cent who are exposed
to the risk of an unwanted pregnancy owing to non-use. Even among
never-married women not cohabiting, the use level is 51 per cent.

While we were aware that sterilization has been increasing in Canada
in recent years, the figures from the CFS reveal that the increase is nothing
short of astounding. Canada may very well be the country with the
greatest prevalence of sterilization in the world, especially in the form
of tubal ligation. Thirty-two per cent of all ever-married women in the
age group 18–49 are sterilized. Among currently married women in this
age group, 31 per cent are sterilized and another 13 per cent are protected
by their husbands' having had a vasectomy. Among currently married
couples where the wife is aged 35 or over, about 65 per cent are protected
by sterilization – 44 per cent by tubal ligation and 21 per cent by vasectomy. It is clear that Canadian couples do not want to take chances
when they have had the desired number of children, usually two.

Next to sterilization, the most popular method is the pill. At the time
of the survey about 19 per cent of all women were using the pill for
birth control. However, this is primarily a method of the young. While
below the age of 30 about 37 per cent of all women were using the pill,
over the age of 30 only 6 per cent were using it, with practically nobody
doing so after 40. Apparently, this non-use is due to concerns about the
pill's negative side-effects on health. Slightly less than 10 per cent of
women were using the IUD or condom, with all other methods having
lost their importance. That there is little difference between Catholics
and Protestants and that the rhythm method has been abandoned by
the Catholics in Quebec are interesting findings.

A comparison with the limited number of earlier studies on contraceptive use in Canada shows that dramatic changes have taken place
in contraceptive practice. Oral contraception, which was very popular
in the sixties, has lost much of its appeal. It has been largely replaced

by sterilization once women have had two children or reached the age of thirty. The IUD, though it first came into use as early as the pill, never became very popular with Canadian women, with use levels always below 10 per cent. Rhythm, which was very popular, especially among the Catholics in Quebec, is no longer relevant. Condom use remains low, at around 10 per cent.

Contraceptive use starts very early in Canada, with two-thirds using even before the first pregnancy, and higher proportions using between the first and second pregnancies. Thus, Canadian women want to control not only the number but the timing of the births and largely succeed in doing so. Extensive use of effective methods across all segments of the population at younger and earlier parities mean that unwanted pregnancies are likely to be low.

Intergenerational relations

It appears that intergenerational expectations have changed substantially from the traditions of the past. Very few of our respondents expect to depend on their children for financial assistance in their old age. A minuscule 1 per cent expect to go and live with one of their children on retirement. They would rather live in a senior citizens' home (6 per cent) or with others (4 per cent) than with their own children. About a fifth were not willing to have their parents live with them for an extended period of time. Thus, though the children are still the prime care givers to their old parents, the level of filial obligations and expectations seems to have been eroded.

Canadian family and childbearing patterns in international perspective

How does Canada compare with other industrialized countries in the area of family formation and childbearing? Our findings from the CFS and the data from the Canadian census and vital statistics show that we are very similar to the United States and most of the western European countries. For example, the total fertility rate in Canada in 1984 stood at 1.80, a figure almost exactly the same as in the United States and somewhere in the middle of the range of 1.4 to 2.2 found in the western and southern European countries (Krótki 1989). The mean number of children for ever-married cohorts of women aged 30–34 and 45–49 in the CFS were 1.82 and 2.59 children, compared with 1.83 and 2.65 in the United States in 1984 (U.S. Department of Commerce 1985).

In such factors as mean age at first marriage and proportions marrying, as well, Canada is very close to the United States and other developed nations in western and southern Europe. Singulate mean age at first marriage* for women in Canada in 1981 was 23.1, compared with 23.3 in the United States, 23.1 in England and Wales, 24.0 in Norway, 27.6 in Sweden, 23.2 in Italy, and 23.1 in Spain. Proportions of women ever marrying by age 50 in Canada around 1981 was 90.1 per cent compared with 90.4 in the United States, 92.0 per cent in England and Wales, 88.6 per cent in Norway, 89.2 per cent in France, 93.8 per cent in Spain, and 68.7 per cent in Sweden (United Nations 1990).

In the area of marital dissolution, the proportion likely to terminate their first marriage among the married women in the CFS was estimated to be around 35 per cent, compared with an estimated figure of close to 50 per cent for the United States (Bumpass 1990). However, Canadian rates are similar to those in the European countries. According to the prevailing rates of divorce in 1981, Roussel estimates that 38.8 per cent of the marriages in England and Wales, 43.4 per cent in Sweden, 24.7 per cent in the Federal Republic of Germany, and 28.6 per cent in the Netherlands will end in divorce (Roussel 1989b).

Cohabitation in Canada has been going up as is evident in the CFS. In the age group 25–29, 11.1 per cent of women in the sample were cohabiting, a figure still somewhat lower than the 16.0 per cent doing so in the United States. For the same age group, the levels of cohabitation in 1986 were 11.3 per cent in France, 16.0 per cent in Norway, and 11.0 per cent in the United Kingdom. Cohabitation figures for women aged 25–29 for an earlier year, 1981, were 23.0 per cent in Denmark and 31.0 per cent in Sweden (United Nations 1990).

Overall contraceptive use among women in the reproductive years in the CFS was 73 per cent. In surveys taken about the same time, the use was 68 per cent in the United States (Bachrach 1984), 78 per cent in Sweden, 83 per cent in Great Britain, and 77 per cent in the Netherlands. Use in other European countries was at the same level (United Nations 1988).

While the overall level of contraceptive use in Canada was similar to that prevalent in the other developed countries, the methods used were quite different. Sterilization in Canada in 1984 was employed by 60 per cent of all current users, the highest among the industrialized countries. The corresponding figures were 41 per cent in the United States in 1982,

---

* Singulate mean age at marriage (SMAM) is the average number of years lived in the 'single' state by those who marry before age 50.

30 per cent in Great Britain in 1983, 4 per cent in Sweden in 1981, and 24 per cent in the Netherlands in 1982. The IUD was not a popular method in Canada. Only 8 per cent in our sample were using the IUD, almost the same as in the United States, at 7 per cent. In contrast, 26 per cent of the Swedish women surveyed relied on this method. Such wide variations can also be found in the use of the pill. Only 15 per cent of the Canadian women were using the pill, compared with 20 per cent in the United States, 36 per cent in Great Britain, 30 per cent in Sweden and 49 per cent in the Netherlands (United Nations 1988).

In many of the attitudes towards marriage and childbearing we are not too different from the Americans. For example, 30 per cent of single women below 30 years of age in the CFS said that it is not necessary for a couple to marry if they want to have a child. The corresponding figure for the United States for single women less than 35 years old is reported to be one-third (Bumpass 1990). Subject to the limitation that the question wordings were not exactly the same, the proportions who said that marriage should be ended only under extreme circumstances amounted to 89.9 per cent in the CFS, compared to 71.8 per cent in the 1988 U.S. survey. The greater incidence of divorces in the United States may reflect this attitude.

It should not be surprising to find that Canadian attitudes and behaviour are similar to those found in the United States and other developed countries. This is because the underlying social changes taking place – such as greater secularization, increased education and female labour-force participation, and changing sex roles – are much the same in all the industrialized countries. To the extent that Canada is not at one end of the spectrum, but rather in the middle, one may surmise that such trends as declining fertility, and increasing cohabitation and marital disruption may continue before levelling off or reversing.

Implications for the future and for public policy

Though the future is hard to predict in this period of turbulent social changes, we may still speculate with caution on family and childbearing patterns. Norms favouring a strong family that includes children as a prerequisite for a happy and fulfilling life are definitely being eroded in Canada as they are in the United States (Bumpass 1990). This is evident in both attitudes and behaviour. The main underlying cause seems to be the tendency for greater individualization in postmodern societies. The pursuit of individual happiness and gratification through personal relationships, work settings, participation in the economy, and so forth takes precedence over societal concerns, traditional values, and filial obligations. The new value systems also put considerable strains on gender relations. Under these conditions the utility of marriage, family, and childbearing is being reassessed. There is no reason to believe that we have reached a turning-point in these trends. Therefore, it is unlikely that we will see reversals in these family or fertility trends in the near future.

Among the demographic phenomena that directly affect the family, fertility was the first to change. The will to reduce family size can be traced back to the end of the nineteenth century. From that time on, the proportion of families having many children has been steadily declining. Furthermore, one has to remember that the high fertility levels observed during the baby boom were largely due to an increase in the proportion marrying and having at least one child, combined with the changing tempo in nuptiality and fertility. The parity progression ratios for births of high order never went up during this century. The availability of modern contraception in the 1960s gave couples an almost perfect control of their fertility. Since then and probably for the first time in history, Western societies are experiencing the effects of individual freedom on one of the most fundamental aspects of human life: the reproductive system. Twenty to thirty years of such freedom seem to be a short period for detecting how society will adjust to this new environment. A reassessment of marriage and of the relationship between men and women, which is certainly related to low fertility and fertility control, has already begun, as we have seen in the 1984 data; the evolution of the last five years shows that the trend is continuing.

The patterns and trends in family and childbearing found in the Canadian Fertility Survey have important implications for public policy. Continued low fertility expectations of younger women, combined with very effective use of contraception, would mean that below-replacement fertility may be with us for several years to come. Should incentives be instituted to encourage childbearing such as cash payments for higher parities, subsidies for child care, and tax rebates? Our finding that fertility behaviour is by and large determined by female work outside the home indicates that policies that make work compatible with childbearing, such as increased child-care facilities and subsidies, flexible work hours, greater job security, liberal maternity-leave provisions, and so on, are likely to be more successful than those that ignore the work milieu.

Sustained low fertility would also mean that the Canadian population will continue to get older. The public-policy interest in increasing immigration levels arises from the notion that more immigrants will not only help in providing a young labour force but contribute towards old-age security programs. While increased immigration may be a short-term solution, the CFS data show that it will not be a long-term solution because the young foreign-born have even lower fertility expectations than the native-born, even though they come predominantly from high-fertility societies. Obviously, this tendency can be traced to the immigrants' selectivity in terms of higher education and socio-economic status.

The CFS data add to what we already know, namely, that the Canadian population will continue to age. The answers to survey questions on intergenerational expectations indicate that many do not expect to live with their children when they get old. This will have policy implications for the support systems or alternative living arrangements needed for many older persons living by themselves.

In the area of family formation and dissolution, the CFS findings on attitudes and behaviour indicate that public policy should not ignore the significant changes taking place. Increased cohabitation and its much wider acceptance would mean that the rights and obligations of individuals in such unions should get greater attention than they have to date. Similarly, the changing attitudes towards expectations in marriage and divorce have implications for legislation in the area of marital dissolution. Further, more and earlier marital separations would mean that the numbers of lone parents with small children are likely to be on the increase. Since many of these lone parents are likely to be women who are also in lower income brackets, greater strains will be placed on public assistance programs aimed at them.

Finally, the changes in the family structure have also to be examined from the point of view of children themselves (Marcil-Gratton 1986; Duchesne 1989). Their family environment has been completely modified by the following: reduction in the number of siblings, increase in the labour force participation of their mother, increase in the number of children having to go through the break-up of their family. In finding new values to accommodate their need for happiness and self-accomplishment, adults of today, both men and women, will have to consider the well-being of the few children to whom they give life. Individuals will need the support of various social systems in order to reach such goals.

Questionnaire:
Canadian Fertility Survey, 1984

University of Montreal, Centre de Sondage

SECTION 1 – RESPONDENT'S BACKGROUND

→ | Exact time now: _____ |

	0 2
	(1–9)

100. To start with, we need some background information. Do you currently live in a city, a small town or on a farm?

City 1
Small town 2
Farm 3

(10–13)

☐ (14)

101. What municipality do you live in?

_____

(name of municipality)

102. Have you always lived in this municipality?

Yes .... 1 ——→ GO TO 109
No 2

☐ (15)

103. How many years have you lived there?

_____

(number of years)

(16–17)

104. Were you born in: _____ ?
(Respondent's province)

Yes .... 1 ——→ GO TO 109
No 2

☐ (18)

105. Were you born in Canada?

| Yes   1 | | No   2 |

☐ (19)

106. In what province?

_____

(province)

↓

GO TO 109

107. In which country were you born?

_____

(country)

(20–21)

108. In what year did you arrive in Canada?

19___

(22–26)

109. Was your father born in Canada?

        Yes 1
        No 2
        Don't know 8   ☐ (27)

110. Was your mother born in Canada?

        Yes 1
        No 2
        Don't know 8   ☐ (28)

111. Up to about age 12, did you live mostly in a rural area, in a small town or in a big city?

        Rural area 1
        Small town 2
        Big city 3
        Don't know 8   ☐ (29)

112. In total how many years of education did you complete?

   _____ If 11 years of education
   (SPECIFY)   or less ⟶ GO TO 115   (30–31)

113. What is the highest degree, certificate, diploma or grade you have obtained?

_____   (32–33)

(SPECIFY)

114. How many years of education had you completed by the time you first started to work (or when you finished regular studying, if you have never worked)?

_____   (34–35)

115. Including yourself how many children did your mother have and which one were you, the oldest, the second oldest, ...?

A) _____ ⟶ B) _____   (36–39)
   (number of children)   (order)

116. To what ethnic or cultural group did you or your male ancestor belong on first coming to North America?

French	01	Ukrainian	07
English	02	Dutch	08
Irish	03	Polish	09
Scottish	04	Jewish	10
German	05	Chinese	11
Italian	06	Greek	12

Other: _____   (40–41)
            (*SPECIFY*)

117. What is your present religion?

Roman Catholic	01	Jewish	09
Protestant		Ukranian	
(no specification)	02	Catholic	10
United Church	03	Pentecostal	11
Anglican	04	Jehovah's Witnesses	12
Presbyterian	05	Mennonite	13
Lutheran	06	Salvation Army	14
Baptist	07	Islam	15
Greek Orthodox	08	No religion	95

Other: _____   (42–43)
            (*SPECIFY*)

118. How often do you attend religious services? Would you say ...

... every week	1
... every month	2
... a few times a year	3
... rarely, or	4
... never	5 (44)

119. What language do you speak most often at home?

English 01
French 02
German 03
Italian 04
Ukrainian 05
Other: _____
        (SPECIFY)

(45–46)

120. What is the language you first learned in childhood and still understand?

English 01
French 02
German 03
Italian 04
Ukrainian 05
Other: _____
        (SPECIFY)

(47–48)

SECTION 2 – OPINIONS AND ATTITUDES ON THE FAMILY

201. In your opinion, when a man and woman decide to live together, is it very important, important, not very important or not at all important for them to get married?

Very important 1
Important 2
Not very important 3
Not at all important 4

(49)

202. In general, would you say you more or less agree or disagree with the following statement: 'Marriage is a permanent union which should only be broken for very serious reasons'?

Agree 1
Disagree 2

(50)

203. When two people decide to get married, is it absolutely necessary, fairly necessary or not necessary that ...

	Absolutely necessary	Fairly necessary	Not necessary	
a) they love each other strongly	1	2	3	☐ (51)
b) there is a strong sexual attraction between them	1	2	3	☐ (52)
c) they want to have children	1	2	3	☐ (53)
d) they feel the same way about wanting to have children	1	2	3	☐ (54)
e) they intend to stay married for the rest of their lives	1	2	3	☐ (55)
f) the couple has the financial means to support itself	1	2	3	☐ (56)
g) they have a similar social background	1	2	3	☐ (57)

204. In order for a couple to live together for a long time, would you say that it is very important, important, not very important or not at all important that ...

	Very important	Important	Not very important	Not at all important	
a) the strong love at the beginning endure forever	1	2	3	4	☐ (58)
b) the strong love at the beginning turn at least into deep affection	1	2	3	4	☐ (59)
c) their sexual life be satisfactory	1	2	3	4	☐ (60)
d) both be faithful to the other	1	2	3	4	☐ (61)

205. Do you find that it is acceptable or not acceptable for a man and woman to decide to live together without marriage ...

	Acceptable	Not acceptable	
a) if they want to make sure that their future marriage will last	1	2	☐ (62)
b) if they are attracted to one another but do not want to make any long term commitments	1	2	☐ (63)

206. A) In your opinion, is it acceptable for young women to have a sexual life before getting married?

Yes 1
No .... 2 ☐ (64)

B) And for young men?

Yes 1
No .... 2 ☐ (65)

207. In order for you to be generally happy in life, is it very important, important, not very important or not at all important ...

	Very important	Important	Not very important	Not at all important	
a) to have a lasting relationship as a couple	1	2	3	4	☐ (66)
b) to be married	1	2	3	4	☐ (67)
c) to have at least one child	1	2	3	4	☐ (68)
d) to be able to take a job outside the home	1	2	3	4	☐ (69)
e) to be free to do as you wish	1	2	3	4	☐ (70)

208. On the whole, would you say that you have had a very happy life, a fairly happy, a fairly unhappy or a very unhappy life up to now?

Very happy life 1
Fairly happy life 2
Fairly unhappy life 3
Very unhappy life 4   ☐ (71)

209. Would you say that being married adds something positive to the relationship that helps couples to get through difficult times?

Yes 1
No 2   ☐ (72)

210. Would you say that being married creates certain obligations which have a negative effect on the relationship?

Yes 1
No 2   ☐ (73)

211. When a couple decide to have children, do you think that it is necessary that they get married?

Yes 1

No 2

☐ (74)

212. Among the people you know, are couples living together accepted in the same way as married couples?

Yes 1

No 2

☐ (75)

213. If you were in the following circumstances, would you be likely to get divorced? Try to put yourself in the situation described.

| 0 | 3 |

(1-9)

	Would be likely to get divorced	Would not be likely to get divorced
a) If the initial strong love no longer exists and there is only friendship and respect left.	1	2
b) If your husband was unfaithful.	1	2
c) If there were no longer any common interests except financial security.	1	2

☐ (10)

☐ (11)

☐ (12)

214. Do you think that divorces should only be granted for the reasons specified in the law or do you think that couples should be allowed to get divorced simply because they want to?

For reasons specified in the law 1

Because the couple want to 2

☐ (13)

215. Do you approve without reservation, approve with reservations or completely disapprove of divorce in the following circumstances ...

	Approve without reservation	Approve with reservation	Completely disapprove	
a) the couple have very young children	1	2	3	(14)
b) the couple have teenagers	1	2	3	(15)
c) the couple have no children	1	2	3	(16)

216. Do you find it acceptable for a divorced woman to live with her children and a new partner without being married to him?

Yes 1
No 2 (17)

217. On the whole, would you say that you strongly agree, agree, disagree or strongly disagree with the following statements:

	Strongly agree	Agree	Disagree	Strongly disagree	
a) Having a child provides a goal in life that nothing else can replace.	1	2	3	4	(18)
b) Having children tends to distance the spouses from one another.	1	2	3	4	(19)
c) Becoming parents means taking on heavy responsibilites	1	2	3	4	(20)
d) Having a child provides an irreplaceable source of affection.	1	2	3	4	(21)

218. Do you think that looking after the children should be done only by the woman, mostly by the woman, equally shared by both partners or done mainly by the man?

       Only by the woman 1
       Mostly by the woman 2
       Equally shared by both partners.........3
       Mainly by the man 4   ☐ (22)

219. Do you think that household chores such as the cooking or the housework should be done only by the woman, mostly by the woman, equally shared by both partners or done mainly by the man?

       Only by the woman 1
       Mostly by the woman 2
       Equally shared by both partners.........3
       Mainly by the man 4   ☐ (23)

220. Do you find that it is a good thing for each partner in a couple to have their own close friends who they each see without the other?

       Yes 1
       No 2   ☐ (24)

221. Do you find it acceptable for a woman to decide to have a child without a husband/partner in the house?

       Yes 1
       No 2   ☐ (25)

222. Could you make such a decision to have a child without the presence of a husband/partner in the house?

       Yes 1
       No 2   ☐ (26)

223. Currently there is a lot of talk about artificial insemination; do you agree with this way of becoming pregnant?

       Yes 1
       No 2
       Don't know about insemination 3   ☐ (27)

224. There is also a lot of talk about couples who cannot have children and who ask another woman to bear a child for them *in exchange for a sum of money.* Do you strongly agree, agree, disagree or strongly disagree with this?

Strongly agree 1
Agree 2
Disagree 3
Strongly disagree 4   ☐ (28)

225. In your opinion, is there a risk that an only child will have more problems than a child in a family with other children?

Yes .... 1 ⟶ *GO TO 227*
No 2   ☐ (29)

226. Do you believe on the contrary that an *only child* will in fact have fewer problems because his parents will be able to devote more time to him?

Yes 1
No 2   ☐ (30)

227. In your opinion, do parents have a second child in order to create a better environment for the children *or rather* for their own personal satisfaction?

Better environment for children 1
Parents' satisfaction 2   ☐ (31)

228. Assuming abortion were legal, would you be for or against a woman having an abortion ...

	For	Against	Don't know	
a) if the pregnancy is endangering the mother's life	1	2	8	☐ (32)
b) if the pregnancy puts the mother's health in danger	1	2	8	☐ (33)
c) if the woman had been raped	1	2	8	☐ (34)
d) if there were good reasons to believe that the child would be physically or mentally handicapped	1	2	8	☐ (35)

	For	Against	Don't know	
e) if the woman was not married	1	2	8	☐ (36)
f) if the household does not have the financial means to support a child	1	2	8	☐ (37)
g) if the woman wants an abortion for a reason she feels is valid	1	2	8	☐ (38)

SECTION 3 – MARRIAGE BACKGROUND

301. Now, I have some questions about your marital status. Are you now married, living with a partner (common law), separated, divorced, widowed or have you never been married?

Married 1
Living with partner .... 2 ⟶ *MARGIN PARTNER/*
      GO TO 320
Separated .... 3 ➤ *GO TO 337*
Divorced .... 4 ⟶ *GO TO 337*
Widowed........................ 5 ⟶ *GO TO 337*
Never married .... 6 ⟶ *GO TO 353*   ☐ (39)

Married only

302. Did you marry in a religious or a civil ceremony?
    (*Current marriage*)

Religious........................ 1
Civil 2
Not a legal marriage .... 3 ⟶ *MARGIN PARTNER/*   ☐ (40)
      GO TO 320

303. Is your husband currently living with you?

Yes .... 1 ⟶ *MARGIN HUSBAND/*
No 2   *GO TO 305*   ☐ (41)

304. Is he away for a short time or for good?

        Short time .... 1 ⟶ *MARGIN HUSBAND/*
        For good .... 2 ⟶ *GO TO 337*   ☐ (42)

305. When did you get married?

       _____   19/ / /
       (month)   (year)

(43–46)

306. Have you been married before?

        Yes 1
        No .... 2 ⟶ *GO TO 313*   ☐ (47)

307. Have you been married before?

        Number of times :   _____

> Note to interviewer: For each of these marriages (excluding the current marriage), ask the following questions, then go to 313.

	... the first time (1)	... the second time (2)	... the third time (3)
308. When did you get married for ...	‾‾‾‾‾‾‾‾ (month) (year)	‾‾‾‾‾‾‾‾ (month) (year)	‾‾‾‾‾‾‾‾ (month) (year)
309. Did this marriage end with your husband's death?	Yes .... 1 *GO TO 310*	Yes .... 1 *GO TO 310*	Yes .... 1 *GO TO 310*
	No .... 2 *GO TO 311*	No .... 2 *GO TO 311*	No .... 2 *GO TO 311*
310. (Husband died) When did he die?	‾‾‾‾‾‾‾‾ (month) (year) *(GO TO NEXT MARRIAGE)*	‾‾‾‾‾‾‾‾ (month) (year) *(GO TO NEXT MARRIAGE)*	‾‾‾‾‾‾‾‾ (month) (year) *(GO TO 313)*

	... the first time (1)		... the second time (2)		... the third time (3)	
311. When did you separate?	(month)	(year)	(month)	(year)	(month)	(year)
312. When did you get your divorce?	(month)	(year)	(month)	(year)	(month)	(year)
					GO TO 313	

313. Have you ever lived with a partner without being married?

    Yes 1   □ (48)
    No .... 2 ⟶ GO TO 400   □ (49)

314. How old were you the first time you started living with a partner?

                _____
                (age at beginning)   (50–51)

315. How long did you live with this first partner?

              _____
              (duration)   (52–53)

316. Did you ever get married to this person?

    Yes .... 1 ⟶ GO TO 400
    No 2   □ (54)

317. Did you live with your current husband before you married him?

    Yes 1
    No .... 2 ⟶ GO TO 400   □ (55)

318. For how long?

              _____
             (duration)   (56–57)

Common-law only

320. When did you and your partner start living together?

_____ 19_____
(month)   (year)

⊞ (58–61)

321. Before this relationship started, had you ever been married?

```
┌───── Yes ............................... 1
│      No ................................. 2 ⟶ GO TO 332          □ (62)
│
▼
```

322. How many times have you been married? _____

┌───┐
│ Note to interviewer: For each of these marriages,   │
│   ask the following questions, then   │
│   go to 328.   │
└───┘

	... the first time (1)	... the second time (2)	... the third time (3)
323. When did you get married for ...	‾‾‾‾‾ ‾‾‾‾‾ (month) (year)	‾‾‾‾‾ ‾‾‾‾‾ (month) (year)	‾‾‾‾‾ ‾‾‾‾‾ (month) (year)
324. Did this marriage end with your husband's death?	Yes .... 1 *GO TO 325*	Yes .... 1 *GO TO 325*	Yes .... 1 *GO TO 325*
	No .... 2 *GO TO 326*	No .... 2 *GO TO 326*	No .... 2 *GO TO 326*
325. (Husband died) When did he die?	‾‾‾‾‾ ‾‾‾‾‾ (month) (year) *(GO TO NEXT MARRIAGE)*	‾‾‾‾‾ ‾‾‾‾‾ (month) (year) *(GO TO NEXT MARRIAGE)*	‾‾‾‾‾ ‾‾‾‾‾ (month) (year) *(GO TO 328)*
326. When did you separate?	‾‾‾‾‾ ‾‾‾‾‾ (month) (year)	‾‾‾‾‾ ‾‾‾‾‾ (month) (year)	‾‾‾‾‾ ‾‾‾‾‾ (month) (year)
327. When did you get your divorce?	‾‾‾‾‾ ‾‾‾‾‾ (month) (year)	‾‾‾‾‾ ‾‾‾‾‾ (month) (year)	‾‾‾‾‾ ‾‾‾‾‾ (month) (year) *GO TO 328*

328. Did you at any time live with another partner without being married?

```
┌──── Yes ............................... 1
│     No ............................... 2 ──→ GO TO 335
↓
```

☐ (63)
☐ (64)

329. How old were you the first time you started living with a partner?

_____
(age at beginning)

☐☐ (65–66)

330. How long did you live with this first partner?

_____
(duration)

☐☐ (67–68)

331. Did you ever get married to this person?

Yes .... 1 ──→ GO TO 335
No .... 2 ──→ GO TO 335

☐ (69)

332. Did you at any time live with another partner?

```
┌──── Yes ............................... 1
│     No ............................... 2 ──→ GO TO 335
↓
```

☐ (70)

333. How old were you the first time you started living with a partner?

_____
(age at beginning)

☐☐ (71–72)

334. How long did you live with this first partner?

_____
(duration)

☐☐ (72–73)

335. Do you plan to get married?

```
      Yes ............................... 1 ──→ GO TO 400
┌──── No ............................... 2
↓
```

☐ (74)

336. Do you intend to live with your partner as long as possible without getting married?

Yes .... 1 ──→ GO TO 400
No .... 2 ──→ GO TO 400

| 0 | 4 | (1–9)

☐ (10)

Separated, Widowed, Divorced only

337. How many times have you been married?　Number of times: ——

Note to interviewer: For each of these marriages, ask the following questions, then go to 343.		
	... the first time (1)	... the second time (2)	... the third time (3)

	... the first time (1)	... the second time (2)	... the third time (3)
338. When did you get married for ...	(month)　(year)	(month)　(year)	(month)　(year)
339. Did this marriage end with your husband's death?	Yes .... 1 GO TO 340	Yes .... 1 GO TO 340	Yes .... 1 GO TO 340
	No .... 2 GO TO 341	No .... 2 GO TO 341	No .... 2 GO TO 341
340. (Husband died) When did he die?	(month)　(year) (GO TO NEXT MARRIAGE)	(month)　(year) (GO TO NEXT MARRIAGE)	(month)　(year) (GO TO 343)
341. When did you separate?	(month)　(year)	(month)　(year)	(month)　(year)
342. When did you get your divorce?	(month)　(year) No divorce ☐	(month)　(year) No divorce ☐	(month)　(year) No divorce ☐ GO TO 343

343. Have you ever lived with a partner without being married?

Yes .... 1 ——→ *GO TO 345*   ☐ (11)

No 2   ☐ (12)

344. Given your personal situation, do you expect to remarry, to live with a partner without getting married again or to stay as you are?

To remarry .... 1 ——→ *GO TO 400*

To live with a partner .... 2 ——→ *GO TO 400*

To stay as I am .... 3 ——→ *GO TO 400*

Other: _____ 4 ——→ *GO TO 400*   ☐ (13)

345. Are you living with a partner now?

Yes .... 1 ——→ *MARGIN/PARTNER*

No .... 2 ——→ *GO TO 348*   ☐ (14)

346. When did you start living with your partner?

_____   19 _____
(month)   (year)   (15–18)

347. Given your personal situation, do you expect to remarry or to continue living with your partner without getting married again?

To remarry .... 1 ——→ *GO TO 349*

To live with a partner .... 2 ——→ *GO TO 349*

Other: _____ 3 ——→ *GO TO 349*   ☐ (19)

348. Given your personal situation, do you expect to remarry, to live with a partner again without getting married or to stay as you are?

To remarry 1

To live with a partner again 2

To stay as I am 3

Other: _____ 4   ☐ (20)

349. Before your first marriage, did you live with a partner?

Yes 1

No .... 2 ——→ *GO TO 400*   ☐ (21)

350. How old were you the first time you started living with a partner?

_____
(age at beginning)

☐☐ (22–23)

351. How long did you live with this first partner?

_____
(duration)

☐☐ (24–25)

352. Did you ever get married to this person?

Yes .... 1 ⟶ *GO TO 400*
No .... 2 ⟶ *GO TO 400*

☐ (26)

Never Married

353. Do you live alone, with your parents, with friends or relatives or with a partner?

With a partner .... 1 ⟶ *MARGIN/PARTNER*
GO TO 359

Alone 2
With parents 3
With friends/relatives 4
Other 5
(SPECIFY)

☐ (27)

354. Have you ever lived with a partner?

Yes 1
No .... 2 ⟶ *GO TO 358*

☐ (28)

355. How many times have you lived with a partner?

_____
(number of times)

☐ (29)

356. How old were you the first time you started living with a partner?

_____
(age at beginning)

☐☐ (30–31)

357. How long did you live with this first partner?

_____
(duration)

☐☐ (32–33)

358. Do you expect to .....

... remain single and live
without a husband/partner   1 ⟶ GO TO 400
... live with a partner and
afterwards get married   2 ⟶ GO TO 400
... get married without living
together beforehand   3 ⟶ GO TO 400
... live with a partner without
ever getting married   4 ⟶ GO TO 400

☐ (34)

359. When did you start living with your partner?

_____ 19 _____
(month)   (year)

☐☐☐☐ (35–38)

360. Before living with your present partner, did you ever live
with another partner?

Yes 1
No .... 2 ⟶ GO TO 364

☐ (39)

361. How many times did you live with other partners?

_____
(number of times)

☐ (40)

362. How old were you the first time you started living with
a partner?

_____
(age at beginning)

☐☐ (41–42)

363. How long did you live with this first partner?

_____
(duration)

☐☐ (43–44)

364. Do you plan to get married?

Yes .... 1 ⟶ GO TO 400
No 2

☐ (45)

365. Do you intend to live with your partner as long as possible without getting married?

     Yes 1
     No 2   □ (46)

SECTION 4 – MATERNITY HISTORY

400. We would like to get a complete record of all the children each woman has given birth to in her life or has adopted; to begin with, have you ever adopted a child?

     Yes .... 1 ⟶ How many? _____   □ (47)
     No 2   □ (48)

401. How many LIVE BIRTHS have you had up to now including those who died <u>after</u> birth or who do not live with you?

– DO NOT INCLUDE CURRENT PREGNANCY, IF APPLICABLE –

     None 0   □□
     1 child......... 1 ⟶ *MARGIN LIVE BIRTHS/GO TO 407*   (49–50)
     2 or more: .... 2 ⟶ *MARGIN LIVE BIRTHS/GO TO 405*
     _____
     (specify number)

402. Are you pregnant now?

     Yes .... 1 ⟶ *MARGIN PREGNANT/GO TO 408*
     Possibly .... 2 ⟶ *MARGIN PREGNANT/GO TO 408*   □ (51)
     No 3

403. Have you had any pregnancies which ended in a miscarriage, stillbirth or abortion?

     Yes .... 1 ⟶ *GO TO 410*
     No 2   □ (52)

404. So you have never been pregnant up to now?

     Never pregnant .... 1 ⟶ *GO TO 500*
     Has been pregnant .... 2 ⟶ *GO BACK TO 401*   □ (53)

405. Have you ever given birth to twins (or triplets or quadruplets)?

    Yes 1

    No .... 2 ⟶ *GO TO 407*   □ (54)

406. How many times?   _____   □ (55)

                         (number of times)

407. Are you pregnant now?

    Yes .... 1 ⟶ *MARGIN/PREGNANT*

    Possibly..... 2 ⟶ *MARGIN PREGNANT*

    No .... 3 ⟶ *GO TO 409*   □ (56)

408. What month is the baby due?

_____

(month)   (57–58)

409. Have you had any other pregnancies which ended in a miscarriage, stillbirth or abortion?

    Yes 1

    No .... 2 ⟶ *GO TO 411*   □ (59)

410. How many of these pregnancies?

_____

('other pregnancies') ⟶ *MARGIN OTHER PREGNANCIES*   (60–61)

411. In summary, you have had in all, including the present pregnancy if applicable:

_____

(total pregnancies) ⟶ *WRITE IN THE MARGIN*

of which: _____ pregnancies ended with live births.
           (times)

        _____ pregnancies ended in a miscarriage,
        (times)   stillbirth or abortion   (62–63)

Note to the interviewer: – If the respondent is pregnant for the first time ⟶ *GO TO 500.*
– If the respondent has had no live births ⟶ *GO TO 413.*
– If respondent has had live births ⟶ *GO TO 412.*

412. Now if you don't mind, we'll try and trace the dates of these pregnancies. Let's begin with the pregnancies that ended with live births.

Interviewer:	Ask the following questions for each live birth; then if 'other pregnancies' go to 413, if 'only live births,' go to 500 after 412.
	A – When was your first (second, etc. ...) child born? B – Was the child a boy or a girl? C – Is this child still alive? If child has died ⟶ When?

(IF TWINS, use one line for each child, and connect the lines on the left with a bracket).

(1st child) A) _____ 19 ____   B) SEX: Boy ☐ Girl ☐
         (birth month)
        C) ALIVE ☐ DECEASED ☐ ⟶ _____ 19 ____
                          (month of death)

(2nd child) A) _____ 19 ____   B) SEX: Boy ☐ Girl ☐
         (birth month)
        C) ALIVE ☐ DECEASED ☐ ⟶ _____ 19 ____
                          (month of death)

(3rd child) A) _____ 19 ____   B) SEX: Boy ☐ Girl ☐
         (birth month)
        C) ALIVE ☐ DECEASED ☐ ⟶ _____ 19 ____
                          (month of death)

(4th child) A) _____ 19 ____   B) SEX: Boy ☐ Girl ☐
         (birth month)
        C) ALIVE ☐ DECEASED ☐ ⟶ _____ 19 ____
                          (month of death)

(5th child) A) _____ 19 ____   B) SEX: Boy ☐ Girl ☐
         (birth month)
        C) ALIVE ☐ DECEASED ☐ ⟶ _____ 19 ____
                          (month of death)

6th child A) _____ 19 ____   (birth month)   B) SEX: Boy ☐   Girl ☐
C) ALIVE ☐ DECEASED ☐ ⟶ _____ 19 ____   (month of death)

7th child A) _____ 19 ____   (birth month)   B) SEX: Boy ☐   Girl ☐
C) ALIVE ☐ DECEASED ☐ ⟶ _____ 19 ____   (month of death)

8th child A) _____ 19 ____   (birth month)   B) SEX: Boy ☐   Girl ☐
C) ALIVE ☐ DECEASED ☐ ⟶ _____ 19 ____   (month of death)

9th child A) _____ 19 ____   (birth month)   B) SEX: Boy ☐   Girl ☐
C) ALIVE ☐ DECEASED ☐ ⟶ _____ 19 ____   (month of death)

10th child A) _____ 19 ____   (birth month)   B) SEX: Boy ☐   Girl ☐
C) ALIVE ☐ DECEASED ☐ ⟶ _____ 19 ____   (month of death)

11th child A) _____ 19 ____   (birth month)   B) SEX: Boy ☐   Girl ☐
C) ALIVE ☐ DECEASED ☐ ⟶ _____ 19 ____   (month of death)

12th child A) _____ 19 ____   (birth month)   B) SEX: Boy ☐   Girl ☐
C) ALIVE ☐ DECEASED ☐ ⟶ _____ 19 ____   (month of death)

13th child A) _____ 19 ____   (birth month)   B) SEX: Boy ☐   Girl ☐
C) ALIVE ☐ DECEASED ☐ ⟶ _____ 19 ____   (month of death)

14th child

A) _____ 19 ___   B) SEX: Boy ☐   Girl ☐
(birth month)

C) ALIVE ☐ DECEASED ☐ ⟶ _____ 19 ___
(month of death)

- -

15th child

A) _____ 19 ___   B) SEX: Boy ☐   Girl ☐
(birth month)

C) ALIVE ☐ DECEASED ☐ ⟶ _____ 19 ___
(month of death)

- -

16th child

A) _____ 19 ___   B) SEX: Boy ☐   Girl ☐
(birth month)

C) ALIVE ☐ DECEASED ☐ ⟶ _____ 19 ___
(month of death)

- -

| 17 children or more | ⟶ Date of birth of last child born live |

_____ 19 ___
(month)

- -

Interviewer: See margin; if 'other pregnancies' ⟶ *GO TO 413*

if no 'other pregnancies' ⟶ *GO TO 500*

413. Let's take a look at those pregnancies which did not end with live births. You told me that you have had _____ such pregnancies.
(Margin)

Interviewer: For each of the pregnancies which did not end with live births, ask the following questions; then after go to 500.

A – Did the first (second, third, etc.) one of these pregnancies end in a miscarriage, stillbirth or abortion?
B – How many months did the pregnancy last?
C – When did it happen?

1st time

A) Pregnancy ended in: Miscarriage ☐ Stillbirth ☐ Abortion ☐

B) Length of pregnancy: _____   C) When: _____ 19 ___
(month)

- -

2nd time A) Pregnancy ended in: Miscarriage ☐ Stillbirth ☐ Abortion ☐

B) Length of pregnancy: _____ C) When: _____ 19 _____
(month)

3rd time A) Pregnancy ended in: Miscarriage ☐ Stillbirth ☐ Abortion ☐

B) Length of pregnancy: _____ C) When: _____ 19 _____
(month)

4th time A) Pregnancy ended in: Miscarriage ☐ Stillbirth ☐ Abortion ☐

B) Length of pregnancy: _____ C) When: _____ 19 _____
(month)

5th time A) Pregnancy ended in: Miscarriage ☐ Stillbirth ☐ Abortion ☐

B) Length of pregnancy: _____ C) When: _____ 19 _____
(month)

6th time A) Pregnancy ended in: Miscarriage ☐ Stillbirth ☐ Abortion ☐

B) Length of pregnancy: _____ C) When: _____ 19 _____
(month)

7th time A) Pregnancy ended in: Miscarriage ☐ Stillbirth ☐ Abortion ☐

B) Length of pregnancy: _____ C) When: _____ 19 _____
(month)

SECTION 5 – KNOWLEDGE AND USE OF CONTRACEPTIVE METHODS

500. Now, I'd like to talk to you about another subject. As
you know, there are various methods to either postpone
or prevent pregnancy. I'm going to mention several
contraceptive methods and I'd like you to tell me
whether you've heard of them and whether you have
used them.

`0 5` (1–9)

	500A. Have you heard of ...		500B. Have you used ...			
	No	Yes	Yes	No	DNK	
1. the pill	2	1 ⟶	1	2	8	(10–11)
2. IUD (intra-uterine device)	2	1 ⟶	1	2	8	(12–13)
3. foam, jelly or cream	2	1 ⟶	1	2	8	(14–15)
4. douching after intercourse	2	1 ⟶	1	2	8	(16–17)
5. condoms (rubbers)	2	1 ⟶	1	2	8	(18–19)
6. diaphragm	2	1 ⟶	1	2	8	(20–21)
7. withdrawal (pulling out)	2	1 ⟶	1	2	8	(22–23)
8. abstinence for a month or more	2	1 ⟶	1	2	8	(24–25)
9. rhythm methods such as temperature or calendar	2	1 ⟶	1	2	8	(26–27)
10. female sterilization (tubal ligation)	2	1 ⟶	1	2	8	(28–29)
11. male sterilization (vasectomy)	2	1 ⟶	1	2	8	(30–31)
12. abortion	2	1 ⟶	1	2	8	(32–33)

Attention interviewer: – If the respondent has never used
a contraceptive method, GO TO 606.
– If the respondent uses or has used
– the pill, ASK QUESTION 501.
For the others, GO TO 503.

---

501. Have you ever stopped using the pill for a reason
other than wanting to get pregnant?

Yes 1
No .... 2 ⟶ GO TO 503.   (34)

502. What was the main reason why you stopped using the pill?

_____

_____

(35–36)

503. | See margin 'total pregnancies':

   If one pregnancy or more ⟶ *GO TO 510*
   Only if no pregnancies at all ⟶ *GO TO 504*

No pregnancies at all

504. At what age did you start using contraception?

_____
(age)

(37–38)

505. Among the contraceptive methods you have used, which one did you use the longest and for how long?

_____   _____
(method)   (duration)

(39–42)

506. Are you or your husband/partner using a contraceptive method now?

   Yes 1
   No .... 2 ⟶ *GO TO 606*

(43)

507. Which contraceptive method are you using and how long have you been using it?

_____   _____
(method)   (duration)

According to the method:

| Respondent or her husband/partner has been sterilized | Other method than sterilization |

(48–49)

GO TO 607   *GO TO 609*

510. Now let's try recalling when you used contraception between each of your pregnancies including, if applicable, current pregnancy, miscarriage, stillbirth or abortion. You told me that you have been pregnant in total: _____ times.
     (see margin)

511. Before your first pregnancy, did you use one contraceptive method, more than one method or no contraceptive method at all?

     One contraceptive method .... 1 ⟶ *GO TO 513*
     More than one method............................ 2
     No contraceptive method .... 3 ⟶ *GO TO 515*
     Can't remember .... 4 ⟶ *GO TO 515*

512. Which method did you use for the longest time before your *first* pregnancy and how long did you use it?

     _____⟶ _____
     (method)   (duration)

513. Which was the last method you used before your *first* pregnancy and how long did you use it?

     _____⟶ _____
     (method)   (duration)

514. When you became pregnant the *first* time, were you still using the contraceptive method, or had you forgotten to use it, or had you chosen to stop using it?

     Still using it 1
     Had forgotten 2
     Had stopped 3

515. When you became pregnant the *first* time ...

     ... did you want to become pregnant
         at that particular time......................... 1
     ... would you have preferred to become
         pregnant at some other time................ 2
     ... would you have preferred not
         to have a child.................................. 3
     ... Don't know 8

```
┌─────────────────────────────────────────────────┐
│  If two pregnancies or more ──▶ GO TO 521         │
│  If only one pregnancy ──▶ GO TO 600              │
└─────────────────────────────────────────────────┘
```

521. Between your *first and second* pregnancy, did you use one contraceptive method, more than one method or no contraceptive method at all?

    One contraceptive method ....1 ──▶ *GO TO 523*
    More than one method............................ 2
    No contraceptive method ....3 ──▶ *GO TO 525*
    Can't remember ....4 ──▶ *GO TO 525*

522. Which method did you use for the longest time before your *second* pregnancy and how long did you use it?

_____ ──▶ _____
(method)   (duration)

523. Which was the *last* method you used before your *second* pregnancy and how long did you use it?

_____ ──▶ _____
(method)   (duration)

524. When you became pregnant the *second* time, were you still using the contraceptive method, or had you forgotten to use it, or had you chosen to stop using it?

    Still using it 1
    Had forgotten 2
    Had stopped 3

525. When you became pregnant the *second* time ...

    ... did you want to become pregnant
    at that particular time.........................1
    ... would you have preferred to become
    pregnant at some other time................ 2
    ... would you have preferred not
    to have a child................................... 3
    ... Don't know 8

> If three pregnancies or more ——➤ *GO TO 531*
> If only two pregnancies ——➤ *GO TO 600*

531. Between your *second and third* pregnancy, did you use one contraceptive method, more than one method or no contraceptive method at all?

    One contraceptive method .... 1 ——➤ *GO TO 533*
    More than one method 2
    No contraceptive method .... 3 ——➤ *GO TO 535*
    Can't remember .... 4 ——➤ *GO TO 535*

532. Which method did you use for the longest time before your *third* pregnancy and how long did you use it?

———————————————➤ ————————————————
(method)   (duration)

533. Which was the *last* method you used before your *third* pregnancy and how long did you use it?

———————————————➤ ————————————————
(method)   (duration)

534. When you became pregnant the *third* time, were you still using the contraceptive method, or had you forgotten to use it, or had you chosen to stop using it?

    Still using it 1
    Had forgotten 2
    Had stopped 3

535. When you became pregnant the *third* time ...

    ... did you want to become pregnant
    at that particular time 1
    ... would you have preferred to become
    pregnant at some other time 2
    ... would you have preferred not
    to have a child 3
    ... Don't know 8

> If four pregnancies or more ⟶ *GO TO 541*
> If only three pregnancies ⟶ *GO TO 600*

541. Before your *third and fourth* pregnancy, did you use one contraceptive method, more than one method or no contraceptive method at all?

  One contraceptive method ....1 ⟶ *GO TO 543*
  More than one method.............................. 2
  No contraceptive method ....3 ⟶ *GO TO 545*
  Can't remember ....4 ⟶ *GO TO 545*

542. Which method did you use for the longest time before your *fourth* pregnancy and how long did you use it?

  ——————————————⟶ ——————————————
  (method)   (duration)

543. Which was the *last* method you used before your *fourth* pregnancy and how long did you use it?

  ——————————————⟶ ——————————————
  (method)   (duration)

544. When you became pregnant the *fourth* time, were you still using the contraceptive method, or had you forgotten to use it, or had you chosen to stop using it?

  Still using it...1
  Had forgotten 2
  Had stopped 3

545. When you became pregnant the *fourth* time ...

  ... did you want to become pregnant
  at that particular time........................ 1
  ... would you have preferred to become
  pregnant at some other time................ 2
  ... would you have preferred not
  to have a child.................................. 3
  ... Don't know..................................... 8

> If five pregnancies or more ———► *GO TO 551*
> If only four pregnancies ———► *GO TO 600*

551. Between your *fourth and fifth* pregnancy, did you use one contraceptive method, more than one method or no contraceptive method at all?

   One contraceptive method .... 1 ———► *GO TO 553*
   More than one method 2
   No contraceptive method .... 3 ———► *GO TO 555*
   Can't remember .... 4 ———► *GO TO 555*

552. Which method did you use for the longest time before your *fifth* pregnancy and how long did you use it?

   _____ ———► _____
   (method)   (duration)

553. Which was the *last* method you used before your *fifth* pregnancy and how long did you use it?

   _____ ———► _____
   (method)   (duration)

554. When you became pregnant the *fifth* time, were you still using the contraceptive method, or had you forgotten to use it, or had you chosen to stop using it?

   Still using it 1
   Had forgotten 2
   Had stopped 3

555. When you became pregnant the *fifth* time ...

   ... did you want to become pregnant
   at that particular time 1
   ... would you have preferred to become
   pregnant at some other time 2
   ... would you have preferred not
   to have a child 3
   ... Don't know 8

If six pregnancies or more ⟶ *GO TO 561*
If only five pregnancies ⟶ *GO TO 600*

---

561. Between your *fifth and sixth* pregnancy, did you use one contraceptive method, more than one method or no contraceptive method at all?

> One contraceptive method .... 1 ⟶ *GO TO 563*
> More than one method.............................. 2
> No contraceptive method .... 3 ⟶ *GO TO 565*
> Can't remember .... 4 ⟶ *GO TO 565*

562. Which method did you use for the longest time before your *sixth* pregnancy and how long did you use it?

_____⟶ _____
(method)   (duration)

563. Which was the *last* method you used before your *sixth* pregnancy and how long did you use it?

_____⟶ _____
(method)   (duration)

564. When you became pregnant the *sixth* time, were you still using the contraceptive method, or had you forgotten to use it, or had you chosen to stop using it?

> Still using it..1
> Had forgotten 2
> Had stopped 3

565. When you became pregnant the *sixth* time ...

> ... did you want to become pregnant
>   at that particular time......................... 1
> ... would you have preferred to become
>   pregnant at some other time................. 2
> ... would you have preferred not
>   to have a child.................................... 3
> ... Don't know...................................... 8

> If more than six pregnancies, use separate sheet for each pregnancy indicating respondent's registration number.
>
> If only six pregnancies ⟶ *GO TO 600*

SECTION 6 – CONTRACEPTION CURRENTLY USED AND FERTILITY EXPECTATIONS

If pregnant now ⟶ *GO TO 614*

600. Are you and your husband/partner using a contraceptive method now?

```
┌──── Yes ............................... 1
│     No .................................. 2 ⟶ GO TO 604          ☐ (50)
↓
```

601. Which method are you using and how long have you been using it?

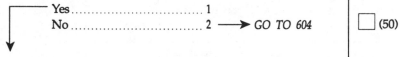

(method)   (duration)   (51–54)

According to the method:

Respondent or her husband/partner has been sterilized (A)	Other method than sterilization (B)

602A. Between your last pregnancy and the time of the operation steriliza tion) did you use a contraceptive method?

602B. Since your last pregnancy have you used other methods of contraception?

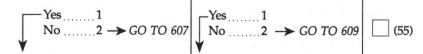

┌─Yes 1   ┌─Yes 1
│ No ....2 ⟶ *GO TO 607*   │ No ....2 ⟶ *GO TO 609*   ☐ (55)
↓   ↓

603A. Which method did you use the longest time and how long did you use it?

(1) _____
     (method)

(2) _____
     (duration)

↓

GO TO 607

603B. Which method did you use for the longest time and how long did you use it?

(1) _____
     (method)

(2) _____
     (duration)

↓

GO TO 609

(56–59)

604. Since your last pregnancy, have you used any method of contraception?

   Yes 1
   No .... 2 → GO TO 606

(60)

605. Which method have you used the longest and how long did you use it?

_____→ _____
(method)   (duration)

(61–64)

606. Have you or your husband/partner, if applicable, had an operation which would make it impossible for you to have children?

   Yes 1
   No .... 2 ⟶ GO TO 608

(65)

607. Among the following operations, which one or ones did you, or your husband/partner if applicable, have and when did they take place?
(Interviewer: Ask each question a, b, c and d)

	Yes	No
a) tubal ligation?	1	2

(66)

_____ 19____
(month)   (year)

If you had the decision to make today, would you make the same one regarding the tubal ligation?

   Yes................................. 1
   No 2

(67–68)
(69–70)
(71)

| 0 | 6 | (1–9) |

	Yes	No	
607. b) hysterectomy?	1	2	☐ (10)

_____ 19_____
(month)   (year)

If you had not had this operation,
would you have had a tubal ligation?

Yes..............................1
No 2

☐☐ (11–12)
☐☐ (13–14)
☐ (15)

c) another operation which made
   you sterile   1   2   ☐ (16)

☐☐ (17–18)

(specify which operation)
_____ 19_____
(month)   (year)

If you had not had this operation,
would you have had a tubal ligation?

Yes..............................1
No 2

☐☐ (19–20)
☐☐ (21–22)
☐ (23)

d) if applicable, has your husband/partner
   had a vasectomy?   1   2   ☐ (24)

_____ 19_____
(month)   (year)

☐☐ (25–26)
☐☐ (27–28)

GO TO 700

608. Since you are not using any contraceptive method at
     the present time, which of the following statements
     best describes your situation? You are not using
     contraception because ...

... you do not have a husband/   1
    partner right now
... you want to become pregnant   2 ——▶ GO TO 610
... you think you are sterile   3 ——▶ GO TO 700
... you think you huysband/
    partner is sterile   4 ——▶ GO TO 700   ☐ (29)

Other reason: _____
              (SPECIFY)

609. Do you expect to have a child in the future?

    Yes 1
    No .... 2 ⟶ *GO TO 613*
    Don't know.............. 8 ⟶ *GO TO 613*

☐ (30)

610. How many children do you expect to have (not counting the children you've already had)?

        Number: _____

☐☐ (31–32)

611. In what year would you like your (next) child to be born?

      19 ___

☐☐ (33–34)

612. Would you like this child to be a boy or a girl?

    Boy........................... 1
    Girl........................... 2
    Either one 3

☐ (35)

613. Do you think you might have an operation for sterilization at some later date?

    Yes .... 1 ⟶ *GO TO 700*
    Maybe...................... 2 ⟶ *GO TO 700*
    No .... 3 ⟶ *GO TO 700*
    Don't know.............. 8 ⟶ *GO TO 700*

☐ (36)

614. Would you like to have children in addition to the one you are expecting now?

    Yes 1
    No .... 2 ⟶ *GO TO 618*
    Don't know.............. 8 ⟶ *GO TO 618*

☐ (37)

615. How many children in addition to your present pregnancy do you expect to have?

    _____
    (number)

☐☐ (38–39)

616. What difference in age would you like to see between the child you are expecting now and the next one?

    _____
    (number of years difference)

☐ (40)

617. Would you like the child you are expecting now to be a boy or a girl?

Boy.............................1
Girl.............................2
Either one 3

☐ (41)

618. Do you think you might have an operation for sterilization at some later date?

Yes 1
Maybe 2
No 3
Don't know.................8

☐ (42)

SECTION 7 – SHARING HOUSEWORK AND PROFESSIONAL LIFE

```
Interviewer:
See margin – Woman living with
                husband/partner  ———→  GO TO 700

             – Woman without
                husband/partner  ———→  GO TO 704
```

700. Would you say that you take part in recreational activities outside the home *without your husband/partner* ...

... more than once a month 1
... once a month 2
... less than once a month 3
... never 4

☐ (43)

701. In your life as a couple, do you often, sometimes or never have problems in the following areas:

	Often	Sometimes	Never	
a) the way you spend money............................	1	2	3	☐ (44)
b) the way you organize your leisure time..............	1	2	3	☐ (45)
c) sharing housework............	1	2	3	☐ (46)
d) your sex life	1	2	3	☐ (47)

702. Would you say that it is **always** you, **mostly** you, **equally** you and your husband/partner or **mainly** your husband/partner ...

	Always you	Mostly you	Equally	Mainly partner	
a) who does the cooking	1	2	3	4	☐ (48)
b) who does the housework	1	2	3	4	☐ (49)

> Interviewer: See margin, if respondent had no live births
> ⟶ GO TO 704

703. Would you say that it is **always** you, **mostly** you, **equally** you and your husband/partner or **mainly** your husband/partner ...

	Always you	Mostly you	Equally	Mainly partner	N/A	
a) who took care of changing the diapers and feeding the baby	1	2	3	4	9	☐ (50)
b) who went shopping for the children's clothes	1	2	3	4	9	☐ (51)
c) who supervised the children's schoolwork	1	2	3	4	9	☐ (52)

704. Let's go on now and talk about your working experience; have you ever worked on a regular basis for *at least six months*, including unpaid work in a family business?

Yes ....1 ⟶ GO TO 706
No 2   ☐ (53)

705. Are you working now?

Yes ....1 ⟶ GO TO 742
No ....2 ⟶ GO TO 736   ☐ (54)

706. When did you start working on a regular basis? (Do not include work during full-time studies or summer jobs)

                   19 _____
     (month)   (year)

(55–56)
(57–58)

707. Since then, have you stopped working for a period of at least a year?

       Yes .... 1 ⟶ *GO TO 715*
       No 2

(59)

708. When you first started working, what type of work did you do and for what type of company?

_____

(type of work)

_____

(type of company)

(60–63)

709. At that time, how many hours per week did you normally work?

_____

(number of hours)

(64–65)

710. At that time, what was your annual gross salary before taxes and deductions?

$ _____ per year

(66–68)

711. Since you started working, have you stopped working fairly often for periods of *less than one year* ?

       Yes 1
       No 2

(69)

712. For this period as a whole, have you worked mostly 30 hours or more a week?

       Yes .... 1 ⟶ *GO TO 714*
       No 2

(70)

713. Why have you mostly worked *less than 30 hours* a week?

_____

_____

(71–72)

714. Are you working now?

Yes _____ 1 ⟶ *GO TO 741*

No _____ 2 ⟶ *GO TO 732*

(73)

0 7 (1–9)

715. When you first started working, what type of work did you do and for what type of company?

_____
(type of work)

_____
(type of company)

(10–13)

716. At that time, how many hours per week did you normally work?

_____
(number of hours)

(14–15)

717. At that time, what was your annual gross salary before taxes and deductions?

$ _____ per year

(16–18)

718. When did you decide to stop working for the first time for a period of *a year or more*?

_____   _____
(month)   (year)

(19–22)

719. Why did you decide to stop working at that time?

_____

_____

(23–24)

720. Did you start working again (either full-time or part-time) after this first interruption?

Yes 1
No .... 2 ⟶ GO TO 732

(25)

721. When did you start working again?

_____   _____
(month)   (year)

(26–29)

722. At that time, how many hours per week did you normally work?

_____
(number of hours)

(30–31)

723. Did you stop working a second time for a period *a year or more?*

Yes 1
No .... 2 ⟶ GO TO 741

(32)

724. When did you stop working this second time?

_____   _____
(month)   (year)

(33–36)

725. Why did you decide to stop working at that time?

_____

_____

(30–31)

726. Did you start working again (either full-time or part-time) after this second interruption?

Yes 1
No .... 2 ⟶ GO TO 732

(39)

727. When did you start working again?

_____   _____
(month)   (year)

(40–43)

728. At that time, how many hours per week did you normally work?

_____
(number of hours)

(44–45)

729. Since then, have you stopped working for periods of *a year or more*?

Yes 1
No .... 2 ⟶ *GO TO 731*

(46)

730. How many times and for how long did you stop working each time?

_____
(number of times)

(47)

_____   _____   _____   _____
(length) 1   (length) 2   (length) 3   (length) 4

(48–51)

731. Are you working now?

Yes .... 1 ⟶ *GO TO 741*
No 2

(52)

732. When you left your last job, were you doing the same type of work as whn you started work for the first time?

Yes .... 1 ⟶ *GO TO 734*
No 2

(53)

733. What type of work were you doing when you left your last job and for what type of company?

_____
(type of work)

_____
(type of company)

(54–57)

734. At that time, how many hours per week were you normally working?

_____
(number of hours)

(58–59)

735. At that time, what was your gross annual salary before taxes and deductions?

$ _____ per year

(60–62)

736. Do you have a personal income now, excluding family allowance?

Yes 1
No .... 2 ⟶ *GO TO 738*

(63)

737. How much is this income?

$ _____
(specify per week, month or year)

(64–66)

738. Why are you not working now?

_____

(67–68)

739. Do you intend to start working in the future?

Yes 1
No .... 2 ⟶ *GO TO 749*

(69)

740. In how many years?

_____ ⟶ *GO TO 749*
(number of years)

(70–71)

741. Are you now doing the same type of work as when you first started working?

Yes .... 1 ⟶ *GO TO 743*
No 2

(72)

742. What type of work are you doing and for what type of company?

_____
(type of work)

_____
(type of company)

(73–76)

0 8 (1–9)

743. How many hours per week are you now working?

_____
(number of hours)   (10–11)

744. What is your gross annual salary now before taxes and deductions?

$ _____ per year   (12–14)

745. Do you now have a personal income that does not come from your work? (Excluding family allowance)

┌──────── Yes 1
│   No .... 2 ──→ GO TO 747   (15)
↓
746. How much is this additional income?

$ _____
(spcecify per week, month or year)   (16–18)

747. Right now, do you intend to work until you are 60?

        Yes .... 1 ──→ GO TO 749
┌────── No 2   (19)
↓
748. Why do you want to stop sooner?

_____

_____
                                                     (20–21)

749. In your opinion, is it acceptable for a woman who has a child *under three* to work outside the home?

        Yes 1
        No 2   (22)

750. When a woman who has a child under three decides to work outside the home, which one of the following three child care solutions *is the best* ...

        ... a babysitter at home 1
        ... taking the child to a
            babysitter's home, or 2
        ... a daycare center 3   (23)

751. For women, do you think that having young children reduces their work opportunities outside the home a lot, a fair amount, not very much or not at all?

> A lot 1
> A fair amount 2
> Not very much 3
> Not at all 4

(24)

752. In general, do you believe that the majority of men accept fairly well that their wife (partner) works outside the home? ...

	Yes	No
... when she has children	1	2
... when she has no children	1	2

(25)

(26)

SECTION 8 – ECONOMIC ASPECTS OF THE FAMILY

(Interviewer ──➤ See Margin)

Live with husband/partner	Live without husband/partner

800A. From a financial stand-point, do you feel that you as a couple have ...

> ... been very successful .. 1
> ... been reasonably successful 2
> ... not been successful 3

800B. From a financial stand-point, do you feel you have ...

> ... been very successful .. 1
> ... been reasonably successful 2
> ... not been successful 3

(27)

801A. Some couples make very precise plans for the future. In general would you say that you as a couple plan things ...

... most of the time 1
... occasionally 2
... rarely 3
... never 4

801B. Some people make very precise plans for the future. In general, would you say that you plan things ...

... most of the time 1
... occasionally 2
... rarely 3
... never 4

(28)

802A. Suppose your household no longer had its normal income, would your household be able to pay all the regular bills for a month without borrowing money?

Yes 1
No 2

802A. Suppose you no longer had the normal income you rely on, would you be able to pay all the regular bills for a month without borrowing money?

Yes 1
No 2

(29)

803A. Do you or your husband/partner participate in a compulsory pension plan not counting the Canada Pension Plan (or Quebec Plan in Quebec)?

Yes 1   ➤ GO TO 804A
No 2   ➤ GO TO 805A
Don't
know 8   ➤ GO TO 805A

803B. Do you participate in a compulsory pension plan not counting the Canada Pension Plan (or Quebec Plan in Quebec)?

Yes 1   ➤ GO TO 804B
No 2   ➤ GO TO 805B
Don't
know 8   ➤ GO TO 805B

(30)

804A. Apart from this compulsory pension plan, do you *as a couple* put money aside on a regular basis, from time to time or practically never?

On a regular basis 1
From time to time 2
Practically never 3

GO TO 806

804A. Apart from this compulsory pension plan, do you put money aside on a regular basis, from time to time or practically never?

On a regular basis 1
From time to time 2
Practically never 3

☐ (31)

GO TO 807

805A. Do you *as a couple* put money aside including retirement savings plans, on a regular basis, from time to time or practically never?

On a regular basis 1
From time to time 2
Practically never 3

805B. Do you put money aside including retirement savings plans, on a regular basis, from time to time or practically never?

On a regular basis 1
From time to time 2
Practically never 3

☐ (32)

806. Does your husband/ partner have life insurance?

Yes 1
No 2

☐ (33)

GO TO 807

GO TO 807

807. Do you have life insurance?

        Yes 1
        No 2   ☐ (34)

808. Do you think that young people who are 18 years or over who are living at home and working should help the family by contributing to household expenses?

        Yes 1
        No 2   ☐ (35)

809. When you were living at home with your parents did you help the family by contributing to household expenses?

        Yes 1
        No 2   ☐ (36)

810. When you retire, do you think you will need financial assistance from your children?

        Yes 1
        No 2   ☐ (37)
        Don't know 8

811. When you retire, do you expect to ...
    (Only one answer)

    go and live with one of your children 1

    live in a senior citizens home 2

    live in your own place 3

    live out your retirement in
    some other way (SPECIFY):

    _____   ☐
                              (38)

    _____ 4

812. Are your parents still alive?

        Yes (one or both) 1
        No (both dead) .... 2 ⟶ GO TO 815
        Don't know .... 3 ⟶ GO TO 815

☐ (39)

813. Do your parents have to count on financial assistance from their children?

        Yes 1
        No 2

☐ (40)

814. If need be, would you be willing to have your parents live with you for an extended period of time?

        Yes 1
        No 2

☐ (41)

815. In what type of building are you living in ...

   ... a single-family house
       (detached, semi-detached,
       townhouse, bungalow, etc.) 1
   ... a duplex or triplex 2
   ... a building with 4 or more
       apartments 3
   ... other: 4

☐ (42)

816. Do you or someone in the household own or rent the dwelling you live in?

Owner .... 1 | Tenant 2

☐ (43)

817A. What is the approximate value of your dwelling?

$_____

817B. How much is your monthly rent (including heating)?

$_____ per month

☐☐☐ (44–46)

If don't know, check ☐   If don't know, check ☐

☐☐☐
(47–49)

818. Approximately, how much do you have left to pay on your mortgage?

$_____

If don't know, check ☐

☐☐☐
(50–52)

If no mortgage, check ☐

| 0 | 9 | (1–9)

Attention Interviewer: See margin:

     If living with husband/partner ——➤ *GO TO 900*

     If no husband/partner ————➤ *GO TO 917*

SECTION 9 – CHARACTERISTICS OF CURRENT HUSBAND/PARTNER

900. When was your husband/partner born?

_____ 19 _____

(month)

☐☐
☐☐
(10–13)

901. How many children did your husband's/partner's mother have?

_____ 19 _____

(month)

☐☐
(14–15)

902. In total, how many years of education has your husband/partner completed?

_____

(number of children)

☐☐
(16–17)

903. What is the *highest* degree, certificate, diploma or grade your husband/partner has obtained?

_____

(SPECIFY)   (18–19)

904. To what ethnic or cultural group did your husband's/partner's male ancestor belong on first coming to North America?

French	01	Ukrainian	07
English	02	Dutch	08
Irish	03	Polish	09
Scottish	04	Jewish	10
German	05	Chinese	11
Italian	06	Greek	12

Other: _____   (20–21)
       (SPECIFY)

905. What is the language your husband/partner first learned and still understands?

English	01
French	02
German	03
Italian	04
Ukrainian	05

Other: _____   (22–23)
       (SPECIFY)

906. What is your husband's/partner's religion now?

Roman Catholic	01	Jewish	09
Protestant (no specification)	02	Ukrainian Catholic	10
		Pentecostal	11
United Church	03	Jehovah's Witnesses	12
Anglican	04	Mennonite	13
Presbyterian	05	Salvation Army	14
Lutheran	06	Islam	15
Baptist	07	No religion	95
Greek Orthodox	08		

Other: _____   (24–25)
       (SPECIFY)

907. What type of work does your husband/partner do and in what type of company? (If he is not working right now, his most recent job)

_____
(type of work)

_____
(type of company)

(26–29)

908. Presently, is your husband/partner self-employed, working on salary, or not working?

Self-employed 01
On salary 02
Not working 03
Other: _____ 04
          (SPECIFY)

(30)

909. In the last 52 weeks, how many weeks did your husband/partner work? (Include full-time, part-time, paid vacations, sick leave, self-employment)

_____
(number of weeks)

(31–32)

910. Would you say that it is mainly you, equally you and your husband/partner, mostly your husband/partner or always your husband/partner who makes the decisions about money?

Mainly the woman 01
Equally shared 02
Mostly partner 03
Always partner 04

(33)

911. In the first three years of your relationship, did you at any time feel financially insecure?

Yes 1
No 2

(34)

912. In the first three years of your relationship, was your husband/partner ever unemployed?

   Yes..................................... 1
   No .... 2 ⟶ *GO TO 914* ☐
                      (35)

913. Were these periods of unemployment particularly trying for you?

   Yes.................................. 1
   No 2   ☐
                 (36)

914. When you got married or when you started living together, was you standard of living better than, the same as, or worse than that of people you knew in your age group?

   Better.............................. 1
   The same 2
   Worse .... 3 ☐
                (37)

915. And now, is your standard of living better than, the same as, or worse than that of people you know in your age group?

   Better.............................. 1
   The same 2
   Worse .... 3 ☐
                (38)

916. What is your husband's/partner's gross annual income before taxes and deductions?

   $ _____ per year ☐☐☐
                 (39–41)

917. In all, what is the gross annual income of your family before taxes and deductions including yourself, your husband/partner and your children?

   $ _____ per year ☐☐☐
                 (42–44)

918. To conclude, did you find that the interview was too long?

> Yes 1
> No 2

(45)

919. Did you find the subjects discussed interesting?

> Yes 1
> No 2

(46)

920. How long do you think this interview lasted?

> _____
> (minutes)

(47–48)

921. Would you rather have been interviewed in person at home?

> Yes 1
> Perhaps 2
> No 3

(49)

⟶ | Exact time now: _____ |

(50–53)

2

| 3 | 3 | 9 |
(55–57)

THANK RESPONDENT AND END INTERVIEW

Further notes on survey methodology

Pre-tests

In the summer of 1982, a pilot study was done on the feasibility of administering a lengthy questionnaire on the subject of fertility in Canada. One of the objectives of the feasibility study was to check the reliability of data gathered over the telephone vis-à-vis that collected in face-to-face interviews. The pilot study was also expected to give relative estimates of cost, time, and other logistics of conducting the survey by the two modes of data-gathering.

In the feasibility study, information was collected from 150 sample women: 50 each in Edmonton, Toronto, and Montreal. Half of these women were interviewed on the telephone and the other half face to face. It was found that it was quite feasible to collect most information on the telephone. The feasibility study was also important in estimating such things as mean interview time, the best sequence of questions, and any sensitive aspects to be considered when the interview is conducted on the telephone.

It was found that the non-response rate was only slightly higher on the telephone, well worth the reduction in cost and time of using the telephone for interviewing. Actual interview time was somewhat shorter on the telephone than face to face. The initial pilot study was largely instrumental in deciding on the telephone mode for the main survey itself.

During the period September 1983 to February 1984, four pre-tests were done, mainly to fine-tune the draft questionnaire and to make sure that the versions in English and French were strictly comparable in question wording and meaning conveyed and that the average length was close to 45 minutes, as a considerable part of the cost of the survey would depend on the interview time on the telephone.

TABLE B.1
Breakdown of the fieldwork: Canada and large regions

Results	Atlantic provinces	Quebec	Ontario	Western provinces	Canada
a. Out of service	677	1123	1744	1929	5473
b. Line trouble	2	27	133	45	207
c. Commercial number	222	521	1135	865	2743
d. Second residence	1	25	46	32	104
e. Language in household	–	19	83	37	139
f. Language of person selected	2	32	105	48	187
g. Not eligible – age/sex	388	1027	1681	1364	4460
h. Illness	5	6	17	15	43
i. No answer	76	268	654	221	1219
j. Household refusal	124	276	614	442	1456
k. Selected person refusal	42	163	207	189	601
l. Incomplete questionnaire	12	19	47	23	101
m. Prolonged absence	4	17	18	39	78
n. Wrong selection	–	1	–	–	1
o. Completed questionnaire	491	1501	1793	1530	5315
p. No result	2	–	39	1	42
Total	2048	5025	8316	6780	22,169

Response rates

The calculation of a response rate always poses problems in the case of a sample that includes ineligible units, since for some of the no-answer categories eligibility status cannot be determined. For example, regrouping the data in table B.1, we find that there were 13,642 residential numbers in the sample (Total minus items a, b, c, and d). Of these, 4829 were clearly ineligible by CFS definitions, even if they contained fertility information (sum of items e, f, g, and h), leaving a total of 8813 numbers. Of these, 2717 (sum of items i, j, and p) could not be contacted to establish eligibility. Of the remaining 6096 eligible respondents contacted, 5315 gave completed interviews. The final response rate of 5315/6096 = 87.2 per cent is deceptive, as many of the 2717 households where eligibility cannot established may have contained an eligible respondent. The estimated total eligible respondents are 7574, for a more appropriate response rate of 5315/7574 = 70.2 per cent.

Table B.2 presents the response rates for the various provinces and the three largest metropolitan areas. The final response rates are comparable to other similar surveys done on the telephone and are probably

TABLE B.2
Response rate: Canada, the provinces, and CMAs

	Estimated number of households containing eligible persons	Number of usable, completed questionnaires	Response rate (%)
Newfoundland / Prince Edward Island	203	161	79.3
New Brunswick	199	143	71.9
Nova Scotia	263	187	71.1
Quebec:	2030	1501	73.9
Montreal CMA	(924)	(648)	70.1
Rest of Quebec	(1106)	(853)	77.1
Ontario:	2742	1793	65.4
Toronto CMA	(1075)	(672)	62.5
Rest of Ontario	(1667)	(1121)	67.2
Manitoba	292	237	81.2
Saskatchewan	267	221	82.8
Alberta	646	503	77.9
British Columbia:	932	569	61.1
Vancouver	(490)	(285)	58.2
Rest of British Columbia	(442)	(284)	64.3
Canada	7574	5315	70.2

not much lower than those found in face-to-face surveys. Considerable variations, however, can be noticed by geographical regions. As is usual, the rates are lowest in the large cities, though Montreal fared quite well with a percentage of 70.1 compared with 62.5 in Toronto and 58.2 in Vancouver. Response rates were significantly higher in the Prairie provinces of Manitoba, Saskatchewan, and Alberta as well as in Newfoundland/Prince Edward Island.

Other aspects of field work

Number and time of calls. It is estimated that 80,000 to 100,000 calls were made, with or without success, in the ten provinces during the survey. This includes calls made to find a household and eligible person as well as those made to complete the interview or for verification purposes. A breakdown of completed questionnaires by number of calls required is shown in table B.3. Out of the 5315 valid questionnaires, less than 25 per cent of the interviews were completed on the first call. Sixteen per cent required six or more calls to complete.

The best time of the day to complete interviews varied. Twenty-two per cent of the interviews were completed in the morning; 43.2 per cent between 1200 and 1800 hours and 34.8 per cent after 1800 hours; and 14 per cent during the weekend. Finally, 2102 questionnaires were completed in April (39.5 per cent), 3205 in May (60.3 per cent), and 8 in June.

Language of interview. For the purposes of the survey, the respondents had to be capable of maintaining a telephone conversation in either French or English. All French interviews were conducted from Montreal. Interviewers working outside of Montreal were instructed to forward the telephone number of respondents in their regions who wanted to do the questionnaire in French. In the project as a whole, 26.7 per cent of the interviews were conducted in French and 73.7 per cent in English. In Quebec, 90.8 per cent of the interviews were conducted in French.

Incomplete questionnaires. When interviewers called respondents back to complete incomplete questionnaires, 101 persons refused to continue with the interview. Compared with the total number of women who participated in full or in part (5315 completed plus 101 incomplete questionnaires), this amounts to a rate of less than 2 percent, which is a low withdrawal rate given the subject matter covered in the interview.

Interview length. One of the important lessons of the Canadian Fertility Survey was that it proved that it is feasible to conduct lengthy telephone interviews with a non-specialized population of diverse backgrounds. The average length of the interview was 36 minutes. This average time is, however, somewhat misleading since the actual time spent, excluding the screening questionnaire, varied between 13 minutes and 115 minutes. Such variations are mainly due to the respondents' diverse backgrounds with respect to fertility as well as work history. It goes without saying that some interviews required more time because of other factors such as the technical quality of the telephone connection, the speed with which certain questions were understood, or the particular characteristics of some respondents. Table B.4 presents the distribution of completed interviews by length.

Verification and call backs. In addition to randomly verifying telephone numbers that did not result in an interview (non-residential numbers,

TABLE B.3
Breakdown of completed questionnaires by number of calls required

Number of calls	Frequency	%
1	1260	23.7
2	1281	24.1
3	877	16.5
4	613	11.5
5	420	7.9
6	257	4.8
7	225	4.2
8	143	2.7
9 and more	239	4.5
Total	5315	100.0

language problems, illness, ineligible households, etc.), each field office was instructed to recontact a minimum of 15 per cent of the respondents in its area. Furthermore, a last verification of the respondent selection criteria was carried out from Montreal once the completed questionnaires were received from Toronto, Regina, Edmonton, and Vancouver. The appropriate corrections were then made. In no case were errors more than marginal. Consequently, no return to the field was necessary and the bulk of the correcting procedure relied on a mild editing process. The purpose of the checks in the regional offices and at headquarters was not to correct such errors as may have been found among the 15 per cent. This would have left errors among the other 85 per cent uncorrected; an unacceptable outcome, if the incidence of errors was considerable. Instead of such a futile exercise, the purpose of the check was to verify that the incidence of errors was small and acceptable. (Actually, the errors discovered among the 15 per cent were corrected, but that was a by-product of the checks, not their purpose.)

The brief assessments provided by the respondents at the end of the interview were clearly positive. Although more than a third of the respondents said that they found the interview too long, 96 per cent mentioned that they were interested in the subjects covered in the interview. When asked whether they would have preferred to be interviewed in person at home, 73 per cent answered no, 17 per cent said they would have preferred an interview at home, and 8 per cent said 'perhaps' they would have preferred such a mode. Two per cent did not provide an answer to this question.

TABLE B.4
Length of interviews

Minutes	Frequency	%
Less than 15 minutes	2	0.0
15 to 29 minutes	1294	24.3
30 to 44 minutes	3052	57.4
45 to 59 minutes	777	14.6
60 to 74 minutes	146	2.7
75 to 94 minutes	35	0.6
95 minutes or more	4	0.1
Not available	5	0.1
Total	5315	100.0

APPENDIX C

Related publications from the Canadian Fertility Survey

T.R. Balakrishnan, Karol J. Krótki, and Evelyne Lapierre-Adamcyk. 'Contraceptive use in Canada 1984,' *Family Planning Perspectives* 17 (Sept./Oct. 1985): 209–15

Evelyne Lapierre-Adamcyk, T.R. Balakrishnan, and Karol J. Krótki. 'Comportement récent des jeunes québécoises en matière de contraception.' In *Actes du Colloque jeunesse et sexualité*, 463–79. Montreal: Editions Iris 1986

T.R. Balakrishnan, K. Vaninadha Rao, Evelyne Lapierre-Adamcyk, and Karol J. Krótki. 'A hazards model analysis of the covariates of marriage dissolution in Canada.' *Demography* 24 (Aug. 1987): 395–406

Evelyne Lapierre-Adamcyk, T.R. Balakrishnan, and Karol J. Krótki. 'La Cohabitation au Québec, prélude ou substitut au mariage? Les attitudes des jeunes Québécoises.' In *Couples et parents des années quatre-vingt*, 27–46. Quebec: Institut Québécois de la Recherche sur la Culture 1987

E. Lapierre-Adamcyk, 'La famille canadienne au XXe siècle: Quelques transformations de son caractère institutionnel.' *Mémoires de la Société royale du Canada*, 5ème série, tome 2 (1987): 109–4

Vijaya Krishnan. 'The relation between income and fertility: The role of immigrant culture.' In *Contributions to Demography: Methodological and Substantive*, 1: 483–504. Essays in honour of Dr Karol J. Krótki. Edmonton: University of Alberta Department of Sociology, 1987

T.R. Balakrishnan, Karol J. Krótki, and Evelyne Lapierre-Adamcyk. 'Attitudes towards abortion in Canada.' *Canadian Studies in Population* 15 (1988): 201–15

T.R. Balakrishnan, K. Vaninadha Rao, Karol J. Krótki, and Evelyne Lapierre-Adamcyk. 'Age at first birth and lifetime fertility.' *Journal of Biosocial Science* 20 (1988): 167–74

K. Vaninadha Rao and T.R. Balakrishnan. 'Recent trends and socio-economic covariates of childlessness in Canada.' *Canadian Studies in Population* 15 (1988): 181–99

T.R. Balakrishnan, K. Vaninadha Rao, Karol J. Krótki, and Evelyne Lapierre-Adamcyk, 'Parametric versus Cox's model: An illustrative analysis of divorce in Canada.' *Proceedings of the Social Statistics Section of the American Statistical Association*, 110–15. Washington: 1987

Vijaya Krishnan. 'Occupational status, earnings, and fertility expectations: Development and estimation of a causal model.' *De Economist* 136/3 (1988): 358–82

K. Vaninadha Rao and T.R. Balakrishnan, 'Age at first birth in Canada: A hazard model analysis.' *Genus* 44/1–2 (1988): 53–72

K. Vaninadha Rao and T.R. Balakrishnan. 'Timing of first birth and second birth spacing in Canada.' *Journal of Biosocial Science* 21 (1989): 293–300

Karol J. Krótki. 'The history and methodology of the Canadian Fertility Survey of 1984.' In *The Family in Crisis: A Population Crisis?*, 17–52. Ottawa: Royal Society of Canada, 1989

David Odynak. 'CFS on MTS using SPSSX at the University of Alberta.' In *The Family in Crisis: A Population Crisis?*, 63–6. Ottawa: Royal Society of Canada 1989

Evelyne Lapierre-Adamcyk.'Le mariage et famille: Mentalités actuelles et comportements récents des femmes canadiennes.' In *The Family in Crisis: A Population Crisis?*, 89–104. Ottawa: Royal Society of Canada 1989

Beatrice Chapman. 'Egalitarian sex roles and fertility in Canada.' In *The Family in Crisis: A Population Crisis?*, 121–40. Ottawa: Royal Society of Canada 1989

T.R. Balakrishnan. 'Changing nuptiality patterns and their fertility implications in Canada.' In *The Family in Crisis: A Population Crisis?*, 229–50. Ottawa: Royal Society of Canada 1989

K. Vaninadha Rao. 'Analysis of first marriage patterns in Canada.' In *The Family in Crisis: A Population Crisis?*, 287–302. Ottawa: Royal Society of Canada 1989

Marianne Kempeneers. 'L'enquête sur la fécondité au Canada: Un privilégié pour l'étude de l'activité féminine.' In *The Family in Crisis: A Population Crisis?*, 311–42. Ottawa: Royal Society of Canada 1989

Vijaya Krishnan. 'Asset accumulation and family size: Insights from recursive models.' In *The Family in Crisis: A Population Crisis?*, 417–38. Ottawa: Royal Society of Canada 1989

Fernando Rajulton, T.R. Balakrishnan, and Jiajain Chen. 'Changes in timing of fertility – A Canadian experience.' *Journal of Biosocial Science* 22 (1990): 33–42

T.R. Balakrishnan and Jiajian Chen. 'Religiosity, nuptiality and reproduction in Canada.' *Canadian Review of Sociology and Anthropology* 27 (1990): 316–40

K. Vaninadha Rao. 'Marriage risks, cohabitation and premarital births in Canada.' *European Journal of Population* 6 (1990): 27–49

Rajulton Fernando and T.R. Balakrishnan. 'Interdependence of transitions among marital and parity states.' *Canadian Studies in Population* 17 (1990): 107–32

C.F. Grindstaff, T.R. Balakrishnan, and David DeWit. 'Educational attainment, age at first birth and lifetime fertility: An analysis of Canadian Fertility Survey data.' *Canadian Review of Sociology and Anthropology* 28 (1991): 324–39

Margaret DeWit and Fernando Rajulton. 'Voluntary sterilization among Canadian women.' *Journal of Biosocial Science* 23 (1991): 263–73

Zheng Wu and T.R. Balakrishnan. 'Attitudes towards cohabitation and marriage in Canada.' *Journal of Comparative Family Studies* 21 (1992): 1–12

References

Andrews, F., J. Morgan, and J. Sonquist. 1969. *Multiple Classification Analysis.*
Ann Arbor: Institute for Survey Research, University of Michigan

Ariès, Philippe. 1980. 'Two successive motivations for the declining birth rate
in the west.' *Population and Development Review* 6(4):645–50

Bachrach, Christine A. 1984. 'Contraceptive practice among American
women, 1973–1982.' *Family Planning Perspectives* 16(6):253–9

Balakrishnan, T.R. 1989a. 'Changing nuptiality patterns and their fertility implications in Canada.' In J. Légaré, T.R. Balakrishnan, and R. Beaujot (eds),
The Family in Crisis, 229–50. Ottawa: Royal Society of Canada

– 1989b. *Recent Trends in Cohabitation in Canada and Its Demographic Implications.* Report to Statistics Canada (unpublished)

Balakrishnan, T.R., G.E. Ebanks, and C.F. Grindstaff. 1979. *Patterns of Fertility
in Canada, 1971.* 1971 Census Analytical Study. Ottawa: Statistics Canada,
Catalogue no. 99–759E

Balakrishnan, T.R., and Carl F. Grindstaff. 1988. 'Early adulthood behaviour
and later life course paths.' Report to the Demographic Review, Health and
Welfare Canada (unpublished manuscript)

Balakrishnan, T.R., J.K. Kantner, and J.D. Allingham. 1975. *Fertility and Family Planning in a Canadian Metropolis.* Montreal: McGill-Queen's University
Press

Balakrishnan, T.R., Karol Krótki, and Evelyne Lapierre-Adamcyk. 1985. 'Contraceptive use in Canada, 1984.' *Family Planning Perspectives* 17:209–15

– 1988. 'Attitudes towards abortion in Canada.' *Canadian Studies in Population* 15:210–15

Balakrishnan, T.R., K.V. Rao, Karol Krótki, and Evelyne Lapierre-Adamcyk.
1987. 'A Hazard model analysis of the covariates of marriage dissolution in
Canada.' *Demography*. 24:395–406

– 1988. 'Age at first birth and lifetime fertility.' *Journal of Biosocial Science*
20:167–74

Balakrishnan, T.R., S. Ross, J.D. Allingham, and J.F. Kantner. 1972. 'Attitudes toward abortion of married women in metropolitan Toronto.' *Social Biology* 19:35–42

Barrett, F.M. 1980. 'Changes in attitudes toward abortion in a large population of Canadian university students between 1968 and 1978.' *Canadian Journal of Public Health* 71:195–200

Barrett, F.M., and M. Fitz-Earle. 1973. 'Student opinion on legalized abortion at the University of Toronto.' *Canadian Journal of Public Health* 64:294–9

Beaujot, Roderic. 1975. 'Ethnic fertility differentials in Edmonton.' Ph.D. dissertation, University of Alberta

Beaujot, R., K.J. Krótki, and P. Krishnan. 1978. 'Socio-cultural variations in the applicability of the economic model of fertility.' *Population Studies* 32(2):319–54

Becker, G.S. 1960. 'An economic analysis of fertility.' In National Bureau of Economic Research, *Demographic and Economic Change in Developed Countries*, 209–40. Princeton: Princeton University Press

– 1981. *A Treatise on the Family.* Cambridge: Harvard University Press

Blake, Judith. 1977. 'The supreme court's abortion decisions and public opinion in the United States.' *Population and Development Review* 3(1–2):45–62

– 1979. 'Is zero preferred? American attitudes toward childlessness in the 1970s.' *Journal of Marriage and the Family* 41(2):245–57

Blake, J., and J.H. Del Pinal. 1981. 'Negativism, equivocation and wobbly assent: Public "support" for the prochoice platform on abortion.' *Demography* 18:309–20

Bower, Donald W., and Victor A. Christopherson. 1977. 'University student cohabitation: A regional comparison of selected attitudes and behavior.' *Journal of Marriage and the Family* 39(3):447–53

Boyce, R.M., and R.W. Osborn. 1970. 'Therapeutic abortion in a Canadian city.' *Canadian Medical Association Journal* 103:461–6

Boyd, M., and D. Gillieson. 1975. 'Canadian attitudes on abortion: Results of the Gallup polls.' *Canadian Studies in Population* 2:53–64

Bumpass, Larry L. 1979, 'The changing linkage of nuptiality and fertility in the United States.' In L.T. Ruzicka (ed.), *Nuptiality and Fertility*, 195–210. Liège: Ordina

– 1990. 'What's happening to the family? Interactions between demographic and institutional change.' *Demography* 27:483–98

Butz, William P., and Michael P. Ward. 1979. 'The emergence of counter-cyclical U.S. fertility.' *American Economic Review* 69:318–28

Caldwell, John C. 1982. *Theory of Fertility Decline.* New York: Academic Press

Card, J.J., and L.L. Wise. 1978. 'Teen-age mothers and teen-age fathers: The impact of early childbearing on the parents' personal and professional lives.' *Family Planning Perspectives* 10:199–205

Catlin, G., Boriss Mazikins, Maureen Moore, and Gordon Priest. 1989. 'The 1984 Family History Survey: An overview.' In J. Légaré, T.R. Balakrishnan, and R. Beaujot (eds), *The Family in Crisis*, 53–62. Ottawa: Royal Society of Canada

Charles, E. 1948. *The Changing Size of the Family in Canada, 1941*. Ottawa: Dominion Bureau of Statistics, Census monograph no. 1

Cherlin, Andrew J. 1981. *Marriage, Divorce, Remarriage*. Cambridge, London: Harvard University Press

Clayton, Richard R., and Janet L. Bokemeier. 1980. 'Premarital sex in the seventies.' *Journal of Marriage and the Family* 42(4):759–75

Collomb, Philippe, and Elizabeth Zucker. 1977. *Aspects culturels et sociopsychologiques de la fécondité française*. Travaux et Documents de l'INED, no. 80. Paris: PUF

Committee on the Operation of the Abortion Law. 1977. *Report*. Ottawa: Minister of Supply and Services Canada

Connidis, Ingrid Arnet. 1989. *Family Ties and Aging*. Toronto and Vancouver: Butterworths

De Boer, Connie. 1981. 'The polls: Marriage – a decaying institution?' *Public Opinion Quarterly* 45(2):265–75

Duchesne, Louis. 1989. 'L'évolution de la famille québécoise vue par les enfants: Le père moins souvent présent, les frères et soeurs moins nombreux.' In J. Légaré, T.R. Balakrishnan, and R. Beaujot (eds), *The Family in Crisis*, 343–58. Ottawa: Royal Society of Canada

Dumas, Jean. 1985. *Report on the Demographic Situation in Canada 1983. Current Demographic Analysis*. Ottawa: Statistics Canada, Catalogue no. 91–209E

Easterlin, Richard A. 1973. 'Relative economic status and the American fertility swing.' In Eleanor B. Sheldon (ed.), *Family Economic Behaviour*, 170–223. Philadelphia: Lippincott

– 1978. 'What will 1984 be like? Socioeconomic implications of recent twists in age structure.' *Demography* 15:397–432

Easterlin, Richard A., and Eileen Crimmins. 1985. *The Fertility Revolution: A Supply-demand Analysis*. Chicago and London: University of Chicago Press

Fawcett, J.T. (ed.). 1972. *The Satisfactions and Costs of Children: Theories, Concepts, Methods*. Honolulu: East-West Population Institute

Festy, Patrick. 1979. 'Ex-nuptial fertility and cohabitation: Recent trends in Western Europe.' In L.T. Ruzicka (ed), *Nuptiality and Fertility*, 175–94. Liège: Ordina

Freedman, R., and John Casterline. 1979. 'Nuptiality and fertility in Taiwan.' In L.T. Ruzicka (ed.), *Nuptiality and Fertility*, 61–100. Liège: Ordina

Freedman, R., and L. Coombs. 1966. 'Childspacing and family economic position.' *American Sociological Review* 31:631–48

Freedman, R., P.K. Whelpton, and A.A. Campbell. 1959. *Family Planning, Sterility and Population Growth*. New York: McGraw-Hill

Fuchs, Ebaugh, Helen Rose, and C. Allen Haney. 1980. 'Shifts in abortion attitudes: 1972–1978.' *Journal of Marriage and the Family* 42(3):491–9

Furstenberg, F.F., Jr. 1976. *Unplanned Parenthood: The Social Consequences of Teenage Childbearing*. New York: The Free Press

Gee, M., and Meredith M. Kimball. 1987. *Women and Aging*. Toronto and Vancouver: Butterworths

Glenn, Norval D., and Charles N. Weaver. 1977. 'The marital happiness of remarried divorced persons.' *Journal of Marriage and the Family* 39(2): 331–7

– 1979. 'A note on family situation and global happiness.' *Social Forces* 57(3):960–7

– 1988. 'The changing relationship of marital status to reported happiness.' *Journal of Marriage and the Family* 50(2):317–24

Goldschieder, Calvin, and Peter Uhlenburg. 1969. 'Minority group status and fertility.' *American Journal of Sociology* 74:361–72

Gove, Walter R., Michael Hugues, and Carolyn Briggs Style. 1983. 'Does marriage have positive effects on the psychological well-being of the individuals?' *Journal of Health and Social Behavior* 24(2):122–31

Granberg, D., and B. Wellman Granberg. 1980. 'Abortion attitudes, 1965–1980: Trends and determinants.' *Family Planning Perspectives* 12:250–61

Grindstaff, C.F. 1984. 'Catching up: The fertility of women over 30 years of age, Canada in the 1970's and early 1980's.' *Canadian Studies in Population* 11:95–109

Hartnagel, T.F., J.J. Creechan, and R.A. Silverman. 1985. 'Public opinion and legalization of abortion.' *Canadian Review of Sociology and Anthropology* 22:411–30

Hendershot, G.E., and E. Eckard. 1978. 'Unwanted teenage childbearing and later life chances: Evidence from the National Survey of Family Growth.' Paper presented at the annual meetings of the Eastern Sociological Society, Philadelphia

Henripin, J. 1972. *Trends and Factors of Fertility in Canada*. Ottawa: Statistics Canada

Henripin, J., P.M. Huot, E. Lapierre-Adamcyk, and N. Marcil-Gratton. 1981. *Les enfants qu'on n'a plus*. Montreal: Presses de l'Université de Montréal

Henripin, J., and E. Lapierre-Adamcyk. 1974. *La fin de la revanche des berceaux. Qu'en pensent les Québecoises?* Montreal: Presses de l'Université de Montréal

Henshaw, S.K., and G. Martire. 1982. 'Abortion and public opinion polls.' *Family Planning Perspectives* 14:53–62

Janssen, Susan G., and Robert M. Hauser. 1981. 'Religion, socialization, and fertility.' *Demography* 18:511–28

Johnson, Nan E. 1982. 'Religious differentials in reproduction: The effects of sectarian education.' *Demography* 19:495–509

Jones, E.F., and C.F. Westoff 1978. 'How attitudes toward abortion are changing.' *Journal of Population* 1:5–21

Kalbach, Warren, and Wayne McVey. 1979. *The Demographic Bases of Canadian Society.* 2nd ed. Toronto: McGraw-Hill Ryerson

Kempeneers, M. 1992. *Le travail au féminin.* Montreal: Presses de l'Université de Montréal (to be published)

Krishnan, P., and K.J. Krótki. 1976. *Growth of Alberta Families Study.* Report to Health and Welfare Canada, Population Research Laboratory. University of Alberta, Edmonton

Krótki, Karol J. 1989. 'The history and methodology of the Canadian Fertility Study of 1984.' In J. Légaré, T.R. Balakrishnan, and R. Beaujot (eds), *The Family in Crisis,* 17–52. Ottawa: Royal Society of Canada

Krótki, Karol J., and Susan McDaniel. 1975. 'Three estimates of illegal abortion in Alberta, Canada: Survey, mail-back questionnaire and randomized response technique.' In *Contributed papers. Contributions libres,* 493–6. Warsaw: International Statistical Institute. Also in *Bulletin of the International Statistical Institute* 46(4):67–70, and in Population Reprint no. 24 (1976), Population Research Centre, University of Alberta

– 1977. 'La technique de réponse rendu aléatoire: Quelques résultats d'une étude à Edmonton, Canada.' *Population et famille* (Brussels) 41(2): 91–119

Kyriazis, N. 1979. 'Sequential fertility decision making: Catholics and Protestants in Canada.' *Canadian Review of Sociology and Anthropology* 16(3):275–86

– 1982. 'A parity-specific analysis of completed fertility in Canada.' *Canadian Review of Sociology and Anthropology* 19(1):29–43

Lapierre-Adamcyk, E. 1981. 'Les aspirations des Québecois en matière de fécondité.' *Cahiers québécois de démographie* 10(2):171–88

– 1989. 'Le mariage et la famille: Mentalités actuelles et comportements récents des femmes canadiennes.' In J. Légaré, T.R. Balakrishnan, and R. Beaujot (eds), *The Family in Crisis,* 89–104. Ottawa: Royal Society of Canada

Lapierre-Adamcyk, Evelyne, T.R. Balakrishnan, and Karol J. Krótki. 1987. 'La cohabitation au Québec, prélude ou substitut au mariage? Les attitudes des jeunes Québécoises.' In Renée B.-Dandurand (ed.), *Couples et parents des années quatre-vingt,* 27–46. Québec: Institut québécoise de recherche sur la culture

Latten, J.J. 1984. 'Marriage and cohabitation among young people. Young people's plans regarding marriage and cohabitation and some related attitudes. In H.G. Moors, R.L. Cliquet, G. Dooghe, and D.J. Van de Kao (eds), *Population and Family in the Low Countries, IV*, 1–2. Brussels: Voorbridge

Lee, R.D. 1980. 'Aiming at a moving target: Period fertility and changing reproductive goals.' *Population Studies* 34:205–20

Légaré, J. 1974. 'Demographic highlights on fertility decline in Canadian marriage cohorts.' *Canadian Review of Sociology and Anthropology* 11(4):287–307

Leridon, Henri, and Catherine Villeneuve-Gokalp. 1988. 'Les nouveaux couples: Nombre, caractéristiques et attitudes.' *Population* 43(2):331–74

Lesthaeghe, Ron, and Dominique Meekers. 1986. 'Value changes and the dimensions of familialism in the European community.' *European Journal of Population* 2(3/4):225–68

Lesthaeghe, Ron, and Johan Surkyn. 1988. 'Cultural dynamics and economic theories of fertility change.' *Population and Development Review* 14(1):1–45

Macklin, Eleanor D. 1980. 'Nontraditional family forms: A decade of research.' *Journal of Marriage and the Family* 42(4):905–22

Marcil-Gratton, N. 1988a. 'Sterilization regret among women in Metropolitan Montreal.' *Family Planning Perspectives* 20:222–7

– 1988b. *Les modes de vie nouveaux des adultes et leur impact sur les enfants au Canada*. Rapport soumis à l'Etude de évolution démographique et de son incidence sur la politique économique et sociale, Santé et Bien-être social Canada

Marcil-Gratton, N., and E. Lapierre-Adamcyk. 1983. 'Sterilization in Québec,' *Family Planning Perspectives*, 15(2):73–8

Marcil-Gratton, N., and J. Légaré. 1988. 'Support networks surrounding future older people: What may we expect from family support?' Report submitted to the Demographic Review, Health and Welfare Canada

Martin, Teresa Castro, and Larry L. Bumpass. 1989. 'Recent trends in marital disruption.' *Demography* 26:37–51

McDaniel, Susan A. 1986. *Canada's Aging Population*. Toronto and Vancouver: Butterworths

– 1988. 'A new stork rising? Women's roles and reproductive changes.' *Transactions of the Royal Society of Canada*. 5th ser. 3:111–22

McDaniel, Susan A., and Karol J. Krótki. 1979. 'Estimates of the rate of illegal abortion and the effects of eliminating therapeutic abortion, Alberta 1973–74.' *Canadian Journal of Public Health* 70:363–98

McKie, D.C., B. Prentice and P. Reed. 1983. *Divorce: Law and Family in Canada*. Ottawa: Statistics Canada, Catalogue no. 89–502E

Menken, J., James Trussell, Debra Stempel, and Ozer Babakol. 1981. 'Proportional hazards life table models: An illustrative analysis of socio-demographic influences on marriage dissolution in the United States.' *Demography* 18:181–200

Millman, S.R., and G.E. Hendershot, 1980. 'Early fertility and lifetime fertility.' *Family Planning Perspectives* 12:139–49

Moore, K.A., and L.J. Waite. 1977. 'Early childbearing and educational achievement.' *Family Planning Perspectives* 9:220–5

Mori, George A. 1987. 'Religious affiliation in Canada.' *Canadian Social Trends* (Statistics Canada), Autumn 1987:12–16

Morsa, J., G. Julemont, and P. Guilmot. 1979. 'Les facteurs socio-économiques de la fécondité et les motivations à la parenté.' *Etudes démographiques* 3 (Conseil de l'Europe)

Mosher, William D., and Gerry E. Hendershot. 1984. 'Religion and fertility: A replication.' *Demography* 21:185–91

Mugford, Stephen, and Jim Lally. 1981. 'Sex, reported happiness, and the well-being of married individuals: A test of Bernard's hypothesis in an Australian sample.' *Journal of Marriage and the Family* 43(4):969–75

Oppenheimer, Valerie K. 1970. *The Female Labour Force in the United States.* Berkeley: Institute of International Studies, University of California

Osborn, R.W., and B. Silkey. 1980. 'Husbands' attitudes towards abortion and Canadian abortion law.' *Journal of Biosocial Science* 12:21–30

Péron, Y., E. Lapierre-Adamcyk, and D. Morissette. 1987. 'Les répercussions des nouveaux comportements démographiques sur la vie familiale: La situation canadienne.' *Revue internationale d'action communautaire* 18(58) 57–66

Population Information Program, Johns Hopkins University. 1982. 'Oral contraception in the 1980s.' *Population Reports*, series A, no. 6

Preston, Samuel H. 1986. 'Changing values and falling birth rates.' In Davis Kingsley, Mikhail S. Bernstam, and Rita Ricardo-Campbell (eds), *Below-Replacement Fertility in Industrial Societies. Causes, Consequences, Policies.* A supplement to *Population and Development Review* 12:176–95

Rao, K.V. 1987. 'Demographic models of age at first marriage and age at first birth.' Ph.D. dissertation, University of Western Ontario

Romaniuc, Anatole. 1984a. *Fertility in Canada: From Baby-boom to Baby-bust. Current Demographic Analysis.* Ottawa: Statistics Canada, Catalogue no. 91–524

– 1984b. *La fécondité au Canada: Croissance et déclin.* La conjoncture démographique. Cqt. 91–524, hors série

Roof, Wade Clarke. 1979. 'Concepts and indicators of religious commitment: A critical review.' In R. Wuthnow (ed.), *The Religious Dimension*, 17–45. New York: Academic Press

Roussel, Louis. 1971. 'L'attitude de diverses générations à l'égard du mariage, de la famille et du divorce en France.' *Population* 26 (numéro spécial): 109–42

– 1975. *Le mariage dans la société francaise contemporaine.* Cahier de l'INED. Paris: PUF

– 1986. 'Le développement de la cohabitation sans mariage et ses effets sur la nuptialité dans les pays industrialisés.' In AIDELF, *Les familles d'aujourd'hui. Démographie et évolution récente des comportements familiaux,* 31–41. Colloque de Genève (17–20 sept. 1984). Paris: AIDELF

– 1987. 'Deux décennies de mutations démographiques (1965–1985) dans les pays industriels.' *Population* 42(3):429–47

– 1989a. *La famille incertaine.* Paris: Editions Odile Jacob

– 1989b. 'Types of Marriage and Frequency of Divorce.' In E. Grebenik, C. Hohn, and R. Mackensen (eds), *Later Phases of the Family Cycle,* 19–36. Oxford: Clarendon Press

Roussel, Louis, 1989c. 'Le seisme démographique des vingt dernières années dans les pays industriels: Sa signification sociologique.' In J. Légaré, T.R. Balakrishnan, and R. Beaujot (eds), *The Family in Crisis.* Ottawa: Royal Society of Canada

Roussel, L., and P. Festy. 1979. 'L'évolution récente des attitudes et des comportements à l'égard de la famille dans les Etats membres du Conseil de l'Europe.' *Etudes démographiques* 4 (Conseil de l'Europe)

Roussel, Louis, and Odile Bourguignon. 1978. *Générations nouvelles et mariage traditionnel. Enquete auprès de jeunes de 18–30 ans.* Travaux et documents de l'INED, no. 86. Paris: PUF

Ryder, N.B., and C.F. Westoff, 1971. *Reproduction in the United States, 1965.* Princeton: Princeton University Press

Simons, John. 1986. 'Culture, economy and reproduction in contemporary Europe.' In David Coleman and Roger Schofield (eds), *The State of Population Theory,* 256–78. Oxford: Basil Blackwell

Singh, B.K. 1980. 'Trends in attitudes toward premarital sexual relations.' *Journal of Marriage and the Family* 42(2):387–93

Sly, David S. 1970. 'Minority group status and fertility: An extension of Goldschieder and Uhlenburg.' *American Journal of Sociology* 76:443–59

Sonquist, John A. 1970. *Multivariate Model Building: The Validation of a Search Strategy.* Ann Arbor: Survey Research Center, Institute of Social Research, University of Michigan

Stafford, Rebecca, Elaine Backman, and Pamela Dibona. 1977. 'The division of labor among cohabiting and married couples.' *Journal of Marriage and the Family* 39(1):43–57

Statistics Canada. 1963. 1961 Census: *Husband-Wife Families*. Catalogue no. 93–520

– 1973. 1971 Census: *Women Ever Married by Number of Children*. Catalogue no. 92–718

– 1973–87. *Vital Statistics*. Catalogue no. 84–205

– 1982. 1981 Census: *Age, Sex and Marital Status*. Catalogue no. 92–901

– 1983a. 1981 Census: *Nuptiality and Fertility*. Catalogue no. 92–906

– 1983b. 1981 Census: *Mother Tongue, Official Language and Home Language*. Catalogue no. 92–910

– 1985a. *Family Income: Census Families*, Catalogue no. 13–208

– 1985b. *Income Distribution by Size in Canada 1983*. Catalogue no. 13–207

– 1986. *Therapeutic Abortions 1983–84*. Catalogue no. 82–211

– 1987. 1986 Census: *Families*. Catalogue no. 93–106

Teachman, J. 1982. 'Methodological issues in the analysis of family formation and dissolution.' *Journal of Marriage and Family* 44: 1037–53

Thornton, Arland. 1985. 'Changing attitudes toward separation and divorce: Causes and consequences.' *American Journal of Sociology* 90(4):856–972

Thornton, Arland, Duane F. Alwin, and Donald Comburn. 1983. 'Causes and consequences of sex-role attitudes and attitude change.' *American Sociological Review* 48(2):211–27

Thornton, Arland, and Deborah Freedman. 1979. 'Changes in the sex-role attitudes of women, 1962–1977: Evidence from a panel study.' *American Sociological Review* 44(5):831–42

– 1982. 'Changing attitudes toward marriage and single life.' *Family Planning Perspectives* 14(6):297–303

Tremblay, Victor, and Guy Trudel. 1984. *Canadian Fertility Survey: Methodological Report*. University of Montreal, Centre de Sondage

Trussell, J. 1976. 'Economic consequences of teenage childbearing.' *Family Planning Perspectives* 8:184–90

Trussell, J., and J. Menken. 1978. 'Early childbearing and subsequent fertility.' *Family Planning Perspectives* 10: 209–18

Turner, J., and A.B. Simmons. 1977. 'Sex roles and fertility: Which influences which?' *Canadian Studies in Population* 4:43–60

United Nations. 1988. *World Population Trends and Policies: 1987 Monitoring Report*. Population Studies no. 103. Department of International Economic and Social Affairs

– 1990. *Patterns of First Marriage: Timing and Prevalence*. Department of International Economic and Social Affairs

United States. Department of Commerce. Bureau of the Census. 1984. *Fertility of American Women: June 1982*. Series P-20, no. 387. Washington

– 1985. *Fertility of American Women: June 1984.* Series P-20, no. 401. Washington

Veevers, J.E. 1980. *Childless by Choice.* Toronto: Butterworths

Weller, Robert H. 1977. 'Wife's employment and cumulative family size in the United States, 1970 and 1960.' *Demography* 14:43–66

Westoff, Charles F. 1984. 'Fertility decline in the west: Causes and prospects.' *Population and Development Review* 9(1):99–104

Westoff, C.F., E.C. Moore, and N.B. Ryder. 1969. 'The structure of attitudes towards abortion.' *Milbank Memorial Fund Quarterly* 47:11–37

Westoff, C.F., and N.B. Ryder. 1977. *The Contraceptive Revolution* Princeton: Princeton University Press

Whelpton, P.K., Arthur Campbell, and John Patterson. 1966. *Fertility and Family Planning in the United States.* Princeton: Princeton University Press

Willis, R.J. 1973. 'A new approach to the economic theory of fertility behaviour.' *Journal of Political Economy* 81:514–64

Wu, Zheng, and T.R. Balakrishnan. 1992. 'Attitudes towards cohabitation and marriage in Canada.' *Journal of Comparative Family Studies* 23(1):1–12

Index

abortion: recent trends, 182; legislation, 182; attitudes towards by situation, 185–7; index construction, 186; index by religion, 186; by religiosity, 187; by education, 187; by age, 187–90; by marital status, 190; by expected number of children, 190; by last pregnancy status, 190; by current method of contraception, 190–1; by attitudes towards marriage, family, and childbearing, 191–2; multivariate analysis, 193–4

age: and children ever born, 22–5; and expected number of children, 22–5; and abortion attitudes, 187–90; and contraceptive use, 202

age at first marriage: by age at interview, 34–5; and children ever born, 35–6; and dissolution probabilities, 127; by socio–economic characteristics, 125–7; hazards-model analysis, 125–7

Allingham, J.D., 53

Alwin, Duane F., 168

Andrews, F., 194

Ariès, Philippe, 157

attitudes towards: marriage, 148–53; cohabitation, 153–7; premarital sex, 155; children, 157–60; divorce, 160–5; role sharing, 168–74; family life and overall happiness, 174–9

Bachrach, Christine A., 9, 242

Balakrishnan, T.R., 7, 8, 25, 38n, 40, 46, 53, 66n, 70, 72n, 74, 105n, 106, 137, 141, 146, 179, 182n, 183, 186, 187, 190, 193, 195, 210, 219

Barrett, F.M., 183

Beaujot, Roderic, 10, 70

Becker, G.S., 10, 92

birth intervals: by age, 47–50; by year of marriage, 47–50; life-table analysis, 50–2

Blake, Judith, 158, 183

Bokemeier, Janet L., 153

Bourgignon, Odile, 148, 153, 157, 158, 165, 180

Bower, Donald W., 157, 180

Boyce, R.M., 183

Boyd, M., 183

Bumpass, Larry L., 106, 141, 242, 243